Sex, Culture and Modernity in China

性、文化與現代化：

民國時期的醫學中性控制

羅星漢題

FRANK DIKÖTTER

Sex, Culture and Modernity in China

Medical Science and the Construction of Sexual Identities in the Early Republican Period

HURST & COMPANY, LONDON

First published in the United Kingdom by
C. Hurst & Co. (Publishers) Ltd.,
38 King Street, London WC2E 8JT

Printed in Hong Kong
ISBN 1-85065-166-3

ACKNOWLEDGEMENTS

I acknowledge with gratitude the Postdoctoral Research Fellowship of the British Academy which allowed me to carry out the research for this book from its very inception to its completion. The Wellcome Trust for the History of Medicine gave me timely support for a research trip to Hong Kong and Taiwan during the summer of 1991; the Universities' China Committee in London also made a contribution towards research expenses. A generous grant from the School of Oriental and African Studies and the British Academy was made in support of fieldwork in China during the winter of 1991–2.

A number of people have been kind enough to discuss research outlines or to comment on the material presented in draft form, and I would like to convey my appreciation to them. They include Bridie Andrews; David Arnold, School of Oriental and African Studies (SOAS), University of London; T.H. Barrett, SOAS; Gregor Benton, University of Leeds; Jean-Francçis Billeter, University of Geneva; Robert Chard, Oxford University; Elisabeth Croll, SOAS; Pamela Crossley, Dartmouth College; Delia Davin, University of Leeds; Glen Dudbridge, Oxford University; Harriet Evans, University of Westminster; Charlotte Furth; University of Southern California; Gail Hershatter, University of California at Santa Cruz; Dorothy Ko, University of California at San Diego; Lars Laamann, British Library; Joseph MacDermott, Cambridge University; Ladislas Mysyrowicz, University of Geneva; Michel Porret, University of Geneva; Roy Porter, the Wellcome Institute for the History of Medicine; W.T. Rowe, Johns Hopkins University; and Kaoru Sugihara, SOAS. I appreciate help received from Charles d'Orban, Assistant Librarian at SOAS until December 1992.

I have pleasure in thanking Martin Lau and Patrick McGinn, who critically followed this project from start to finish. I especially wish to thank Claude Bouguet and Martin Jelenic, since an idea of this project, then still unfocused, first emerged during our year in Canton, 1986–7. Christopher Hurst, the publisher, suggested a number of modifications to the first draft of the manuscript, which I accepted with gratitude. The responsibility for the views expressed in this book, as for errors and omissions, is mine alone.

London, May 1994 F.D.

CONTENTS

ILLUSTRATIONS

INTRODUCTION

I

The revolution of 1911 profoundly altered the political structures of imperial China. In its aftermath, another revolution soon challenged the sexual order maintained by Confucianism: sex shook the large cities in early Republican China. Open talk of sex rapidly became a sign of liberation from the 'shackles of tradition' among modernizing élites. Under the guise of medical science, literary writers exposed their personal sexual experiences to the public, young intellectuals clamoured for sexual equality, educationalists campaigned for the enlightenment of youth through sexual instruction, and social improvers undertook to reform the sexual habits of the nation. Urban culture was increasingly sexualized, and such diverse topics as prostitution, venereal disease and birth control became issues of public concern. Anxiety over sexuality was expressed by the educated public in letters to specialized periodicals, confessions to daily newspapers and inquiries to medical journals.

Sex was indeed a profitable item for popular consumption. Many new periodicals had titles like *The sex periodical (Xing zazhi)*, *The sexual desire weekly (Xingyu zhoubao)*, *The sex journal bi-weekly (Xing sanrikan)* and *The sex journal (Xingbao)*.[1] The media were keenly aware of the profits to be made in this new cultural domain, and publishing houses deployed sophisticated marketing methods and editorial strategies in their competition for the allegiance of readers. In an era of intense nationalism and rapid state-building, however, the interest in sex reflected far more than a desire for sexual indulgence and commercial exploitation. Educated groups were convinced that the proper

1 See Pan Guangdan, *Renwen shengwuxue luncong* (Writings on human biology), Shanghai: Xinyue shudian, 1939, p. 89.

control of sexual desire was the key to restoring the strength of the nation and achieving modernity. Since the rise of evolutionary theories in the late nineteenth century, reformers like Kang Youwei and Liang Qichao had consistently explained national weakness as the result of an inadequate knowledge of human sexuality and reproduction. For the modernizing élites in Republican China, individual sexual desire had to be disciplined and evil habits eliminated, and couples were to regulate their sexual behaviour strictly to help bring about the revival of the nation. The survival of the social group, represented in biologizing terms of 'race', was thought to be founded on a sense of self-discipline and restraint: 'To strengthen the country, one should first strengthen the race; to strengthen the race, one should first improve sex education.'[2] The threat of racial degeneration could only be thwarted by the social control of carnal impulses. Biological goals were heralded: reproduction was to be regulated by eugenics, and marriage disengaged from the tyranny of Confucianism. Sexual enlightenment was the bright light on the path to national wealth and power.

Medical science, it was proclaimed, would provide a rational guide to the regulation of sexuality. The pre-World War II period in China was generally characterized by an intense faith in the capacity of 'science' to dismantle 'tradition' and to achieve its opposite, dubbed 'modernity'. 'Science' was a talisman for universal truth, used with what has been called a 'crusading zeal' to regenerate culture and society.[3] A new generation of intellectuals, searching for social renovation, invoked the authority of medical science to scrutinize the anatomy of the reproductive system, the physiology of internal secretions, the determination of sexual differences, and other related issues.

2 Wang Chengpin, *Qingchun de xingjiaoyu* (Sex education for youth), Shanghai: Xiongdi chubanshe, 1939, p. 1.

3 E.Z. Sun, 'The growth of the academic community, 1912–1949' in J.K. Fairbank and A. Feuerwerker (eds), *The Cambridge history of China*, vol. 13, part 2, Cambridge University Press, 1986, p. 382; see also D.W.Y. Kwok, *Scientism in Chinese thought, 1900–1950*, New Haven: Yale University Press, 1965.

The investigation of human sexuality and reproduction was not only carried out by a few radical thinkers: major universities started setting up courses in human biology during the 1920s and '30s, and institutions for advanced research were founded with financial support from the government, from overseas Chinese entrepreneurs and from the urban élites of the coast.

II

This book is based on an analysis of over 350 publications produced by the new presses of Republican China. From the medical treatise on sexual differentiation to the pamphlet on birth control, it reflects a variety of different registers of medical discourse. Scholarly literature is represented by scientific journals on human biology, university textbooks on evolution and publications on genetics. Availability of this type of literature to the average reader was made easier by a growing circulation network. Printed material belonging to more popular registers includes teach-yourself manuals, books of medical remedies, family handbooks, marriage guides and primers on sexual hygiene. Many were written in vernacular Chinese, produced as cheaply as possible, and made widely available in all major cities. Some of these primers, guides or outlines were slender volumes that were sold for a few dozen cents; by means of this small expenditure, it was claimed, one could come to understand a science in half an hour: a contemporary commentator called them 'snacks to nourish the soul'.[4] The scientific popularization of human sexuality can also be traced in periodicals, vernacular newspapers and commercial advertisements. A wide variety of periodicals, managed by established publishing companies or by independent associations, were introduced during the New Culture Movement (1915–1924). In general, the spread of these different types of literature on sex was made easier by the rise of publishing houses, the introduction of modern printing

4 Lu Xun, *Selected works*, Beijing: Foreign Languages Press, 1980, vol. 4, p. 56.

methods, the growth of a modern education system after the abolition of the imperial examination system in 1905, and by a general increase in functional literacy.

Private printing houses profited most from increased demand for new books and the general growth in literacy after the fall of the empire, and they rapidly grew into huge publishing companies. The Commercial Press in particular started to compile textbooks and to introduce new knowledge after 1902.[5] It was to remain the most important publishing house in China until 1949, and increased its yearly production from fifty-one titles a year to 352 titles between 1903 and 1920. Some of the most influential periodicals were also published by the Commercial Press, such as the *The Eastern Miscellany* (*Dongfang zazhi*, 1904–48), *The Ladies' Journal* (*Funü zazhi*, 1915–31), *The Educational Review* (*Jiaoyu zazhi*, 1909–48) and *The Students' Magazine* (*Xuesheng zazhi*, 1914–47). Other influential publishing houses included the Shijie shuju, founded in Shanghai in 1921, the Zhonghua shuju, founded in 1912, and the Zhengzhong shuju, which was the biggest official publishing house of the Republican period to come under Guomindang control after 1933. The printed pages which poured forth from the vernacular press made new cultural modes much more accessible to a large public of consumers. Shared consumption of cultural products which heralded the advent of modernity also contributed to the spread of new structures of knowledge about human sexuality. If anybody was responsible for the proliferation of modernizing discourses on sexuality, it was the handful of directors of the publishing houses who promptly responded to the requests of the reading public in a highly competitive market.

5 Jean-Pierre Drège, *La Commercial Press de Shanghai, 1897–1949*, Paris: Presses Universitaires de France, 1978; Jean-Pierre Drège and Hua Changming, *La révolution du livre dans la Chine moderne. Wang Yunwu, éditeur*, Paris: Publications Orientalistes de France, 1979.

III

Journalists, social reformers, professional writers, sex educators, university professors, political ideologues, and cultural popularizers were some of the more important groups that participated in medical discourses about sexuality. No unified interest group or distinct class of people had pre-eminence in this, and these discourses were articulated around a multiplicity of points in the social field and anchored in a variety of cultural locations. Different individuals in these groups also differed markedly in their appeal to medical science, a reflection of the contradictory forces which existed in the new social formations of early Republican China. The dispersion of knowledge and the de-centred nature of power continued to be an important feature of modernizing discourses even after Jiang Kaishek established a central government in 1927, when people with a modern education were in charge. From the warlord period, an era of political division between 1918 and 1927, to the Nanjing decade, when the Guomindang succeeded in imposing a measure of national unity, these discourses were not fundamentally changed: neither provincial warlords nor a central government were able to curb intellectual diversity or exert effective control over the central agencies of cultural life in the big cities of the coast. 'State power' did not simply incorporate intellectuals with a modern worldview; it was built upon a variety of professional groups and social formations who manipulated new bodies of knowledge to further their own careers and impose their own representations of social reality. Modernizing discourses in China were not generated by an integrated scientific community under state control, as in Germany during the same period, but by a loose association of more or less independent intellectuals from a variety of disciplines, particularly medical science and human biology, but also fields like education and sociology. These groups represented the vanguard of modernity, the agents of change whose discursive practices, in the long term, would have a momentous impact on the whole of society. An overemphasis on institutions and 'the state' would therefore be dangerous.

Many individuals certainly had a desire to strengthen the power of the state, not only in exchange for the protection of professional privileges, but also for the achievement of nationalist ideals. The Republican era in China was one of great commitment to the nation, but this only reflected a degree of self-mobilization which had little to do with state manipulation. Although many individuals were linked in one way or another to state-supported institutions that promoted scientific research, few links can be established between the interests of 'the state' and the discursive practices of different writers. Population control, for instance, was considered an important aspect of state policy by a majority of authors, but the official ideology of the Guomindang was openly in favour of increasing population. Conflicts between modernizing discourses and state policy were common, and there is little evidence of a strong and unambiguous link between science, medicine and the state before the establishment of a socialist regime in 1949.

Although many intellectuals were active in the prestigious universities of the big cities or held positions of power in other institutions, a flow of more or less unremarkable writers participated to an equal extent in the production of discourses on sex. Any meaningful analysis of discursive practices in modern China should transcend the insights of a few individuals and uncover the common conceptions of the many. It is dangerous to reduce the cultural categories of a period to the expressions of a dozen authors, and the hagiographic conventions which endlessly parade figures such as Hu Shi, Cai Yuanpei and Chen Duxiu through the pages of the history of ideas have to be discarded. With the uncovering of deeper layers of change, historical analysis gets much closer to the pulse of cultural life: observations on adolescent masturbation by general medical practitioners, self-help guides to sexual hygiene compiled by professional writers, research proposals for the study of eugenics by geneticists, pamphlets on childbirth written by local welfare groups. Hence the object of this study is not so much to explore the ideas of a few writers, or identify the attitudes of social formations or institutions, but to elicit evidence of new structures of knowledge and meaning that transcended the individual author.

New structures of knowledge were created, maintained and perpetuated through texts, which can be interpreted as semiotic encounters through which meanings that constitute social reality are exchanged. By these acts of meaning, social reality is continuously created, shaped and modified: texts both reflect and act upon the environment.[6] Symbolic struggles over different definitions of the social world were grounded in modernizing discourses, including important issues such as the meaning of sexual reproduction, the nature of gender relations, the position of young people in society and the treatment of people afflicted with venereal diseases. Texts about sexuality and science symbolically expressed an allegiance to modernity, and the reform of human sexuality became a symbol used to identify enemies of 'progress'. 'Science' conferred the authority to impose a different vision of the social world and became the central aspect of a new cultural frame of reference. 'Enlightened' professional groups made use of their new knowledge of sexuality to further their claims for social status. New cultural norms were used by modernizing groups to oppose the values of the traditional élites, much like the bourgeoisie attacked the nobility in France at the end of the eighteenth century. In the texts analysed, sexuality and reproduction are treated as symbols created and invested with meaning by social groups, and used to legitimize an alternative vision of power structures and prestige systems. Discursive formations, however, are not only a tool for the expression of a person's ideas; they are more than the representation and symbolization of authority and power and constitute a normative system independent of the individual.

6 M.A.K. Halliday, *Language as social semiotic: The social interpretation of language and meaning*, London: Edward Arnold, 1978; Pierre Bourdieu, *Language and power*, London: Polity Press, 1991.

IV

Modernizing discourses on sex, produced by the new print culture of Republican China, formed an interconnected textual network, a relatively coherent web which can be analysed as a whole. Sex as a form of discourse was the intersection of a variety of cultural locations; it was the point of convergence through which different agents could represent themselves as an integrated group with a separate identity ('progressive intellectuals', 'radical thinkers'). The texts analysed in this study, in other words, were not merely the product of a certain field, but the focal point of socially dispersed voices, a factor of social integration, a practice which created and gave shape to the field itself: the professional physician in Hong Kong with his treatise on the evils of self-abuse and the Beijing professor of literature with his piece on the national significance of the male organ came together in their promotion of 'modernity' in medical discourses.

Sexual discourses, moreover, may have encompassed a vast register of representations, but they also shared a distinct number of integrating features, notably an appeal to evolutionism, nationalism and scientism. In their use of medical science, new modes of writing about sexuality represented an epistemic shift away from Confucian discourse. An important aspect of this shift was the dichotomy between 'nature' and 'culture'. Previously imagined as a purposeful whole, a benevolent structure which could not exist independently from ethical forces, 'nature' was now conceptualized as a set of impersonal forces which could be objectively investigated. While medical science increasingly became the main source of reference, appeals to the authority of 'nature' were made for prescriptive claims about the social order. No longer were physical bodies thought to be linked to the cosmological foundations of the universe: bodies were produced by biological mechanisms inherent to 'nature'. With the decline of conformity to the moral imperatives enshrined in a canon of Confucian texts, a growing number of people believed 'truth' to be encoded in a nature which only science could decipher: identity, ancestry and meaning were buried deep inside the body. Embryology or genetics could establish truth, not philology or paleography. Human biology replaced Confucian philosophy as the epistemological foundation for social order.

Other important aspects of this epistemic disjunction can be identified, although the exact reasons for its appearance still need to be investigated. The concept of time underwent drastic change, as evolutionism replaced ideas about cyclical alternations. The rise and fall of dynasties, thought to reflect the mandate of Heaven, was replaced by a biological mandate of progress. Evolution was interpreted as an inevitable ascent through a preordained hierarchy of developmental stages on a ladder, and even the embryo was thought to develop in a purposeful way towards maturity. Modernizing élites in early Republican China not only deployed racial hierarchies in which 'savage tribes' were represented as throwbacks on the evolutionary scale,[7] but also portrayed women and children as the lower stages of evolutionary growth. The social roles of women and men were thus thought to be firmly grounded in biology: gender hierarchy was now represented as 'natural' and 'progressive'. Instead of invoking the social duties of mothers, sisters, widows or orphans, writers debated the anatomical function of the womb in 'women', the physiological effects of menstruation in 'females', the nature of sexual desire in the 'opposite sex'. With the rise of medical science, differentiation between other groups of people also became more important: through an investigation of their sexuality, people were more rigidly classified according to their gender, age and social position. Measurement and quantification further boosted claims to scientific exactness. Embryological growth, female intelligence, menstrual flows, even the size of the penis came to be measured in great detail. In these compilations of arbitrary selected facts, biomedical data

7 Frank Dikötter, *The discourse of race in modern China*, London: C. Hurst/ Stanford University Press, 1992.

were stressed at the expense of social and emotional factors: nature mattered more than nurture. The individual, moreover, became the focus of biologizing discourses. A clearer delineation of the boundaries of the body and an increased sense of personhood become important. The causes of disease were located inside the body, and belief in the relative autonomy of the individual spread. Health was said to be determined by the individual's own actions, an approach which was bolstered by notions of bodily resistance and weakness. Human agency and causality were underlined in medical discourses which constituted the individual as a site of sexual desire and as a crucial node for its proper control: the regulation of sexuality, rather than its suppression, was a constant concern in a period of intense nationalism.

V

Based on the assumption that 'Chinese culture' must be fundamentally different from 'Western culture', an essentializing approach would reject the primary sources of this book as 'Westernized' and not representative of China. The construction of an ontological dichotomy between 'West' and 'East' is indeed pervasive in the field of Chinese studies. As Rey Chow forcefully underlines, 'cultural studies are predicated on an opposed set of imperatives':[8] 'Chinese women' are counterposed to 'Western women', and an insistence on 'Chinese tradition' leads to the representation of China as a radically different entity. The idealization of otherness, the desperate search for 'authenticity', the quest for a 'real' China not yet 'Westernized', is coupled with the systematic rejection of aspects of contemporary life in China which are too much like the West. The tendency to look for particularities, to ignore commonalities, to idealize otherness is widespread, and its consequences for historical research are devastating: the experience of modernity by other peoples is

8 Rey Chow, *Woman and Chinese modernity: The politics of reading between West and East*, Minneapolis: University of Minnesota Press, 1991, p. xiv.

rejected outright as 'Westernization'. While the study of sexuality and modernity in the history of France, Spain or Russia is generally seen to be a fruitful and necessary enterprise, the same type of research in the recent history of China is not thought to deserve any credit: research into the very roots of cultural transformations in one of the most populous countries of the world is denied relevance.

Orientalist discourses on China have other consequences too. They represent 'the West' as an amorphous and homogeneous entity, and overlook the cultural differences between countries like France and England, and the historical changes of the nineteenth and twentieth centuries. Between the 1880s and the 1930s in particular, medical science in Europe exploded into a multiplicity of theories and hypotheses that could hardly be described as 'a' system. Many of the medical concepts that were invented in this period, such as 'hereditary syphilis', 'masturbatory insanity', 'organotherapy' or 'biological recapitulation', would be considered absurd by scientists today, and it is against this variety of competing bits of knowledge that developments in Republican China have to be assessed.

China was not a static entity called 'tradition' either, and its history cannot be reduced to a 'response' to another ahistorical entity called 'the West'.[9] The 'Western impact – Chinese response' approach not only introduces Eurocentric distortions, it also fails to take into account historical transformations which took place in parts of China before its prolonged exposure to foreign ideas. Gender relations, for instance, had undergone drastic changes during the late imperial period, including the emergence of an ideal of 'companionate marriage' in which both partners were similarly cultivated. Increased concern for women's reproductive health became prominent during the seventeenth and eighteenth centuries, including medical specializations in female disorders. The nature of scholarship itself

9 Paul Cohen, *Discovering history in China: American historical writing on the recent Chinese past*, New York: Columbia University Press, 1984.

changed, as discontent among Qing literati with imperial orthodoxy led to the flourishing of alternative trends of thought in the eighteenth century. The evidential research movement (*kaozhengxue*) in particular was characterized by a concern with precise scholarship and practical matters: 'important scientific research did take place, and the institutions required for precise scholarship were already in place,' notes Benjamin Elman.[10] It is in this context of change that elements from a foreign repertoire were introduced. Cultural disparities between different countries, in other words, have to be placed within a broader framework of historical convergence: it is not so much a 'shock of encounters' between 'East' and 'West' we attempt to trace, but rather the emergence of a plurality of intertwined modernities that have diverse origins and many directions.

If any artificial opposition between 'China' and 'the West' should be treated with deep suspicion, dualities between 'tradition' and 'modernity' should also be avoided, since no homogeneous entities such as 'traditional medicine' or 'modern science' ever existed in early Republican China. The changes which occurred in the discursive field we analyse cannot be described as a conflict between two 'systems', in which both would be seen as distinctive, integrated and self-determining 'frameworks'. Modernizing discourses of sex were not 'hybrids' of 'Chinese' and 'Western' ideas, nor can they be interpreted as some sort of survival of 'traditional' cultural values underneath a veneer of 'modern' scientific ideas. What emerged was a type of 'latticed knowledge', to borrow a term from the anthropologist David Parkin,[11] a body of knowledge in flux, characterized by interactions, overlaps and echoes, by constant change and endless combinations. It is precisely this variety of discourses that makes Republican China fertile terrain for the

10 B.A. Elman, *From philosophy to philology: Intellectual and social aspects of change in late imperial China*, Cambridge, Mass.: Harvard University Press, 1984, p. 84.

11 David Parkin, 'Latticed knowledge and the impossibility of eliminating dispersal', manuscript, May 1993.

historian. Below the surface of political events, moreover, beyond the cycles of social and economic change, an analysis of these discourses may help to uncover the deeper historical shifts which have transformed culture and society in China in the twentieth century.

2

THE PASSIVE SEX: THE NATURALIZATION OF GENDER DISTINCTIONS

THE EMERGENCE OF 'WOMANHOOD'

The authority and prestige of neo-Confucian knowledge, on which prescriptive claims about gender hierarchy were founded, gradually eroded during the last decade of the nineteenth century and finally disintegrated with the disappearance of the last dynasty in 1911. Natural sciences were introduced instead to represent gender distinctions as biologically determined structures. The shift from metaphysics to science in discourses about gender differences was particularly evident in the dozens of childbirth manuals, gynaecological treatises, books of medical remedies, family handbooks, marriage guides and primers on sexual hygiene which proliferated in the 1920s and 1930s. In these modernizing discourses of sexuality and reproduction, physical bodies were no longer thought to be linked to the cosmological foundations of the universe: bodies were said to be produced by biological mechanisms inherent in 'nature'.

Although the shift from Confucianism towards the natural sciences in prescriptive claims about the social order was important, it would be wrong to underestimate the extent to which new social and economic realities had already transformed gender relations in late imperial China. The economy of the coastal regions was gradually commoditized after the late sixteenth century, foreign trade became prominent and fuelled regional specialization in export commodities, and a high rate of urbanization created new opportunities that altered the quality of gender relationships. Greater contact between both sexes in workplaces and recreational sites fuelled a far-reaching debate about the position of women and the role of the family.[1] Cri-

1 W.T. Rowe, 'Women and the family in mid-Ch'ing social thought: The case of Ch'en Hung-mou', *Late Imperial China*, 13, no. 2 (Dec. 1992), p. 8.

ticism of the subordinate position of women was increasingly articulated by orthodox scholars and writers of fiction. Yu Zhengxie (1775–1840), a celebrated scholar and official, wondered 'Why does the world make a distinction between men and women?'[2] A new ideal of 'companionate marriage', evoking the myth of a predestined attachment between two lovers, appeared in some Qing novels,[3] while polygamy was criticized in a number of erotic stories. Official campaigns also promoted a common ideal of domestic life during the same period, a classical revival which emphasized the privileged role of wives and stressed domestic harmony. Like Victorian writings on the subject of women, mid-Qing authors accorded great value to woman's role as a wife, manager and guardian of the 'inner apartments'; the idea of complementarity between spouses became prominent in writings on the family.[4] Even divorce became a contentious issue, and a historian and expert in evidential scholarship (*kaozhengxue*), Qian Daxin (1728–1804), overtly argued in its favour on the grounds that marriage was not a natural bond but a human institution.[5] A result of economic and cultural affluence, rising literacy rates led to the development of a highly literate women's culture.[6] Guidebooks for the education of women proliferated, printed in affordable editions

2 Paul Ropp, 'The seeds of change: Reflections on the condition of women in the early and mid-Ch'ing', *Signs*, 2, no. 1 (1976), p. 15.
3 Keith McMahon, 'A case for Confucian sexuality: The eighteenth-century novel, *Yesou puyan*', *Late Imperial China*, 9, no. 2 (Dec. 1988), pp. 32–55.
4 Susan Mann, 'Grooming a daughter for marriage: Brides and wives in the mid-Ch'ing period' in Rubie S. Watson and Patricia B. Ebrey (eds), *Marriage and inequality in Chinese society*, Berkeley: University of California Press, 1991, p. 205.
5 Yuasa Yukihiko, 'Shindai ni okeru fujin kaiho ron', *Nippon Chugoku gakkai ho*, no. 4 (1952), p. 115, quoted in W.T. Rowe, 'Women and the family in mid-Ch'ing social thought: The case of Ch'en Hung-mou', *Late Imperial China*, 13, no. 2 (Dec. 1992), p. 17.
6 Dorothy Ko, 'Pursuing talent and virtue: Education and women's culture in seventeenth- and eighteenth-century China', *Late Imperial China*, 13, no. 1 (June 1992), pp. 9–39.

characteristic of a new commercial print culture.[7] A shift in gender arrangements also led to a heightened concern about women and children in the neo-Confucian family. From the late Ming onwards, Charlotte Furth notes, medical thought advocated common erotic goals for both men and women and supported the social status of women as wives and dependants in the family. Increased concern for women's reproductive health became prominent during the seventeenth and eighteenth centuries. Medical specialization in female disorders, in other words, developed in imperial China well before any 'impact of the West'.[8]

Social and cultural changes were also reflected in some scholarly reorientations. The evidential research movement in particular was characterized by a concern with precise scholarship and practical matters. Although inquiries into natural phenomena remained ancillary to philosophical concerns, important scientific research began to be conducted, and the institutions required for precise scholarship were gradually established. In a shift away from numerological explanations towards empirical induction, the development of mathematics, astronomy and archaeology in Confucian discourse transformed intellectual life in the Qing dynasty.[9] Previously thought to be connected with events in human society, Heaven was increasingly seen by a number of scholars as a physical entity devoid of will or aim. Correlative thinking, which provided a cosmological validation for the prescription of social roles in imperial China, also came under attack by a minority of seventeenth-century scholars.[10]

7 Evelyn S. Rawski, *Education and popular literacy in Ch'ing China*, Ann Arbor: University of Michigan Press, 1979.

8 Charlotte Furth, 'Rethinking van Gulik: Sexuality and reproduction in traditional Chinese medicine', paper presented at the Conference on Engendering China, Harvard University, Feb. 1992.

9 Benjamin A. Elman, *From philosophy to philology: Intellectual and social aspects of change in late imperial China*, Cambridge, MA: Harvard University Press, 1984, pp. 84, 180–1.

10 John B. Henderson, *The development and decline of Chinese cosmology*, New York: Columbia University Press, 1984.

Despite these momentous changes, the prevalence of correlative thinking and the belief that gender roles were preordained by Heaven remained largely intact throughout the Qing dynasty. The three bonds (*sangang*), linchpin of a hierarchical order centred around the relations between ruler and subject, father and son, and husband and wife, continued to be seen as the reflection of a cosmic order between Heaven and Earth which was sacred and unalterable. Only in the late nineteenth and early twentieth centuries did the authority of a hierarchical family system come under assault.

The Taiping rebellion (1851–64) first brought women on to the agenda of political and social reform, a shift in attitudes which also became prevalent within scholarly circles after the Sino-Japanese War of 1895. As the result of a long trend of relative secularization which had started in the late sixteenth century, the 1898 reformers championed a radical transformation of imperial institutions and orthodox ideology. In contrast to their precursors, they promoted an alternative body of knowledge which derived its legitimacy independently from the official examination system. The product of a fusion between different indigenous strains of knowledge[11] and foreign discursive repertoires, the principal object of political attention was the species. The scientific category of 'race' and the administrative category of 'population' were heralded as objects worthy of systematic investigation. The interest in the mechanisms of human reproduction was intimately linked to a political end, and many reformers, particularly Yan Fu, considered national wealth and power to be based on the physical strength of the population. Gender relations were no longer considered to be only a question of social ethics, as human sexuality and reproduction were thought to be tied to the power of the state. The woman had a duty to the body politic, social reformers claimed, since careless procreation would lead to the production of unfit people and degenerates. In a memorial to the throne, Kang Youwei argued

11 Chang Hao, *Chinese intellectuals in crisis: Search for order and meaning, 1890–1911*, Berkeley: University of California Press, 1987.

that foot-binding 'weakened the race hereditarily' and impeded the 'increase of military strength';[12] he envisaged the replacement of the Confucian bond between husband and wife by consensual unions between equal partners.[13] The emancipation of women, in the opinion of Liang Qichao, would 'strengthen the race': healthy mothers bred healthy offspring. Despite political support from some sectors of the imperial government, the reformers failed to secure the power necessary to implement their vision of change. Their critique of the established social order, however, was to culminate after the fall of the empire in 1911, a momentous political event which undermined the authority of neo-Confucian knowledge.

Another striking feature of the early twentieth century, according to William Rowe, was the rapid transformation of the traditional gentry into powerful new élites, such as factory managers, bankers, lawyers, doctors, scientists, educators and journalists.[14] The gradual emergence of new social formations, a consequence of new economic opportunities created through contacts with Western traders and the closer integration of the country into a global economy, was particularly pronounced in the large metropoles of the coast. The First World War in particular was a prosperous period for the economy of the Chinese coastal regions, which benefited both from the replacement of the imperial system by a Republican one and from the decline of European world trade. During this 'golden age' of economic expansion,[15] cities like Tianjin, Nanjing, Shanghai, Wuhan and Canton became the outposts of modernization.

12 Kang Youwei, 'Qing jin funü chanzu zou' (Memorial with a request for a ban on the binding of women's feet), in Jian Bozan *et al.* (eds), *Wuxu bianfa* (The Hundred Days), Shanghai: Shenzhou guoguang she, 1953, vol. 2, pp. 242–4.

13 Kang Youwei, *Datongshu* (One World), Beijing: Guji chubanshe, 1956.

14 W.T. Rowe, 'Modern Chinese social history in comparative perspective' in Paul Ropp (ed.), *Heritage of China: Contemporary perspectives on Chinese civilization*, Berkeley: University of California Press, 1990, p. 260.

15 Marie-Claire Bergère, *The golden age of the Chinese bourgeoisie, 1911–1937*, Cambridge University Press, 1989.

Students and businessmen in particular gained a prolonged and practical experience with the realities of the modern world abroad, and both groups were imbued with a sense of cultural renewal. Based on a common ground of social values, a sophisticated network of relations webbed intellectuals, urban notables and financial élites together into a modernizing avant-garde.[16]

Social and economic changes altered the structure of the family system. Rapid growth of the industrial sector attracted young people into factories and offices, increasing their economic independence and cultural distance from the older generations. Isolation in the cities further weakened the structure of the extended family, and there was a great contrast between middle-class rooms and apartments and the overcrowded working-class dormitories. The barriers between men and women started to erode, and consensual unions became the norm of the educated urban groups. Ideally, if not necessarily in reality, polygamy was abandoned for the conjugal family model; the so-called 'civilized wedding ceremony' (*wenming jiehun*) replaced more customary marriage rituals. These changes reflected the higher social status gained by women: unmarried girls started to pursue higher education, participate in public activities and engage in politics.[17] Away from home, young people rapidly acquired a modern outlook through formal education and extracurricular reading of books and magazines. They too were producers and consumers of discourses on sexuality which thrived on the creation of a mass-market for books.

Central to the attack on the epistemological foundation of

16 Marie-Claire Bergère, 'The Chinese bourgeoisie, 1911–37' in J.K. Fairbank (ed.), *The Cambridge history of China*, vol. 12, part 1, Cambridge University Press, 1986, p. 758.

17 For an introduction, see Sally Borthwick, 'Changing concepts of the role of women from the late Qing to the May Fourth Period' in D. Pong and E. Fung (eds), *Ideal and reality: Social and political change in China (1860–1949)*, Lanham: University Press of America, 1985, pp. 63–92; Charlotte L. Beahan, 'In the public eye: Women in early twentieth-century China' in R.W. Guisso and S. Johannesen, *Women in China: Current directions in historical scholarship*, New York: Philo Press, 1981, pp. 215–38.

the traditional family system, the meanings attributed to the category 'women' (*funü*) were heatedly debated during the early Republican period. Following similar developments in other secular nations, male and female bodies were imagined to be autonomous entities which could be analysed independently from any metaphysical context. In contrast to medical thought in late imperial China, the modern-educated élites of the coast no longer believed the physiology of the human body to reflect the order of a universe. Cut adrift from analogies with a metaphysical order, characteristic of discussions about gender hierarchy in imperial China, social roles of women and men were now thought to be grounded in nature: bodies dictated different but complementary social roles, not imperial cosmology. Biological distinctions between male and female, which rarely assumed a primary function in imperial China, became essential. Modernizing discourses appealed to science in order to posit distinct if complementary differences between male and female bodies.

THE BODY AS A MACHINE

'Medical practitioners in China have a theory that men and women both have an orgasm. This theory is so excellent that it ought to be known by everybody. Those who have also investigated sexology in Western medical science have examined in detail the movement of the muscles and the state of saliva during intercourse. They have illustrated their description with drawings and have left nothing undiscussed. They have also made wax models of the human body which can be dismantled for the purpose of examination. They have established many research institutes devoted to the study of sex and they widely circulate books on sex theories so that everybody knows what sex is all about and understands that the very matter on which they have vainly spent their lifetime is nothing more than a mechanism.'[18]

18 Tan Sitong, *Renxue* (A study of benevolence), Shanghai: Zhonghua shuju, 1958, p. 17; translation with modifications based on Chan Sin-wai, *An exposition of benevolence: The Jen-hsüeh of T'an Ssu-t'ung*, Hong Kong: Chinese University Press, 1984, pp. 86–7.

A pioneer among the 1898 reformers in his concern for male and female bodies,[19] Tan Sitong (1865–98) boldly proclaimed that science could remove the veil of mysticism which Confucianism had cast over human sexuality. He described sexual relations as a physiological mechanism, a natural act between two equal lumps of flesh and blood. His comparison of sexual intercourse with the mechanics of a machine had two important implications: first, sex was a relatively simple mechanism which could be understood by scientists and secondly, the key to this understanding was believed to be located in the body itself. Like a machine, the body functioned independently from any external reality; a collection of intricately assembled parts, it was imagined to be self-contained.

Spurred by new knowledge about human anatomy, the mechanical metaphor became current among the modernizing élites of the urban centres. The modern body was seen as a structure of finely attuned cogs and wheels, an intricate machinery which could be adjusted and regulated;[20] one writer even compared the mechanics of the body to the machinery of a motorcycle.[21] Other authors compared the body to a modern building. For Chen Yucang (1889–1947), a foreign-educated doctor who became director of the provincial hospital of Hubei province, director of the Medical College of Tongji University and a secretary to the Legislative Yuan, the ears were the telephones of the soul, the eyes corresponded to a camera, the head was the general headquarters, the backbone was the central pillar. Bellows pumped air into the body, while fuel was proceeded towards the furnace, eliminated by the water trough.[22]

19 Ono Kazuko, *Chinese women in a century of revolution, 1850–1950*, edited by Joshua A. Fogel, Stanford University Press, 1989, p. 38.

20 See David Le Breton, *Anthropologie du corps et modernité*, Paris: Presses Universitaires de France, 1990.

21 Tang Zhou, 'Renti jixie yu motoche de bijiao' (A comparison of the mechanics of the body to the motorcycle), *Xuesheng zazhi*, 15, 12 (Dec. 1928), pp. 19–25.

22 Chen Yucang, *Renti de yanjiu* (Research on the human body), Shanghai: Zhengzhong shuju, 1937.

By analogy, the body was integrated into an industrialized landscape: Modern Man became a factory. Shen Junqi, researcher at the Department of Medicine of the Central University in Beijing and secretary of the Chinese Association of Physiology, constantly referred to a 'factory' in his textbook on human physiology published in 1946. The circulation of blood corresponded to the 'irrigation works' of a watercourse, whereas the digestive system was analogous to the 'processing' of raw material. Excrement simply became 'waste material' mechanically expelled by the human factory. The administrative centre 'naturally' corresponded to the brain, and the reproductive system was seen as the 'preparation for the construction of a new factory': 'the female and the male factory both reach completion in order to set up branch factories'.[23]

As was noted above, gender boundaries were thought to be only partly dependent on biological markers until the end of the nineteenth century: according to Patricia Ebrey, 'Chinese writers did not argue for women's subordination based on women's childbearing capacity or men's larger bodies and stronger muscles'.[24] The mechanical metaphor, which invaded representations of the body in early Republican China, entailed that the pursuit of knowledge had to be directed on to the body itself. No longer the expression of a metaphysical hierarchy which transcended individual bodies, nature was conceptualized as a set of impersonal forces which could be objectively investigated. Physical bodies were no longer thought to be linked to the cosmological foundations of the universe: bodies were produced by biological mechanisms inherent in nature. Gender differences were thought to be found in almost every part of the body.

An epistemological foundation for claims about gender hierarchy, bodies were thought to reveal that man and woman

23 Shen Junqi, *Jixie rensheng* (Mechanic life), Shanghai: Wentong shuju, 1946, p. 629.

24 Patricia Ebrey, 'Women, marriage and the family in Chinese history' in Paul Ropp (ed.), *Heritage of China: Contemporary perspectives on Chinese civilization*, Berkeley: University of California Press, 1990, p. 204.

were different but complementary in structure and physiology. Human biology was invoked to suggest that woman was endowed with physical characteristics which marked her as the passive counterpart to the more active constitution of man. In an attempt to reconcile the need for gender hierarchy and the desire to underline the kinship of men and women, different authors imagined her reproductive system to be similar to that of man: the vagina was portrayed as an interior penis, the womb was depicted as a scrotum, the ovaries were represented as the testicles. Woman was man turned outside in, containing a topological inversion of the male penis within her body. It was common for anatomical and gynaecological treatises in Republican China to stress how the male was *wai*, or exterior, in opposition to the female, who was *nei*, or interior. 'The most striking difference between the reproductive organs of both sexes is that the male sex is for the greatest part exterior whereas the female sex is for the greatest part interior. (. . .) The female sex is exactly the opposite of the male sex.'[25] The two ovaries were thought to correspond naturally to the two testicles: both exuded secretions which were vital for the health of the individual. The clitoris, or 'sexual pit' (*yinhe*), was isolated as a separate part of the female reproductive system and was compared to the penis, or 'sexual stalk' (*yinjing*). In analogy to the penis, it was presented as composed of three parts, a 'head', a 'foot' and a 'body': like the male member, it was made of spongy tissue and was presented as an erectile member, the female rod; it was also compared to the cavernous bodies of the penis. *Faluopiaoguan*, a transliteration of 'fallopian tube', was quickly abandoned for *shuluanguan* ('duct transporting the ovary', or uterine tube), which stood in perfect symmetry to the vas deferens, called *shujingguan* ('duct transporting sperm'; few treatises made a distinction between the vas deferens and the ejaculatory duct): the ovaries (*luanchao*) thus became the perfect opposite of the testicles (*jingchao*). Invoking terms which were

25 Wang Chengpin, *Qingchun de xingjiaoyu* (Sex education for youth), Shanghai, Xiongdi chubanshe, 1939, pp. 103–6.

current in ancient medical texts, woman was said to be concave (*ao*, a square character with an indented top), man convex (*tu*, a square character with a protruding top); they were 'opposite and complementary to each other' (*xiangfan er xiangcheng*). Gu Mingsheng, an expert in Chinese medicine and founder of the *Journal of Chinese and Western Medicine* (*Zhong Xi yixuebao*), put it unambiguously: 'The reproductive organs of the male and the female sexes appear to be opposite but are in reality similar. Let us examine their general structure. The testicles produce semen like the ovaries produce eggs. The spermatic duct transports semen like the uterine tube transfers eggs. The scrotum stores sperm like the uterus nurtures the embryo. The glans of the penis becomes erect after friction just as the clitoris becomes excited when it is touched. The fluids of the urethral glands which are secreted as a result of copulation are like the vaginal fluids secreted during sexual congress.' Gu Mingsheng even detected the vestigial traces of a female equivalent to the epididymis (*fugaowan*) in the uterus (not surprisingly, he called it *fuluanchao*).[26] First published in 1916 by the Wenming shuju, Gu Mingsheng's *Medicine for the bedchamber* was in its fifteenth edition in 1930, a testimony to the huge success enjoyed by medical discourses on the human body. Although different authors did not all emphasize physical similarities between men and women in the same way, these new representations of gender differences were widely circulated in a variety of texts, ranging from popular self-help guides on sexual hygiene to university textbooks on anatomy. Scientific notions of gender in Republican China thus revealed profound ambiguities about the nature of masculinity and femininity, and many writers even explored hermaphroditism to highlight the basic kinship between man and woman.[27] In contrast to some medical writings in England,

26 Gu Mingsheng, *Fangzhong yi* (Medicine for the bedchamber), Shanghai: Wenming shuju, 1916 (1930, 15th edn), p. 130.
27 Frank Dikötter, 'The neuter sex: Hermaphroditism, medical science and gender boundaries in China' in Leslie Hall and Frank Dikötter (eds), *The body and beyond: The creation and violation of bodily boundaries* (forthcoming).

France and Germany, woman was rarely thought to be a different species with incommensurably different organs and functions.[28] On the contrary, the idea that both genders were the two extremes of a neuter body allowed medical writers to express their belief in a continuity of male and female and their faith in the universality of human nature. Biologizing discourses of the body in Republican China reflected a tension between the idea of gender hierarchy, in which female bodies were the passive counterparts of active male bodies, and a vision of modernity in which men and women were undifferentiated members of an equal society. Male and female bodies were thought to be different in degree, not in kind.

If gender boundaries were ambiguous, cultural representations of male activity and female passivity governed accounts of reproductive anatomy. Testicles were thought to actively 'manufacture' (*zhizao*) sperm on a ceaseless production line, according to the mechanized vision of Shen Yong: 'Its use is infinite, and from puberty to old age it is an inexhaustible source of semen.'[29] The symbol of masculinity, sperm had a 'head', a 'body' and a 'tail', just as the penis had a 'head' and a 'neck' followed by a 'main body'. Called 'essence insect' (*jingchong*), at times even 'small insect' (*xiaochong*), the spermatozoon was described as an autonomous organism endowed with life. Sperm was compared to the tadpole (*kedou*), since it would metamorphose itself into a fully formed human being like the larva of the amphibian. The engendering agent of life, it actively 'penetrated' the passive egg just as the man took the woman. The penis was described in anthropocentric terms: it was 'valiant', 'vigorous', 'hard as wood'; failure forced the penis to 'shrink back', 'cower', or 'flinch'. A military terminology, reminiscent of some traditional notions of war between *yin* and *yang*, was also used in medical texts. The foreskin protected 'the

28 Thomas W. Laqueur, *Making sex: Body and gender from the Greeks to Freud*, Cambridge, MA: Harvard University Press, 1990.
29 Shen Yong, *Xingyuan* (The origin of sex), Shanghai: Dadong shuju, 1931, p. 191.

killing instrument' 'like the sheath protected the sword'; the tip of the penis was referred to as a 'control centre' (*zhunao*): it 'pierced' and 'plugged into' the vagina; it 'shot' or 'fired' like a cannon, and sperm 'hit' the egg; ejaculation was compared to 'firing a cannon' (*dapao*), a term still current in contemporary slang. In medical terminology, the ejaculate was 'injected' into the vagina, the woman 'received a shot' or 'received semen'. The penis thus fulfilled a vital role for the 'replication of the individual, the strength of the race and the rise of the state [. . .] a sacred, solemn and dutiful obligation', Chen Yucang proudly proclaimed.[30] Quantification, an essential part of modernizing discourses of the body, became important, in particular the size of the penis. Some authors estimated a 'normal' size to be four *cun* (approximatively 13 centimetres). For Shen Yong, who studied medicine in Japan in the 1920s, sizes varied according to 'race', the 'yellow race' generally measuring three to four *cun* (equivalent to 10–13 centimetres).[31] In 1897, as we have seen above, the pioneer Tan Sitong had heralded sexual equality by emphasizing that the only difference between men and women was a few inches in the human genitals. These few inches of flesh had become a focus of medical attention in twentieth-century China.

In a lexicon of Chinese terms used in midwifery during the 1850s, Benjamin Hobson listed 'tubes at the right and left of the womb' (*zigong zhi zuoyou guan*) for the fallopian tubes and 'pits at the right and left of the womb' (*zigong zhi zuoyou he*) for the ovaries:[32] female organs were seen as a collection of indistinct functions gathered around the uterus, and different sexual

30 Chen, *Renti*, p. 168.

31 Shen, *Xingyuan*, p. 193; obsession with length has not disappeared in communist China: the author of a recent book on sexology reported having measured the length and circumference of 1,412 penises in the 1950s, the result of which are classified in a table; Shi Chengli, *Xingkexue zixun* (Sexological counselling), Shenyang: Liaoning renmin chubanshe, 1988, pp. 12–13.

32 Benjamin Hobson, *A medical vocabulary in English and Chinese*, Shanghai: Shanghai Mission Press, 1858, p. 55.

parts were conflated together. Although Hobson compiled and translated an illustrated outline of anatomy and physiology in 1850,[33] new knowledge only acquired cultural meaning after neo-Confucian prescriptions of gender roles were permanently undermined by the fall of the Qing dynasty. New anatomical knowledge was deployed by modernizing élites to represent the womb as a biological marker of female passivity. The uterus remained a warm place to nurture sperm: 'its function is to receive and nurture the fertilized egg' and it existed 'waiting' for sperm. Portrayed as a replicator, the womb was in the service of the 'preservation', the 'progress' and the 'development' of the 'race', while more mechanized versions of the human body presented it as a factory for the 'production' (*shengchan*) of offspring (see illustration 1), with 'pipes' or 'tubes' which 'transported' eggs (*shuluanguan*).[34] Previously represented as the more hidden recesses of a poorly defined anatomy, the vagina became a clear organ distinct from the womb. It was represented as a unitary counterpart to the male penis, a 'sheath' into which the 'sword' was made to fit. Medical texts usually mentioned a

33 Anatomical treatises which included the reproductive system had been translated into Chinese in the second half of the nineteenth century. Benjamin Hobson, who opened a hospital in Canton in 1848, compiled a series entitled *Chinese textbooks on medical subjects* from various well-known English works. The first volume, published in 1850, was an illustrated outline of anatomy and physiology which also included a short chapter on the reproductive system (Benjamin Hobson and Chen Xiutang, *Quanti xinlun* [Outline of anatomy and physiology], 1850). This book remained a standard work in Chinese for several decades, followed by many editions and reprints. A reprint of Shen Youpeng's eighteenth-century treatise on gynaecology in 1850 included an appendix on 'Various Western Theories' based on Benjamin Hobson: see Shen Yaopeng (*zi* Yaofeng), *Nüke jiyao* (Essentials of gynaecology), orig. 1764, 1850 edn, first *juan*, pp. 60–1. Other treatises on human anatomy were published after the abolition of the traditional examination system in 1904–5, for instance Dezhenzigu (D.W. Osgood), *Quanti tongkao* (Anatomy), 1886 and Ke Weiliang (J.G. Kerr), *Quanti chanwei* (Treatise on anatomy of the complete body), 1906.

34 On the womb as a factory, see Emily Martin, *The woman in the body: A cultural analysis of reproduction*, Milton Keynes: Open University Press, 1987, pp. 44 ff.

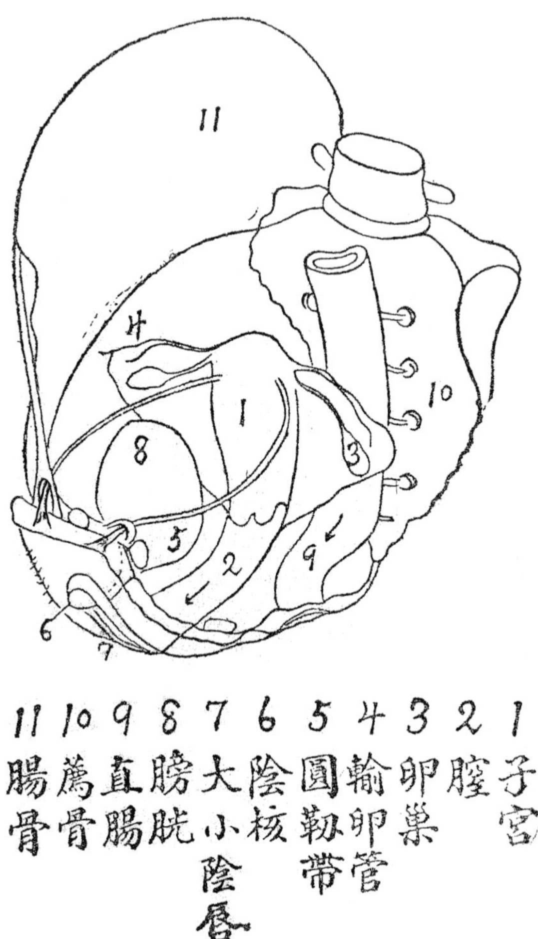

1. A mechanized representation of the female reproductive system. Su Yizhen, *Funü shengyu lun* (About women bearing children), Shanghai: Zhonghua shuju, 1922.

'female duct' (*yindao* or *zihu*), and the vagina was seen simply as a passage from the uterus to the external parts, a channel through which fluids had to transit, a part of the machinery which was often thought to be devoid of sensitivity. Biomedical texts also continued to emphasize the bewildering amount of folds, wrinkles, protuberances and bulges of the female reproductive organs: despite increased anatomical understanding, the geography of the female organs remained 'complicated', 'complex', 'difficult to understand' or even 'mysterious': there were many things which a male 'could not understand', a *Sex education for youth* (1939) claimed.[35]

THE SEXUALIZATION OF THE HUMAN BODY

The new conjugal relationship which was established by modernizing discourses implied complementarity between husband and wife: human anatomy was claimed to sanction the new division of duties in which man was the brain, the worker in the public domain, and woman was the womb, the wife and mother of the private sphere. New anatomical drawings, spread by the printing industry in the big cities, for instance made the female skeleton look smaller and more frail (illustration 2). Drawings exaggerated the size of the pelvic bone, identifying it as a biological marker which assigned women a primary responsibility over reproduction.[36] The size of her skull also appeared to be proportionally smaller, as if man only had been designed for the higher functions of the intellect.

Drawing on a variety of theories from evolutionary biology and human genetics, many writers imagined men and women to be two complementary extremes of a neuter body. Textbooks on embryology underlined that the female features gradually atrophied and degenerated in the male embryo, whereas the

35 Wang, *Qingchun*, p. 147.

36 Londa Schiebinger, 'Skeletons in the closet: The first illustrations of the female skeleton in nineteenth-century anatomy', *Representations*, 14, no. 2 (Spring 1986), pp. 42–82.

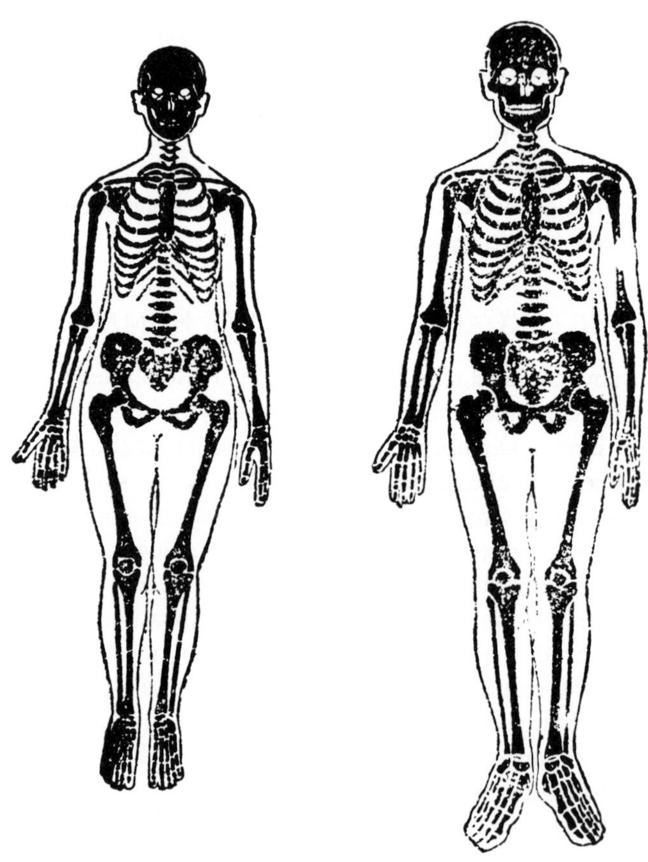

2. New representations of the body spread by the print culture of Republican China made the female skeleton look more fragile compared to that of the male. Chen Yucang, *Renti de yanjiu* (Research on the human body), Shanghai: Zhengzhong shuju, 1937.

outer male organ disappeared in the female embryo. The emphasis on a shared embryological development even led a number of writers to claim that the male foetus was also initially endowed with breasts. A sign of arrested development, they were though to have 'degenerated' (*tuihua*) during the last month in the womb. Much as the human foetus had evolved out of an apish embryo, the male transcended the female in the last stage of growth, wrote Chen Yucang in his popular *Life and physiology*.[37] In line with the theory of recapitulation, which held that embryological growth passed through the earlier stages of evolution, analogies were thus established between the woman and the infant: 'The shape of woman resembles a child. The original physical characteristics of the child are a long torso, short legs and abundant fat. The torso of man is short, his legs are long and his muscles are developed.'[38] Children and women were pictured as the vessels of evolutionary traits which had disappeared with 'modern man'. The repository of a lost phylogeny, woman was a man not fully evolved.

In a very different vein, the theory of neoteny (the retention of juvenile features in adult form) was appropriated by some writers to portray woman as the representative of a perfect stage of evolution: the male had degenerated after childhood, similar to the gorilla who developed bestial features only with pubertal growth. Purity was enshrined in womanhood, while decline was thought to set in with the development of male sexual characteristics.[39] Despite an emphasis on gender hierarchy, a variety of evolutionary theories were thus deployed in efforts to establish a continuity between male and female bodies.

Gender differences were also claimed to be contained in the blood, described as more 'watery' in women, who suffered from a smaller quantity of red corpuscles. The embodiment of activity

37 Chen Yucang, *Shenghuo yu shengli* (Life and physiology), Taibei: Zhengzhong shuju, 1958, pp. 208–9.

38 Li Baoliang, *Xing de zhishi* (Sex knowledge), Shanghai: Zhonghua shuju, 1937, p. 41.

39 Zhang Ziping, *Renlei jinhualun* (The theory of human evolution), Shanghai: Shangwu yinshuguan, 1930, p. 43.

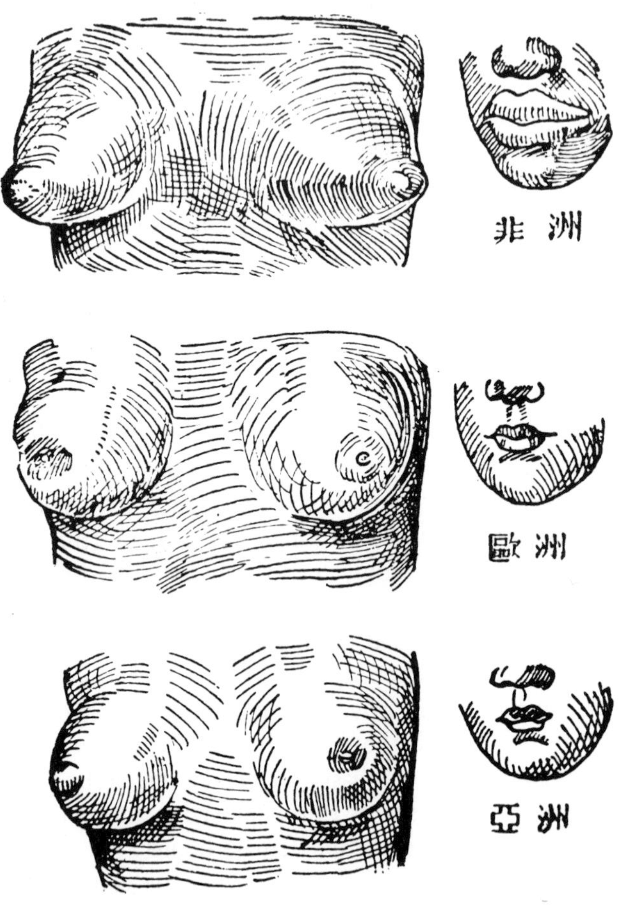

3. Breasts became a favourite object of speculation in the modern constructions of 'race' and 'sex'. This illustration comes from a popular book on human physiology last reprinted in 1965 and still widely available in public libraries in Taiwan. The 'black race' was described as having breasts with protruding nipples, so that the baby had to hold the whole teat in its

mouth. The big and thick lips of the black baby were shaped during the time of suckling. The 'white race' had mammary glands with inverted nipples, leading to the tight lips characteristic of the European: 'Generally, civilized people have thinner lips than savage races. Africans have particularly thick lips.' Only the Chinese people approached perfection: their elegantly shaped chests and beautiful lips were the source of a noble language and a brilliant civilization. Handicapped by thick lips, the African could only speak a language characterized by clicking and flat sounds. Europeans spoke languages equally rich in consonants and vowels, 'hence we know that the shape of the mother's breast not merely exerts a tremendous influence upon the type of language a race speaks and the pronunciation of each individual, but also on the whole of life.' Such illustrations promoted three core beliefs of modernity: (1) mankind could be divided into a small number of biologically distinct groups which were unequally endowed; (2) the reproductive organs were one of the most important parts of individual bodies; (3) biology determined culture. Chen Yucang, *Renti de yanjiu* (Research on the human body), Shanghai: Zhengzhong shuju, 1937.

and creativity, men were fuelled by a redder type of blood with a higher specific gravity. In their representation of woman as the passive and weaker counterpart to man, many medical texts insisted that she had only 4,500,000 red corpuscles per square millimetre as against 5,000,000 in men, a magic figure which even appeared in more sophisticated university textbooks such as Dai Qiling's *General physiology* (1931).[40]

If scholarly endeavours to quantify memory remained relatively rare in late imperial China, the measurement of cranial capacity and the sexualization of the brain became important tendencies among prominent intellectuals and more popular writers in Republican China. Selectively appropriating theories in craniology, which had flourished in Europe after 1860, the intelligence of women was frequently claimed to be inferior to that of men.[41] Differences in intelligence between male and female infants, Chen Jianshan casually observed in his *The evolution of the human brain* (1947), gradually increased after the age of four to become incommensurable at puberty. The male brain continued to increase in size until the age of forty, but the female one had a tendency to decrease in volume until it reached a low point at fifty-four. Motherhood, it was boldly asserted, diverted resources to other parts of the body: 'After the onset of puberty, the heavy burden of reproduction takes its toll on the physical strength of women, and their cranial capacity inevitably tends to decline.'[42] Jiang Xiangqing (1899–1981), head of the Physical Education Department at various institutes of higher education like Fudan University, Central University and Dongyang University, also identified the brain as a biological feature which assigned a responsibility to women over reproduction. In his popular introduction to the 'science of body measurements', he

40 Dai Qiling, *Shenglixue dayi* (General physiology), Shanghai: Shangwu yinshuguan, 1931, p. 9.

41 Elisabeth Fee, 'Nineteenth-century craniology: The study of the female skull', *Bulletin of the History of Medicine*, 53, no. 3 (1979), pp. 415–33.

42 Chen Jianshan, *Renlei naosui zhi jinhua* (The evolution of the human brain), Shanghai: Zhengzhong shuju, 1947, p. 88.

drew on popular representations of the female body as a vessel which conserved fat to nurture offspring. Jiang Xiangqing, who was to become deputy president of the Shanghai Sports Training School in communist China, thus discerned an inverted relationship between 'intelligence' and 'weight' in women, since the heavier ones were also the least brainy.[43] Female bodies, it seemed, 'naturally' channelled energy away from the brain towards the reproductive function.

The hypothesis of male genius and female mediocrity, widespread in European scientific literature until the 1920s,[44] was very popular with modernizing writers in the early Republic. Hereditary variability, it was sometimes argued, was greater in men than in women: frontiers of idiocy and genius were crossed by men alone, and women remained confined to the regions of mediocrity. Excellence could only be achieved by the male organism, the spearhead of evolution and progressive energy; the female mind was conservative. Similar to the position of her reproductive organs in relation to her body, the woman was depicted as a more balanced organism. Gu Shi observed: 'It is common to say that women are inferior to men, but this is a great mistake. The ways in which men and women differ from each other are grounded in their particular evolutionary functions. From a physiological point of view, there can be no question of superiority or inferiority. Man is inclined to consume his energy easily whereas woman conserves it. Hence the body of man has been shaped for movement, whereas that of woman is made for reproduction. Man is dominated by action, woman by patience. Man has a tendency to go to extremes: he can become a genius, a psychotic or a moron. Women are generally more constant and are not subject to extreme changes. These are due to the structural differences which exist between male and

43 Jiang Xiangqing, *Renti celiangxue* (The science of body measurements), Shanghai: Qinfen shuju, 1935, pp. 97–8 and 130–1.

44 Stephanie A. Shields, 'The variability hypothesis: The history of a biological model of sex differences in intelligence', *Signs: Journal of Women and Culture in Society*, no. 7 (1982).

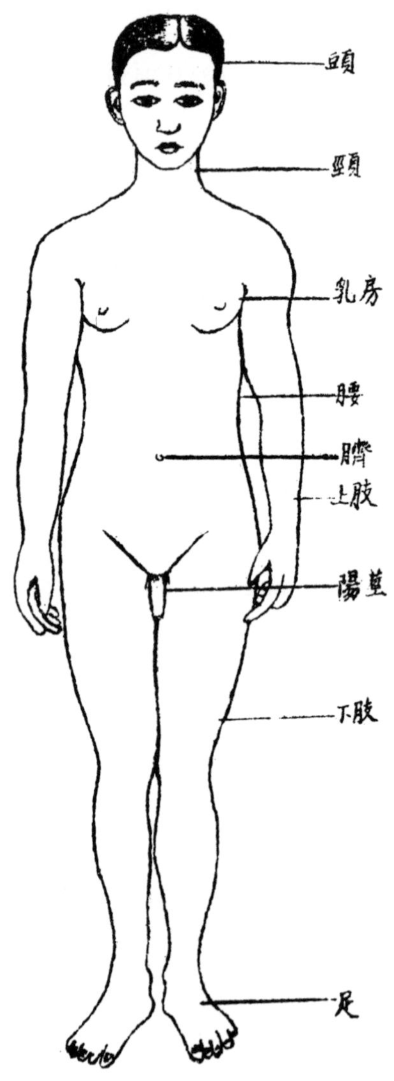

4. Male and female bodies. Chen Yucang, *Renti de yanjiu* (Research on the human body), Shanghai: Zhengzhong shuju, 1937.

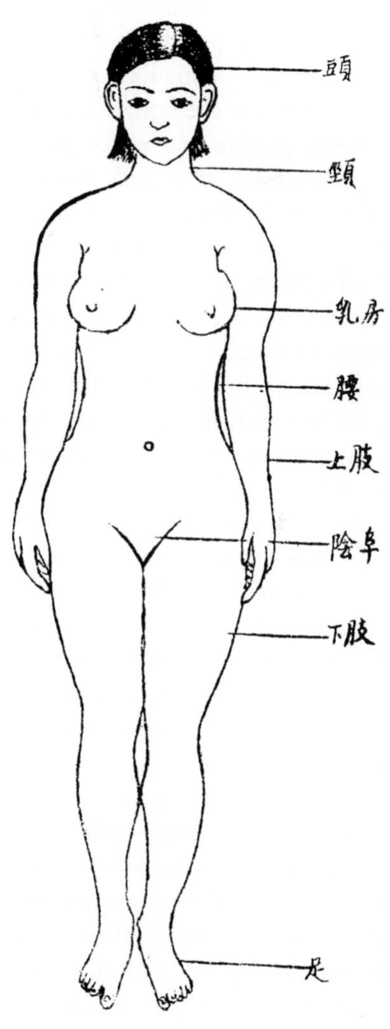
頭
頸
乳房
腰
上肢
陰阜
下肢
足

female.'[45] Gu Shi, author of *Man may live two hundred years* (1916), which was published in its sixth edition in 1929 by the popular Commercial Press, also thought that gender differences could somehow be compared to the boundaries separating animals from vegetables. Man, like animal, was an active consumer of energy, whereas the female was more like a vegetable: inert, unconscious, passive and nurturing. Different biological endowments predestined men and women to fulfil different social roles. New gender distinctions, based on presumed biological characteristics, thus established a conjugal relationship in which both husband and wife were theoretically complementary partners, although women were assigned responsibility only over the spheres of domesticity and reproduction.

Other examples can be found in the work of Zhou Jianren (1888–1984), the brother of the famous writer Lu Xun. A professor of human biology in various universities in Republican China, he is still remembered in the People's Republic as a staunch defender of women's rights (he joined the communists in 1948 and became governor of Zhejiang Province at the end of his life).[46] As the science editor of the Commercial Press in Shanghai, moreover, Zhou Jianren occupied a key position to exert influence over the new print culture of Republican China. Actively responding to the requests of a new public of consumers, he was personally responsible for the publication of dozens of books on human sexuality and reproduction. Zhou Jianren made the relationship between his political commitment to the emancipation of women and his scholarly interest in human biology clear: like other self-proclaimed feminists in the early Republic, he believed that gender differences were rooted in an immutable organic constitution which had to be investigated. Different biological endowments between man and woman, science was claimed to demonstrate, resulted in com-

45 Gu Shi, *Rensheng erbainian* (Man may live two hundred years), Shanghai: Shangwu yinshuguan, 1929 (1st edn 1916), pp. 132–3.
46 Xie Dexian, *Zhou Jianren pingzhuan* (A critical biography of Zhou Jianren), Chongqing: Chongqing chubanshe, 1991.

plementary social roles: 'Physiologists tell us that women's pulmonary capacity is relatively small, their blood gravity is relatively small, their red blood vessels [*sic*] are relatively thin. Yet their production of fresh blood is stronger than that of men, and stored fat is also more abundant in comparison to men. These differences are very interesting. The lungs are the organ of respiration, whereas the red corpuscles transport the nutrient energy of life [*yangqi*, a concept derived from traditional medicine]. If the pulmonary capacity is small, the nutrient energy which is conveyed into the body through respiration will be small; if the red corpuscles are thin, the energy transported will be small. This not only indicates that combustion is not vigorous, and unfit for strenuous physical exercise, but proves that slow combustion has a negative effect on metabolism. As the production of blood is stronger in women and the body is apt to accumulate fat, it becomes clear that the structural functions of the female are vigorous and stand in contrast to the male, who has vigorous disruptive functions. In conclusion, the man is relatively lively, whereas the female is relatively obtuse [*chidun*]; these characteristics are comparable to the differences which exist between sperm and ovum.'[47] Almost half a century after the publication of *The evolution of sex* (1889) by Patrick Geddes and J. Arthur Thomson,[48] the discredited theory of 'anabolic' and 'katabolic' gender differences was thus popular with some of the most influential popularizers of science in China. As a justification for the division of responsibilities in the new conjugal relationship, masculinity and femininity were polarized into complementary and mutually dependent roles. Symbol of the passive and receptive female, the ovum was produced by quiescent and well-nourished anabolic cells: described as 'motionless' (*jingzhi bu dong*), it held in store the nutrients for the embryo. The sperm, on the contrary, was the expression

47 Zhou Jianren, *Xingjiaoyu* (Sex education), Shanghai: Shangwu yinshuguan, 1931, p. 48.
48 See Cynthia E. Russett, *Sexual science: The Victorian construction of womanhood*, Cambridge, MA: Harvard University Press, 1989, pp. 89–102.

of the small and active katabolic cell, symbol of the active male. Prescriptions for social order, in other words, were thought to have been discovered at the level of the cell.

METAPHORS OF FEMALE PATHOLOGY: MENSTRUATION AND MENOPAUSE

Traditional medical theories in China represented male and female bodies as structurally similar. Bodies were all structured around a certain number of meridians (*jingluo*) through which vital energy (*qi*) and blood (*xue*) circulated, contained a system of solid and hollow organs (*zangfu*) and were based on the interdependence of *yin* and *yang*. Male and female bodies were correlated to a higher order in medical theory and were thought to be controlled to a large extent by cosmological forces. Physiological processes like menstruation and lactation, moreover, were considered part of a common economy of humours as between male and female. Despite an emphasis on similarities between male and female bodies, gynaecological works (*fuke*) from the tenth century onwards gradually started emphasizing that blood defined female difference.[49] Menstrual disorders were elaborated on the basis of *yin* and *yang* categories, and menstruation, represented as a key to health and fertility, became a central concern of gynaecology. Medical theory also increasingly focused on the inner workings of bodies to the detriment of external influences from the environment or the cosmos, in particular after the sixteenth century. Although it is difficult to make generalizations on the basis of a few gynaecological treatises only, it seems probable that female blood was increasingly identified as the bodily sign of female generative power, as Charlotte

49 Charlotte Furth, 'Blood, body and gender: Medical images of the female condition in China, 1600–1850', *Chinese Science*, 7 (Dec. 1986), pp. 43–66; Charlotte Furth, 'Talk on Ming-Qing medicine and the construction of gender', paper presented at the Institute of History and Philosophy, Taibei, 26 November 1992; see also Angela K. Leung, 'Autour de la naissance. La mère et l'enfant en Chine aux XVIe et XVIIe siècles', *Cahiers Internationaux de Sociologie*, 76 (Jan.–June 1984), pp. 51–70.

Furth has suggested. 'When woman starts her period', wrote Li Shizhen (1518–1593) in his famous sixteenth-century treatise, 'her evil juices are full of stench and filth, hence the gentleman should keep his distance; as they are not clean, they will harm his male essence and invite disease'.[50] Although Li Shizhen was warning his reader against the use of menstrual blood as a medicine, its image as a filthy substance to be avoided was very powerful. Gynaecological texts of the Qing period related these images to representations of female weakness. Our understanding of the emergence and development of gynaecology from the tenth to the nineteenth century, however, remains diffuse and inconclusive. The current state of the field, moreover, does not allow the historian to make any meaningful comparisons between Ming, Qing and Republican China.

The gynaecological treatises, outlines of obstetrics and other self-help books on sexual hygiene produced by the new publishing houses after the fall of the empire represented menstruation as a pathological process which symbolized female weakness. Physiological cyclicity indicated female instability. The bleeding female, it was claimed, quickly became tired and irritable, was easily excited and might withdraw into a state of depression, only to suddenly come out of it and wander about in high spirits. The swelling of the thyroid gland was sometimes seen to be responsible for the 'agitated mood' of the menstruating female.[51] Mental instability also fuelled social unrest. Cesare Lombroso (1836–1909), the Italian founder of criminology who developed a theory of female criminality, was popular in Republican China, and special studies dedicated to the relationship between sex and crime, based on the assumption that women were ruled by emotions and suffered from an inferior intelligence, continued to appear even after the Second World War.[52] Drawing on the

50 Li Shizhen, *Bencao gangmu* (Compendium of materia medica), Beijing: Renmin weisheng chubanshe, 1981.
51 Zhang Qiutao, *Qingnian jiankang zhidao* (Health guide for youth), Shanghai: Dadong shuju, 1933, p. 97.
52 Zhou Guangqi, *Xing yu fanzui* (Sex and crime), Shanghai: Zhengzhong shuju, 1946, p. 40 in particular.

theory of recapitulation, menstruation was thought to bring out the darker tendencies of female nature. Loss of blood threw the woman back to more primitive levels of biological development, giving scope to the hidden forces of evil. A woman who was 'normally' shy and submissive 'committed ruthless and harsh crimes'. The faithful wife started to lie or steal without any shame. Under a veneer of civilization lay a wasteland of brute instincts, which could suddenly emerge to disrupt social order: 'I have seen many women who suffer from mental disorders. These disorders emerge in an extreme form during menstruation, hence even if it is a disease, normal women also have this tendency, which simply becomes more apparent in those who are diseased.'[53]

Although some guides to sexual hygiene indicated that the tip of the womb would open widely when a woman had her period and would facilitate fertilization, most modernizing discourses proscribed sexual union during menstruation and underlined the pathological consequences of any transgression: the reproductive organs were fragile, the womb became replete with toxic blood, and the penis could become infected. Even the iconoclast Zhang Jingsheng, who was usually quite outspoken about gender equality, thought that the prohibition against intercourse during menstruation was justified. He judged the period of menstruation to be 'unaesthetic' and 'devoid of interest'.[54] Although it is difficult to assess the extent to which sexual practices were affected by modernizing discourses, readers' letters tend to confirm that notions of sexual hygiene had an actual impact, as the following question from a reader demonstrates: 'Now there is one thing I would like to ask you, in the hope that you will be able to answer me. When the woman has her period, can man and woman kiss? It is said that this is not hygienic, is that true?'[55]

53 Cao Guanlai, *Qingchun shengli tan* (Chats about the physiology of youth), Taibei: Zhengzhong shuju, 1982 (1st edn 1936).
54 Zhang Jingsheng (Chang Ching-sheng), *Sex histories: China's first modern treatise on sex education*, tr. by H.S. Levy, Yokohama: Levy, 1967, p. 99.
55 'Tongxun' (Letters from readers), *Xinwenhua*, 1, no. 2 (Feb. 1927), p. 112.

The representation of menstruation as a pathological process contributed to claims about female emancipation being confined to the domains of reproduction and domesticity. Instead of a social relationship of absolute superiority and inferiority, conjugal harmony was described as a natural relationship of relative complementarity. Women were thought to contribute in equal measure to marital stability and were given a special responsibility over the domain of reproduction. A flourishing literature of advice stressed personal discipline and restraint, since health was thought to be determined by the individual's own actions, not by higher forces beyond individual control. Notions of bodily resistance and weakness became important, and the use of soap, warm water and daily baths was increasingly prescribed. At the time of their periods, women were advised to follow a balanced diet and to eliminate faeces regularly in order to avoid 'obstruction' (*zhang'ai*). The concepts of expulsion of menstrual blood by the female (*paichi, paishui*) and expulsion of semen by the male (*paijing*) were sometimes constructed in symmetry. Expulsion became a key term in the description of bodily functions: in modern terminology, the ovaries 'expelled the egg' (*pailuan*, ovulation), the urinary duct 'expelled urine' (*painiao*, urination) and the bowels 'expelled dung' (*paifen*, excretion); 'to drain' or 'to excrete' was one and the same movement (*paixie*). Mechanical metaphors of expulsion promoted a clearer delineation of the boundaries of the body and an increased sense of personhood: the egg was 'expelled outside of the body' (*paichu yu shenti zhi wai*) or 'expelled to the outside' (*paichu yu tiwai*). Failure to monitor one's bodily fluids individually had medical consequences which were depicted in stark biological terms. Leucorrhoea corrupted the flesh (*fulan*) and gave off an evil stench (*echou*), a *Home medicine* (1930) in its eighth edition underlined.[56] After a few weeks, it would cause the skin to turn pallid, the digestive system to falter and the body to wither away. Reminiscent of the seventeenth-century medical work of Fu Shan (1607–84)

56 Chen Jiwu, *Jiating yixue* (Home medicine), Shanghai: Shangwu yinshuguan, 1930 (1st edn 1915), p. 220.

which distinguished between white, green, yellow, black and red vaginal discharges,[57] some modernizing manuals evoked the different tints of fluids which could leak out of an unregulated organism.[58] In the imperial period, however, the five discharges were correlated to the five phases and the disorders of the five organs; in the Republican era, the existence of pathological fluids was more indicative of a lack of self-control. Medical representations of menstruation, in other words, not only contributed to the cultural construction of women as a weaker gender, but also as relatively autonomous individuals who were given a responsibility over their own bodily secretions for the sake of reproductive health.

A number of publications on sexual hygiene attacked rural beliefs and practices, reflecting a more fundamental change in the relationship between the city as a site of modernity and the countryside as the repository of 'tradition'.[59] It was 'benighted' and 'backward', whereas the city was depicted as 'enlightened' and 'progressive'. 'Civilized' girls used disinfected cotton during menstruation, it was underlined, in contrast to 'peasant' girls who used rough straw paper causing infections. The alien sensibility of 'peasants' (*nongmin*, a new term), represented as an amorphous and undifferentiated category, was stressed in order to highlight the 'progressive' worldview of the coastal cities. The cover of one popular *Hygiene for women* (1933), which castigated the peasants' use of straw, represented a high-heeled girl in modern dress against a background of tower blocks glowing in the night (see illustration 5).[60] It was edited by the 'Research Committee for the Education of the Common People'; mean-

57 Fu Shan, *Fu Qingzhu nüke* (Fu Shan's gynaecology), Shanghai: Shanghai kexue jishu chubanshe, 1991, pp. 1–6 (orig. 1827).
58 Zhu Kongzhao, *Funü weisheng* (Hygiene for women), Shanghai: Shijie shuju, 1933, p. 46.
59 Myron L. Cohen, 'Cultural and political inventions in modern China: The case of the Chinese "peasant"', *Daedalus*, 122, no. 2 (1993), pp. 151–70; see also Charles W. Hayford, *To the people: James Yen and village China*, New York: Columbia University Press, 1990.
60 Zhu, *Funü weisheng*, p. 14.

5. Cover of a popular *Hygiene for women* (1933) with a girl posing against a modernist urban scene with glowing skyscrapers. Zhu Kongzhao, *Funü weisheng* (Hygiene for women), Shanghai: Shijie shuju, 1933.

while, reprints of gynaecological manuals from the Qing dynasty, printed by the Buddhist Philosophy Press in Shanghai, continued to cater to a wide audience.[61]

Medical discourses also represented menopause as a pathological and degenerative process. Ovulation was generally thought to cease between the ages of forty and forty-five, the beginning of the 'period of old age' (*laonian shidai*), but nature could retract its mandate at any time: writers pointed to cases of premature menopause striking at the age of thirty, while some women continued to menstruate into their eighties. Popular newspapers continued to bring marvellous cases to the attention of the public, very much in the tradition of the official records which carefully noted all extraordinary events for posterity: in 1934, a woman aged seventy gave birth to twins, according to one newspaper, and a Singapore daily proudly announced that Xu Tianlang was finally ready to give birth after a pregnancy of seventy-five years.[62] The medicalization of menopause, however, dominated publications produced for city people by the new print culture. The 'first omen of decline',[63] it was interpreted as the exact reversal of puberty: pubic hair became 'rare', the clitoris 'degenerated' or 'receded', the vagina 'slackened', the uterus 'retracted' and the breasts 'shrivelled' or 'shrank'. The deregulated body could suffer from thin blood and would start hoarding fat tissues in compensation, leading to a pathological state of obesity (*feipangbing*). Memory declined until amnesia set in. The aged woman was singled out as an object of fear, and Chen

61 For instance *Dashengbian* (Obstetrics), Shanghai: Foxue shuju, 1934 (orig. 1715).

62 'Shengli qitan – qishi lao'ou luansheng erzi' (Strange tales of physiology – old woman gives birth to two sons at age seventy), *Dagongbao*, 2 April 1934, 2:5; 'Heyuan liushisi sui lao'ou Deng Chen shi chan zi' (Old lady Deng born Chen from Heyuan gives birth to a son at the age of sixty-four), *Xianggang gongshang*, 3 May 1936, 2:4; 'Yibailingqi sui lao Huafu Xu Tianlang huaiyun qishiwu nian jin shi yu chan' (Old Chinese woman aged one hundred and five pregnant for seventy-five years and about to give birth), *Xingzhou ribao*, 30 March 1936, 2:5.

63 Zhuang Weizhong, *Jiankangshu wenda* (Questions and answers on the art of health), Shanghai: Dahua shuju, 1934, p. 165.

Jianshan even observed in his *Evolution of the human brain* (1947) that 'at the age of sixty, the brains of old women can again increase in weight, which is indeed a most incomprehensible phenomenon'.[64] Similar to the menstruating girl, 'the spirit becomes sluggish and obtuse, and irregular behaviour can occur, such as lying, cheating and irrational swearing'. The idea of menopausal madness or 'involutional melancholy', which gained some currency in nineteenth-century Europe, also appeared in Republican China: 'Her mind gets easily agitated, the face reddens, becomes congested with blood and breaks into a sweat; some even faint, and children should look after post-menopausal women with particular care.'[65] Arrested development, or the idea of a biological reversion to a previous level of evolution, became a popular way of explaining senescence. On the threshold of death, the old woman was thought to return to the mental stage of the child.

Medical texts endowed post-menopausal women with a sexuality which was thought to be irresistible and dangerous. Sexual deprivation caused 'old girls' (*laonü*) to become bitter, jealous and intolerant. Spinsters never had the opportunity to absorb the invigorating male secretions which were so vital in enhancing health and prolonging life. They were thought to suffer frequently from 'neurasthenia' and 'anaemia', much as their pallid faces were traditionally explained to be due to a functional disharmony between *yin* and *yang*. 'This explanation is wrong', corrected Wang Chengpin, specifically writing about aged women, 'as those who have sunk to this condition have recourse to unnatural practices when they are unhappy in their sex lives, or indulge excessively in imagination, trying to picture obscene postures in order to satisfy their lecherous desires.'[66] According to an *ABC of sexology*, the 'sex centre' (*seqing zhongshu*), thought to be part of the nervous system, could subsist in some old

64 Chen, *Renlei naosui*, p. 88.
65 Guo Renji and Li Renlin, *Nüxing yangsheng jian* (Mirror of health for women), Shanghai: Shangwu yinshuguan, 1928 (1st edn 1922), p. 95.
66 Wang, *Qingchun*, p. 114.

women, who would 'imagine sexual life'.[67] Lower levels of culture also stressed the perverted nature of aged women, and an article in a Beijing daily paper, to take only one example, reported how an aged widow had given birth to a loaf of flesh suspiciously shaped 'like a bottle gourd'[68] (the *Medicine for the bedchamber*, on the other hand, noted how middle-aged women used vegetables and strange objects to satisfy their desires).[69] Sexuality, with its secret fantasies and dangerous excesses, was represented as the very essence of individual identity by these discourses, and their target extended to post-menopausal women.

THE MEDICAL DISCOURSE OF HYSTERIA

The sexualization of the female body in biologizing discourses was particularly prominent in medical concepts of hysteria,[70]

67 Chai Fuyuan, *Xingxue ABC* (ABC of sexology), Shanghai: Shijie shuju, 1928, p. 46.
68 'Shaoxing yi laoshuang chansheng huluxing rouqiu' (Old widow from Shaoxing gives birth to flesh loaf shaped like bottle gourd), *Beiping chenbao*, 5 June 1935, p. 3.
69 Gu, *Fangzhong yi*, p. 167.
70 The special term *ji*, invented by a team of Western doctors in 1904 for 'hysteria', never appeared in medical texts, a testimony to the degree of cultural independence of modernizing writers in Republican China (see P.B. Cousland, *An English-Chinese lexicon of medical terms compiled for the terminology committee*, Shanghai: Medical Missionary Association, 1908, p. 173). A number of medical writers in the Republican period, on the other hand, claimed that traditional medicine in China had an equivalent to hysteria called 'visceral unrest' (*zangzao*) or 'running pig' (*bentunqi*). Described as a paroxysmal state of distress due to deficiency of heart- and liver-blood and mental depression, *zangzao* was said to be characterized by loss of control over behaviour and emotions. For these medical experts, the term *xiesidiliya*, a transliteration of 'hysteria', was no more than a 'modern alternative name' (*jindai biecheng*) for *zangzao*. Were these nationalist writers entirely inventing a tradition in order to legitimize the appropriation of a foreign medical concept, or, like the savants of the European enlightenment, were they forging new names for conventional symptomatologies? The prevalent opinion among experts on the history of *fuke* seems to be that *zangzao* as a nosological category did not exist in any ancient or modern text of Chinese medicine: it would be no more than a twentieth-century invention. However, the classic

of medicine *Jinkui yaolüe fanglun* (Synopsis of prescriptions of the golden chamber), an important text which contained special sections on gynaecology and obstetrics, clearly discussed both *zangzao* and *bentunqi* (see *Zhongguo yixue da cidian* [Encyclopedia of Chinese medicine]), Shanghai: Shangwu yinshuguan, 1921, vol. 2, p. 4383). It would be far-fetched, of course, to hypothesize that an ancient text written in the Eastern Han period (25 to 220 AD) could have exerted any kind of influence on medical terminology in the twentieth century. More directly relevant to our purposes, however, is the fact that at least a dozen commentaries appeared on this ancient text during the seventeenth and eighteenth centuries, many written by medical writers from the Jiangnan region. As part of cultural reorientations which permanently shattered the foundations of orthodox Cheng-Zhu Confucianism – notably evidential scholarship (*kaozhengxue*) and a movement in favour of a return to antiquity (*fugu*) – these commentaries were critical of medical theories which had flourished since the Song. Some commentators on the *Jinkui*, such as Xu Bin's *Jinkui yaolüe lunzhu* (Annotated comments on the Golden Chamber, orig. 1671), were influenced by Yu Chang (about 1585–1664), a well-known practitioner from Jiangsu province who openly attacked the teachings of the old masters and reinterpreted the classics. Shen Mingzong (*zi* Munan) added his own observations on *zangzao* in his *Jinkui yaolüe benyi* (The basic meaning of the Golden Chamber), explaining that it was caused by blood-deficiency of the uterine cavity. His comments were incorporated in the *Jinkui yaolüe xindian* by You Yi (d. 1749), a work which was highly praised by Xu Dachun, a notorious scholar of Han learning from Jiangsu province who criticized the medical works published since the Song dynasty and favoured a return to the most ancient medical texts in order to reconstruct the classical tradition (You Yi, *Jinkui yaolüe xindian* [Commentaries on the Golden Chamber], orig. 1726, reprint 1881, *juan* 3:60ab). *Zangzao*, in other words, was a common nosological category for medical writers of Han learning in late imperial China.

Of even greater interest is the observation that a number of nineteenth-century commentators – for example, Tang Zonghai's *Jinkui yaolüe qianzhu buzheng*, published in 1893 – explicitly attempted to combine Western and Chinese medicine (Wang Jintao (ed.), *Zhongguo yiji tiyao* [Essential of Chinese books on medicine], Changchun: Jilin kexue jishu chubanshe, 1984, vol. 1, pp. 245–6). The meanings assigned to the concepts of hysteria and *zangzao*, of course, have changed considerably over time and space, and it would be absurd to assume that a traditional disorder corresponds one to one to a modern disease. Nonetheless, this examples illustrates the hypothesis, formulated in the introduction to this book, that important cultural reorientations in the late imperial period may have made the appropriation of foreign medical notions in modern China significantly easier: it also shows how much more thorough work remains to be done in the field of gynaecology in particular and medicine in late imperial China in general before meaningful comparisons with the twentieth century can be attempted.

thought to be a hereditary disease which found expression between the age of fifteen and twenty-five. The diagnosis was wide enough to incorporate all sexual deviations thought to be peculiar to the female gender. Unlike some psychiatric discourses in Europe,[71] writers in Republican China did not identify nymphomania and erotomania separately: all were pathological phenomena classified under the label of hysteria. 'The characteristics of this disease [called *zangzaozheng*] are neuroticism, violent affectional changes, emotional instability, a tendency to be jealous, frequent depressions, a poor memory, excessive apprehension, readiness to hold superstitious beliefs and deliberate exaggerations', claimed an *Elementary knowledge of female hygiene* (1935).[72] Hysteria became a catch-all for irregular female behaviour. The hysterical woman lacked self-control and often indulged in improper thoughts or wild fancies. Like the menstruating girl or the post-menopausal woman, she was inclined towards crime, wandering about in a state of altered consciousness. 'Her sense of self-restraint is weak and she often harbours vain thoughts', wrote Cao Guanlai in a popular book still displayed in some public libraries in Taiwan and Hong Kong, 'hence she easily commits crimes; she will offend the law with cruel criminal acts while she is in a state of somnolence. The changes are particularly acute when she has her periods or when she is pregnant, so one should be especially vigilant.'[73] Like a number of other publications referred to in this chapter, Cao Guanlai's *Chats about the physiology of youth* was published by the Zhengzhong shuju, the biggest official publishing house

71 For historical surveys of shifting conceptions of hysteria in Europe, see Étienne Trillat, *Histoire de l'hystérie*, Paris: Seghers, 1986; Gladys Swain, 'L'âme, la femme et le corps. Les métamorphoses de l'hystérie à la fin du XIXe siècle', *Le Débat*, no. 24, March 1983; see also Mark S. Micale, 'Hysteria and its historiography: A review of past and present writings', 2 parts, *History of Science*, 27 (1989), pp. 223–61 and 319–51.

72 Su Yizhen, *Nüxing weisheng changshi* (Elementary knowledge of female hygiene), Shanghai: Zhonghua shuju, 1941, (1st edn 1935), p. 42.

73 Cao Guanlai, *Qingchun shengli tan* (Chats about the physiology of youth), Taibei: Zhengzhong shuju, 1982 (1st edn 1936), p. 60.

under the control of the Propaganda Department of the Guomindang. Books published by the Commercial Press, which retained its independence from government control until 1941,[74] equally focused on female hysteria. Cheng Hao's gynaecological textbook, for instance, claimed that her system was deregulated and she could become hypersensitive, particularly in the ovaries and the womb. On the other hand, the private parts could suffer from numbness and insensitivity. Structural extremities like the head and the 'tail' (*sic*) also endured intermittent waves of pain, while the hysteriac could engage in frenzied sex only to become withdrawn and passive the next moment.[75] Hysteria was represented as a 'women's disease': heralded as a sign of civilization; journals like the *Ladies' Journal* dedicated a number of articles to this 'disease of modernity'.[76]

Similar to representations of menstruation, notions of hysteria were couched in biomedical terms which stressed the physical causes of female pathology. Neurasthenia, the reduction in internal secretions at the end of the menstrual cycle, puerperal psychosis after giving birth and more obscure gynaecological disorders became popular ways of explaining the deregulated woman. Sexual frustration was also seen as a cause of hysteria. The hysterical woman was compared to the unmarried woman and the widow, desperately seeking vivifying semen. Male impotence and premature ejaculation were highlighted in the

74 Jean-Pierre Drège, *La Commercial Press de Shanghai, 1897–1949*, Paris: Presses Universitaires de France, 1978.

75 Cheng Hao, *Fukexue* (Gynaecology), Shanghai: Shangwu yinshuguan, 1950 (9th edn; 1st edn 1939), pp. 183–6.

76 For instance Ye Zuozhou, 'Funü yu xiesidiliya' (Women and hysteria), *Funü zazhi*, no. 10 (Sep. 1927), pp. 8–11; Early publications for women, such as the *Ladies' Journal*, often had a male authorship and readership; see Jacqueline Nivard, 'L'évolution de la presse féminine chinoise de 1898 à 1949', *Études Chinoises*, 5, nos 1–2 (1986), pp. 164 and 176 n. 36; see also Jacqueline Nivard, 'Histoire d'une revue féminine chinoise: Funü zazhi 1915–1931', Paris, EHESS, Ph.D. dissertation, 1983; the management of feminist literature by men is a characteristic which can also be found in eighteenth-century France and Meiji Japan.

pathogenesis of female insanity, a notion which reinforced the idea that women were dependent on male sexuality.

With the rise of the conjugal family model and the bringing of women into a theoretically equal partnership with men, female satisfaction became a cause for medical concern. Dr Zhang Jingsheng wrote: 'It has been my frequent observation that women who were bright and active in their girlish days suddenly lose their vitality when they get married. In middle age considerable numbers of them contract hypochondria and most often the hysteria which is caused by unsatisfied sexual desires.'[77] Lin Yutang (1895–1976), once professor of English literature at Beijing Girls' Normal University, even wondered whether women had really been suppressed in China. Was it not true that 'the primeval urge for motherhood – formless, wordless and vague and strong – fills their whole beings?' There seemed to be no escape from the maternal instinct, as if biology dictated motherhood: 'I have seen selfish, mean little wights blossom forth into gentle, all-loving and self-sacrificing mothers, who are models of perfection and virtue in their children's eyes. I have also seen beautiful girls who do not marry and who shrivel up in their thirties and never reach that second period of woman's beauty, glorious like the autumn forest, more mature, more human, and more radiant, best seen in a happy wife three months after her confinement.'[78] Sexual desire, with its frustrations, deviations and excesses on the one hand and its need for control and regulation on the other, seemed to be the core of female identity in modern China and other secular nations.

FRAIL BRIDES AND WICKED WIVES: THE REGULATION OF MARITAL SEXUALITY

Whether disparaged as a bundle of uncontrolled sexual impulses, or idealized as a vessel of purity and innocence, woman was

77 Chang, *Sex histories*, p. 62.
78 Lin Yutang, *My country and my people*, New York: John Ray, 1935, pp. 140 and 145.

defined through her sexuality. Marriage guides and handbooks of advice for couples all promoted sex as the most central aspect of married life. The wedding night in particular became a ritual in which the woman's personal identity, the control of marital behaviour and the future health of the population were all at stake. Successful defloration would ensure the sexual harmony of the couple and the health of their offspring; failure to discipline desire would lead to infidelity and the irregularity of marital behaviour. Sex educators of the early Republic believed that the 'modern husband' should first be taught the pain felt by his bride during the wedding night. The *Secrets of the Bedchamber* (1938) explained: 'Merely because of this wedding night, many brides develop all kinds of fears which eventually lead to vaginismus, frigidity and other sexual disorders. Hence it is best if the husband is able to exercise self-control, even though the sexual instinct is violent and can hardly be held back. Only a display of gentleness and consideration will convince the kind and pure bride that the husband is warm, loving and full of affection. Her fears will diminish and she will be pleased. A few warm and tender words will fill her heart with joy and arouse her sexual instinct. On the other hand, one should discreetly check whether or not her private parts are in a normal state, for at this stage, although her desire has been aroused, one still cannot drive straight in like a madman. Absolute calm has to be maintained, kisses should be tenderly exchanged and a hand furtively pressed on the breasts to excite her sexual desire to the utmost. The Bartholin's glands will then secrete an abundant fluid which lubricates the vagina and moistens the hymen. If the member is anointed with a little bit of Vaseline in order to smooth the vagina even better, the pain felt at the moment when the penis penetrates the vagina and breaks the hymen can be lessened.'[79] Represented as self-contained machines that could be regulated in the interests of marital harmony, male and female bodies had to be adjusted to each other. Man was gendered as

79 Xu Zheshen, *Xingfang mijue* (Secrets of the bedchamber), Shanghai: Xinxin shudian, 1938, pp. 8–9.

an essential category endowed with a powerful sexual desire which was inherent and uncontrollable. If sexuality was the steam that fuelled human bodies, the husband was the engine-driver in charge of his wife's sexual drives, represented as a passive and responsive counterpart.

New codes of behaviour were also prescribed during the 1920s and '30s: the 'honeymoon' was now thought to impose a tremendous stress on frail brides, and was to be discarded in favour of the prophylactic journey to the countryside. The mountains and the seaside became the privileged places where the 'modern couple' could start their journey of initiation into sex at leisure. Virgin landscapes became the ideal scenes for the ritual of defloration.[80]

Represented as the seal of the female sexual organs, the fragile proof of virginity, the diaphanous partition between the outer world and the inner recesses of the womb, the hymen was to be broken only during the ritual of defloration in imperial China. With the emergence of a new sexual morality constructed around the idea of mutual love in the Republic, the hymen lost much of its symbolic power. Excessive attention paid to the virginal membrane was denounced as a 'superstition': sexual harmony was the aim of monogamous marriage. Zhu Xi (1900–62), a notorious cytologist who obtained his Ph.D. in France and taught at Zhongshan University in the 1930s, was one of the most outspoken opponents of the hymen as a sign of virginity in Republican China. In his detailed physiological analysis of the membrane, supported by illustrations of all the possible forms and shapes it could assume, he dismissed it as a mere hindrance. An 'obstructive object' (*zhang'ai wu*), it could only impede the expulsion of polluted blood during periods, cause infections and lead to 'chlorosis'. Even his attitude remained ambivalent, however, and he still professed his belief that defloration could cure young virgins of anaemia.[81] (The

80 Zhao Shifa, *Geren weishengxue* (Personal hygiene), Shanghai: Nanjing shuju, 1933, p. 198.
81 Zhu Xi, *Danshengren yu renshengdan* (The evolution of sex), Shanghai: Wenhua shenghuo chubanshe, 1939, pp. 195–6.

belief in the power of semen, shared by many other writers, is discussed in chapter 6.) The idea that the female reproductive organs carried the mark of virginity, however, continued to pervade medical texts within more conservative circles. For Shen Yong, virginity was important from the point of view of 'medical science': firm breasts shaped like two little hemispheres, light red nipples, tight rose labia, a narrow vagina and an intact hymen were the key features which betokened the virgin, and all were discussed in minute detail. A sign of woman's purity, virginity contributed to the eroticization of the female body. In a further section, tellingly entitled 'The Physical Beauty of the Virgin', free rein was given to the mystification of virgins, thought to have 'an extraordinary charm' and an 'incomparable beauty'; they were portrayed as the embodiment of tenderness, the 'sweet grass of spring'. After this passionate interlude, the author returned to the more austere tasks of science with a detailed account of hormones.[82] Virginity and female chastity were judged differently by different authors, but all of them contributed to the construction of womanhood through the prism of sexuality. Their lengthy discussions of the hymen sustained the myth that the core of woman's identity resided in her sexuality.

Sexuality was constructed as a powerful and pervasive force, and it was in the interest of the individual to control its dangerous potential. A discourse of discipline supported the idea that sexuality was a mysterious instinct which could engulf the individual who lacked the proper knowledge and power to control and monitor himself. Disentangled from a web of obligations and duties specific to Confucian social ethics, the individual became responsible for a potentially destructive drive called 'sexuality': he was at once liberated from the pressure of social control and given the burden of self-restraint. Similar to the traditional sex handbooks which discussed in great detail the number of times males of varying ages could afford to ejaculate every month, new books on sex education always ordered the

82 Shen, *Xingyuan*, pp. 80–2, 87–93.

frequency of intercourse: twice a week was generally considered normal for young people, and once a week was a limit for people up to the age of forty. The prescription of coital frequency, however, was more than an outgrowth from classical sex handbooks, since normative texts promoted the construction of sexuality as an instinct comparable to food, a natural drive which needed a regular and measured release.

Instead of a capacity which could be used creatively in various ways at different times, sexuality became a dangerous force which demanded strict supervision. Female sexuality was seen as dangerous to men, and too many demands upon the male would lead to the weakening of the nervous system; it would 'dry up the spring of life'.[83] Conservatives advised young people to inhibit their sexual instincts, pointing out their duties with regard to the future of the race: 'If the sexual desire is not curbed, the sexual organs will weaken through wear and tear. This in turn will affect the physical strength of our sons and grandsons, eventually leading to the disappearance of our race.'[84] Too much excitement would wear the fallopian tubes and lead to barrenness, and it was thought that loose women and prostitutes could not have children.[85] Judging from the notes left behind in the margins by concerned readers, these prescriptions were taken very seriously. 'The male must experience spiritual excitement each time in order to copulate, hence he cannot last as long as the female', one popular *Sex knowledge* of the 1930s underscored, while also claiming that 'the brain can easily be flooded with blood during the time of sexual excitement'. Undesirable results of intercourse included sexual neurasthenia, physical decay, anaemia, psychosis, indigestion, respiratory problems and impotence: 'To consider sexual intercourse a means of pleasure is the most harmful and unproduc-

83 Wang, *Qingchun*, p. 97.
84 Jerome Ch'en, *China and the West: Society and culture, 1815–1937*, London: Hutchinson, 1979, p. 388.
85 *Nannü xingbing zhinan* (Guide to venereal diseases), Hong Kong: Xianggang shuju, n.d. (1920s), p. 7.

tive thing under heaven!' was the succinct conclusion of one manual.[86] Even the sex revolutionary Zhang Jingsheng thought that sleeping in separate beds or rooms was desirable in order to lessen the frequency of intercourse.

Sex educators mapped out new sexual itineraries. Within the conjugal family model, orgasm became the symbolic representation of married intimacy, and sexuality was seen as the most fundamental force which could unite two individuals. The more traditional rhetoric of struggle over *yin* and *yang* fluids between male and female was abandoned, since the wife was now seen as a complementary partner. Partners should first engage in 'love talk' before kindling the 'lower instincts' into activity by fondling the breasts and the body. The temperature of the room should be properly preserved. The husband should carefully observe the facial expression of his wife and 'proceed in a calm and unhurried way' in order to achieve climax simultaneously. This kind of 'pleasant feeling' (*kuaigan*) was called 'orgasm' in English, the reader was told (foreign terms, with which literature of advice was littered, lent an aura of scientific authenticity).[87] 'Orgasm' became a 'process' (*chengdu*) which was carefully located within a structure that was both temporal and spatial. The married couple could enter together the 'realm of bliss' (*jiajing*, a classic term in erotic vocabulary), or the 'boundaries' (*jingjie*) of 'orgasm', after which the male would enter the 'realm of sleep' (*shuixiang*). The husband was required to find out the period of female sexual activity and initiate intercourse in response to her sexual 'impulse'. Desire was quantified, and sophisticated graphs charted the progression of both sexes to allow the reader to absorb the need for mutual adjustment.[88] As in traditional manuals, the man was given the responsibility for the management of bodily fluids: he initiated, conducted and

86 Li, *Xing de zhishi*, p. 156.

87 Ru Qiu, 'Kuaigan de shengli' (The physiology of orgasm), *Xuesheng zazhi*, 15, no. 12 (Dec. 1928), pp. 15–18.

88 Gui Zhiliang, *Nüren zhi yisheng* (A woman's life), Beijing: Zhengzhong shuju, 1936, p. 83.

concluded the process of intercourse. Cultural representations of female sexual passivity, perhaps the most consistent and least contested feature of modernizing discourses of sexuality in Republican China, were part of efforts to legitimize a vision of social order in which women were confined to the spheres of domesticity and reproduction. Based on ideas of racial degeneration and the physical health of offspring, the control of marital sexuality was also seen as the foundation of the regulation of collective reproductive strategies in which male and female had clearly defined responsibilities (more on this in chapter 4).

Constructed as a powerful drive for which the husband was mainly responsible, sexuality became a fundamental notion which replaced the three bonds of Confucianism in the maintenance of gender hierarchy. Intimate drives instead of ethical norms were thought to weld the husband and his wife together. Medical texts described women as 'attractive', 'alluring' and 'charming', and sexuality was described as a powerful and attractive force. Women were represented both as objects of male desire and as subjects of a powerful sexuality in tales of unknown pleasures. The vagina was a site of power which could incite desire in men. The suction of the vagina, the 'sex revolutionary' Zhang Jingsheng even claimed, increased during intercourse, giving the male a feeling of extreme pleasure. The labia minora would also draw the male organ into a zone of delight: 'If a woman becomes fully agitated sexually during intercourse, even though there is much secretion in the vaginal passage through its heat, suction power and other characteristics, the male and female organs are able to harmonize most perfectly.'[89] Older notions of *yin* and *yang* were also rescued from the past in Zhang Jingsheng's promotion of marital harmony: 'positive' (*yang*) and 'negative' (*yin*) 'currents' (*dian*), he claimed, would be released during orgasm. Other authors appropriated foreign theories to support a vision of gender hierarchy in which male activity was thought to complement female passivity, and Marie Stopes's *Married love* was twice translated in the

89 Chang, *Sex histories*, p. 90, altered translation.

1920s. Her fifth chapter on 'mutual adjustment' was particularly welcomed.

If passions were idealized in modernizing discourses of sexuality, even their expression was supposed to conform to a strict gender hierarchy: the only advisable position during intercourse was with the man on top and the woman underneath. Other positions were judged 'incorrect', 'against nature' (*fan ziran*) and having 'strange names used by prostitutes to allure customers', according to an *ABC of sexology* (1928).[90] As in the penitentials in the medieval Christian world, emissions *extra vas* were condemned, as was the use of sterile orifices. Following theories of 'mutual harmony', the husband was advised to comb his hair, shave his beard 'like the overseas Chinese in America', and dress sharply to remain 'attractive'. Promoting a vision of modernity in which the bond between husband and wife was thought to be based on mutual intimacy, some marriage guides even codified private behaviour: when the wife awoke, the husband was advised to approach her gently and say 'good morning'; a 'tender kiss' was also encouraged. Nuances could be complex to master, and it was explained to 'modern man' that to stay in the room and observe her dishevelled hair would be very improper. New strategies of winning the wife's affection were called 'control methods' by Zhang Jingsheng, and his *Sex histories* listed seven different techniques of control over the spouse, ranging from al fresco dinners and gifts of flowers to the sharing of household duties.[91] The 'kiss', symbol of marital intimacy, became a popular topic for debate in vernacular newspapers, although enthusiastic writers felt obliged to warn the uninitiated reader against its heady effects: some hospitals, according to a Hong Kong daily newspaper, even warned patients who suffered from high blood pressure or a weak constitution against kissing.[92] Although the normative pressures exercised by new modernizing

90 Chai, *Xingxue*, p. 65.
91 Chang, *Sex histories*, pp. 79–80.
92 'Tan jiewen' (About the kiss), *Xianggang gongshang*, 10 Feb. 1935, 2:1, followed by a 'Wen' (The kiss), *Xianggang gongshang*, 1 Feb. 1936, p. 7.

discourses in real life may be difficult to assess, the historian Yeh Wen-hsin has observed that new notions of sexual behaviour rarely emancipated students from the inhibitions of traditional families, and often increased their awkwardness and anxiety in courtship: 'fictional writing, journalistic reports and personal biographies of this period gave ample evidence of the emotional cost accompanying such protracted anxiety.'[93] The actual anxieties generated by modernizing discourses, which may be observed through a very different type of historical source (for instance letters written to journals), would clearly be a very fruitful topic for further investigation.[94]

'A wolf at thirty, a tiger at forty' was a common saying, and it was sometimes thought that the sexual instinct could surge again in middle-age.[95] The sudden thrust of the lower instincts was a menace to conjugal bliss. In its search for an outlet, the sexual urge could trample upon marital harmony: adultery, prostitution and concubinage – dreaded enemies of the new social norms – were likely to emerge again. But under what was called a 'correct line of guidance' (*zhengdang de zhidao*), these raw energies could be directed into the proper channels. According to Chai Fuyuan, old age started at thirty-one for women, but sexual desire could surge violently between forty and forty-five and had to be 'correctly' satisfied.[96] Some women were less subject to such renewed vigour, and for those busy with their household duties, the sexual drive did not press

93 Yeh Wen-hsin, *The alienated academy: Culture and politics in Republican China, 1919–1937*, Cambridge, MA: Harvard University Press, 1990, p. 256.
94 On the quest for sexual enlightenment within the frame of marriage in England, analysed on the basis of readers' letters written to Marie Stopes, see Lesley A. Hall, *Hidden anxieties: Male sexuality, 1900–1950*, Oxford University Press, 1991.
95 Zhang Jingcheng, 'Sishi sui yihou aiqing de huoyan zai chi' (The flame of love will blaze again after the age of forty), *Dagongbao*, 1 March 1936, 3:12, translation from Peter Brunt; 'Yige Meiguo yisheng de jianjie sishi sui you kaishi shi lian'aiqi' (According to an American doctor the period of love begins again at the age of forty), *Zhongyang ribao*, 29 July 1936, 3:3.
96 Chai, *Xingxue*, p. 45.

itself with the same sense of urgency. Where it did manifest itself, it was thought to be unconsciously diverted to nourish the inner realm of thought: a tortured imagination and hypochondria were the results of excess energy. In a similar vein of logic, sex educators attacked the taboo on the remarriage of widows: an unsatisfied 'sexual impulse' would lead to 'improper sexual relations' (*fei zhengshi zhi yixing*).[97] Women of all ages were constituted both as sites of sexual desire and as crucial nodes for its proper control: the regulation of sexuality, rather than its suppression, was a constant concern of modernizing discourses. Assertive sexual desire in women was seen in negative terms, and young women were seen as dangerous to men. Attractive women were compared to evil flowers which developed into full bloom through contact with men: 'Most criminals among young women are pretty. This is because their moral education is not yet completed, while there are too many opportunities to meet men.' Ugly women were equally a source of crime: left unsatisfied by their husbands, they easily enticed other men into illicit sexual relations. Jealousy was another characteristic of ugly women, so one should not be surprised to find that they indulged more often in pyromania and murder, claimed Cao Guanlai's *Chats about the physiology of youth* of 1936.[98] Frail brides or wicked wives, each of these representations constructed female identity and womanhood through the prism of sexuality. Dependent and responsive to the more direct and instrumental expressions of 'male sexuality', 'female sexuality' was constructed as a 'maternal instinct' mainly geared towards reproduction.

97 Zhang Xichen, 'Du *Funü wenti zatan*' (Reading *Talks about women's problems), Xinnüxing*, 1, no. 6 (June 1926), p. 433.
98 Cao, *Qingchun*, pp. 94–5.

3

SEXUAL DESIRE AND HUMAN PROCREATION

With the sexualization of the body by modernizing élites in early Republican China, gender distinctions were represented as biologically determined structures: the passive woman was seen as a 'natural' complement to the active man. The construction of sexual desire as a dangerous drive which formed the very core of the individual also led to the emergence of a range of female identities such as the menstruating girl, the hysterical housewife and the menopausal harpy. Medical discourses, moreover, closely associated the personal identity of the woman with the future health of the nation. From learned gynaecological treatises to self-help manuals on childbirth, different discursive registers all stressed that better knowledge of human sexuality was a matter of individual as much as of collective interest. Women were given increased personal and social responsibilities, since the careful monitoring of their bodies and regulated procreative behaviour would contribute healthy offspring to the nation. Failure to master and implement the proper knowledge of sexuality could lead to a sickly and degenerate population being produced. Individual women, married couples and political bodies were thus linked through a common knowledge promoted by modernizing discourses on sex. Conception and gestation in particular became a major focus of such knowledge. The discursive link between sex and procreation, however, had little to do with contemporary developments in medical science in Europe.

THE NATURALIZATION OF 'SEXUAL DESIRE'

The construction of 'sex' as a natural and fixed need occurred in Europe at a particular historical time. Increasingly removed from religious categories of debauchery, sin and excess, sex gradually became an integrated object of medical knowledge in Europe during the first half of the nineteenth century. Isolated as an 'instinct', a powerful 'drive' or a natural impulse, sexual desire was conceptualized as a biological essence which culture could not alter. Medical works like Heinrich Kaan's *Psychopathia sexualis* (1846) assigned a new significance to the 'sexual' as a unified domain for investigation, and the positing of a sexual instinct enabled a group of professional people who posed as scientists to inquire and explore human sexuality. In an age of protracted anxiety about prostitution, venereal disease, homosexuality, masturbation, degeneracy and other social issues, it also allowed sex reformers to advocate state intervention in sexual matters.[1] A variety of acts, sensations and capacities – disparate forms of eroticized behaviour – were integrated through medical concepts and isolated by biologizing discourses which had as their object the normalization of the individual. More important, however, was the psychiatrization of 'sex' in the space of a new theoretical construction called 'sexuality'. In its unprecedented attention to sexual disorders, abnormality and deviance, the emphasis in nineteenth-century medical discourse was shifted from descriptions of sexual *acts* towards sexual *preferences*. The notion of 'sexuality', together with new categories like 'homosexuality' and 'heterosexuality', closely connected the individual to the object of desire. Instead of describing 'sodomy' as a category of forbidden acts, for instance, 'homosexuality' became an essentially different type of behaviour associated with a particular personage called 'the homosexual'. The gradual appearance of a notion of 'sexuality' in Europe had at least three consequences. First, 'sexuality' became detached from reproduction. Earlier treatments considered sexual intercourse to be a bodily need primarily designed for the perpetuation of the human species. Discourses about 'sexuality', on the other hand, no longer established strict distinctions between procreative and

1 Michel Foucault, *The history of sexuality*, Harmondsworth: Penguin, 1984, p. 118.

nonprocreative sex: if 'homosexuality', for instance, could be an alternative to 'heterosexuality', pleasure was no longer subordinated to procreation but could be seen as an end in itself. Secondly, 'sexuality' was interpreted as an individual matter, concerned less with procreation than with hidden pleasures and secret fantasies thought to determine an individual's personality. Thirdly, discourses of 'sexuality' contributed in promoting the individual as a site of desire which should be regulated as well as a bearer of rights to self-expression. The sexualization of individuals and the recognition of perversions as simple variations, in the words of Lawrence Birken, were part of a process of democratization.[2] Heavily dependent on notions of natural law and human rights, the individual's particular and unique preferences became significant with the consolidation of a notion of 'sexuality' during the late nineteenth and early twentieth century. Although a conception of sexual desire (*xingyu*) as a natural need emerged in China and remains fundamental to this day, no similar conception of 'sexuality' ever appeared.

Given the dearth of reliable studies on sexuality in late imperial China, however, it remains a matter of conjecture whether or not the articulation of sexual desire as a powerful and natural drive in the Republican period had historical precedents. Closely related to our concerns, it can at least be hypothesized that 'desire' in general became increasingly an object of philosophical discourse during the Qing period. Promoted by a specific academic community, the evidential scholarship movement represented a fundamental departure from Cheng-Zhu Confucian concepts and attitudes. Its adherents engaged in philological reconstructions of philosophical texts to criticize and reject the officially sponsored Confucian orthodoxy.[3] Dai Zhen (1724–77) was one of the most brilliant and iconoclastic scholars interested in evidential research. Although the extent to which current sinological interpretations of Dai Zhen have been influenced by

2 Lawrence Birken, *Consuming desire: Sexual science and the emergence of a culture of abundance*, 1871–1914, Ithaca: Cornell University Press, 1988, p. 12.
3 Elman, *From philosophy to philology*, pp. 17–22.

earlier nationalist narratives (Hu Shi) still remains to be assessed, it seems clear that his *Evidential analysis of the meanings of terms in the 'Mencius'* had broader political implications. A philological examination of key concepts in Confucian philosophy, this work attacked the metaphysical dualism of mainstream Confucianism which opposed principles (*li*) to desires (*yu*). By positing principles as the source of moral values which were incompatible with desires, Dai Zhen believed that Cheng-Zhu Confucian philosophy had led to a debilitating asceticism and an inhumane social order. Building on the naturalist approach of important seventeenth-century philosophers like Wang Fuzhi (1619–92), Yan Yuan (1635–1704) and Li Gong (1659–1733), Dai Zhen compared human desires to a river which could not be stopped and had to be regulated into the correct channels. His followers in the early nineteenth century used the terms 'regulation of desires' (*jieyu*) and 'regulation of nature' (*jiexing*).[4]

Although a discourse about 'desire' became widespread in philosophical circles in the Qing period, 'sex' as an integrated category of analysis probably remained elusive. The term *se*, which often appeared in these debates, is generally translated as 'sex'. When it was used in philosophical discourse, however,

4 Ruan Yuan, *Yanjingshi ji* (Collected works of Ruan Yuan), Shanghai: Shangwu yinshuguan, 1937, pp. 191–214; see also Chen Guying *et al.* (eds), *Ming Qing shixue sichao shi* (The history of practical scholarship under the Ming and the Qing), Shandong: Qilu shushe, 1989, vol. 3, pp. 1711–14; see also Benjamin A. Elman, 'The revaluation of benevolence (*jen*) in Ch'ing dynasty evidential research' in Richard J. Smith and D.W.Y. Kwok (eds), *Cosmology, ontology, and human efficacy: Essays in Chinese thought*, Honolulu: University of Hawaii Press, 1993, pp. 59–80. Jiao Xun (1763–1820) compared man to an animal in his desires for food and women, which were thought to be part of human nature (*xing*); Jiao Xun, *Diaogu ji* (Collected works of Jiao Xun), Shanghai: Shangwu yinshuguan, 1936, pp. 127–8. The shift of emphasis away from principles (*li*) towards the acceptance of desires (*renyu*) as a fundamental part of human nature was even noticeable among early Qing Cheng-Zhu Confucianists like Li Guangdi (1642–1718); see On-cho Ng, '*Hsing* (nature) as the ontological basis of practicality in early Ch'ing Ch'eng-Chu Confucianism: Li Kuang-ti's (1642–1718) philosophy', *Philosophy East and West*, 44, no. 1 (January 1994), pp. 79–109.

se was often compared to morally reprehensible aspirations for food, fame or status. While *shi se xing ye*, an apophthegm attributed to the ancient philosopher Gaozi in the *Mencius*, is often translated as 'food and sex are part of nature', *shi* and *se* might be better interpreted as 'gluttony' and 'lust'. In these texts, those two elements were probably meant as categories of excess, broadly comparable to moral sins like pride and vanity chastised in the Christian world, rather than appetite and sexual desire as medical categories. On a very different level of discourse, however, it is difficult to avoid the impression that a notion of 'sex' as a natural need was relatively common. A cursory reading of medical texts from the late imperial period reveals that detailed discussions of sexuality, fertility, longevity and health circulated widely in Ming and Qing China. Sun Simo (581–682), the medical master whose work was reprinted several times in late imperial China, stressed that 'A male cannot live without a female, nor can a female live without a male.'[5] Called *yangsheng* ('nourishment of life'), this relatively new type of medical literature – which still remains to be fully investigated – insisted on the control of sexual acts for the health of the self, the couple and posterity. *Yangsheng* authors, it would appear, envisaged *se* as a medical category which transcended the moral meanings of lust. Some authors isolated *seyu* as a need distinct from other desires: 'No human desire is stronger than the desire between men and women (*nannü zhi yu*)', casually observed Chu Renhuo in his seventeenth-century collection of jests and jottings.[6] Similar comments can be found again and again in late imperial China. Cao Tingdong (1699–1785), author of a guide to health for elderly people, saw copulation between male and female (*nannü goujing*) as the 'natural way of *yin* and *yang*' (*yinyang ziran zhi dao*), although he urged his readers to restrain this natural desire.[7] Even before Qing evidential

5 Sun Simo, 'Fangzhong buyi', *Beiji qianjin yaofang* (Book of remedies), orig. 652, 1805 edn, *juan* 27:29a.

6 Chu Renhuo, 'Renyu', *Jianhuji* (Collected writings of Chu Renhuo), orig. 1690, *miji, juan* 3:14a.

7 Cao Tingdong, *Laolao hengyan* (Health manual for elderly people), orig. 1784, 1878 edn, *juan* 2:10a.

scholars criticized Cheng-Zhu Confucian philosophy, the distinguished late Ming paediatrician Wan Quan (1488–1578?) referred to Mencius in his use of the notion of 'regulation of desire' (*jieyu*). Like other *yangsheng* authors, Wan Quan urged his male readers to monitor carefully a reproductive economy in which finite quantities of semen should be economized in the interests of longevity and posterity: 'The male's *jing* [semen] and the female's *xue* [blood] mingle to generate a foetus, and its shape resembles its parents [. . .]. Hence in seeking a child, the male should increase his *jing* and regulate his desire [. . .] and the female should nurture her blood and calm her *qi*.'[8] Dissipated (*jinghao*) through excessive intercourse, waste of semen could bring about bodily decay and a decline in generative power; mingled with female blood, it could lead to new life. Represented as homologous and complementary to men, *yangsheng* and *fuke* texts also advised women to observe continence and to nurture their blood through menstrual regulation and the use of medical remedies. Described as a heterosexual drive, suppression of sexual urges could cause various disorders, including spermatorrhoea in the male and amenorrhoea in the female: Shen Jin'ao (1717–1776), a notorious medical writer, claimed that 'the menses become deregulated if the female has no intercourse with a male for ten years. Even within a period of ten years she may suffer from deregulated menses if she has pined for intercourse without actually having it.' He went on to underline how nuns and widows suffered amenorrhoea when their 'urge' (*yudong*, a term which implies an active impulse) was not satisfied.[9] Lack of copulation with women, numerous medical treatises in turn underlined, would cause spermatorrhoea (*huajing*) and potentially lethal nocturnal emissions (*yijing*) in the male.[10] Although these

8 Wan Quan, 'Peihe bian', *Guangsi jiyao* (Essentials for multiplying offspring) in *Wan Mizhai yixue quanshu* (The collected medical works of Wan Quan), orig. 1549, 1778 edn.

9 Shen Jin'ao, 'Yuejing', *Fuke yuchi* (Health manual for women), orig. 1773, 1784 edn, *juan* 1:11a.

10 Ming and Qing medical cases provide ample evidence for the widespread concern with nocturnal emissions; see for instance *Song Yuan Ming Qing mingyi lei'an* (Cases from famous physicians from the Song, Yuan, Ming

examples can hardly be accepted as sufficient evidence for a shift in the conceptualization of sexuality, they could well testify to the emergence of a social subject endowed with natural needs that had to be carefully deployed for individual longevity and reproductive health. Governed by natural urges, sex and reproduction were closely linked in these medical texts.

The terms *xing* ('nature') and *yu* ('desire'), which had been at the centre of philosophical debates in the Qing period, were conflated in early Republican China into a notion of 'sexual desire' which could also be interpreted as 'natural desire', 'natural urge' or 'inherent urge': *xingyu* was a notion which essentialized sexuality as a natural need meant to ensure procreation. The older term *seyu* ('lust', 'passion', 'desire for feminine beauty'), with its connotations of excess and lust, gradually disappeared. *Xing*, which generally meant 'nature', 'disposition', or 'temper' in classical Chinese, acquired a new meaning as 'sex' in Republican China. Represented as a powerful drive towards heterogenitality, sexual desire was seen as a 'primeval and destructive force' or a 'barbaric instinct' (*yeman benneng*).[11] As an instinctual urge, a biological drive for procreation, 'sexual desires' (*xingyu*) needed to be properly disciplined: during the early twentieth century, sex education was called the 'education of the sexual desire' (*xingyu jiaoyu*).[12] 'Sex' (*xing*) and 'nature' (*xing*) eventually became homonymous, encapsulating the notion of sexual desire as a powerful drive which conferred a social respon-

and Qing dynasties), Taibei: Da Zhongguo tushu gongsi, 1971, pp. 42, 70–4 and 102; medical concern with spermatorrhoea is clearly expressed, for instance, in Wan Quan, *Wan shi jiachuan yangsheng siyao* (Four essentials of Wan Quan's family notes on nourishing life), Wuhan: Hubei kexue jishu chubanshe, 1984, pp. 43–4, and Chen Shiduo, *Shishi milu* (Writings of Chen Shiduo), orig. 1687, 1805 edn, *juan* 2:18a–20b and 53a–55b.

11 Wang, *Qingchun*, p. 3.

12 On sex eduction in China, see Chen Yongsheng, 'Qingmo minchu woguo xuexiao xingjiaoyu shulüe' (Brief account of sex education in China's schools during the early twentieth century), *Zhonghua yishi zazhi*, 23, no. 1, (Jan. 1993), pp. 6–11; see also Sheng Langxi, 'Xingjiaoyu zai xinxuezhi kechengshang de weizhi' (The position of sex education in the curriculum of the New Learning system), *Jiaoyu zazhi*, 15, no. 8 (Aug. 1923), p. 17.

sibility on the individual. Contrary to 'sexuality', a concept which became overwhelmingly important in Europe from the late nineteenth century onwards, 'sexual desire' was not dissociated from procreation. In their conflation with reproduction, moreover, 'sexual desires' were seen as 'natural' drives that should be regulated in the name of a higher entity, be it 'the race', 'the state', or 'future generations': they did not confer any rights to pleasure upon individuals. Finally, modernizing discourses in China continued to focus on procreative acts in relation to fertility, not on sexual preferences as an expression of individual variation. No term for or conception of 'sexuality' appeared in twentieth-century China, and the use of that term to translate *xingyu* would be misleading. Constructed in parallel to the notion of *shiyu* ('appetite', 'desire for food', 'urge for food'), *xingyu* is thought of as universal and natural: 'sex' is essentialized into a biological drive for heterogenital intercourse. The discursive formations which emerged in Republican China, in other words, cannot be reduced merely to a 'derivation' from the 'West'. Although superficially similar, the structure, contours and targets of discourses of sexual desire were in many ways different. As much as their counterparts in Europe, however, modernizing élites in China were masters in the selective appropriation of the language of medical science to endow their ideas about discipline and control with the necessary authority.

EGG AND SEMEN: MEDICAL REPRESENTATIONS OF CONCEPTION

As an expression of allegiance to 'modernity', biologizing discourses denounced the 'superstitions' (*mixin*, [a neologism]) and 'popular errors' which impeded the 'rational' understanding of human conception by the 'general public'.[13] Proper knowledge of sexual generation, it was claimed, would empower married

13 On these customary beliefs, see the excellent chapters on popular culture in M. Leutner, *Geburt, Heirat und Tod in Peking: Volkskultur und Elitekultur vom 19. Jahrhundert bis zur Gegenwart*, Berlin: Reimer, 1989.

couples to control their procreative behaviour and contribute to the strength of the nation. Customary accounts which interpreted conception as the mixture of female blood with male semen, folk beliefs in demons that could find their way into the womb, popular tales about the appearance of unearthly creatures impregnating the woman in dreams and visions, theories of retribution and reincarnation were all denounced as 'benighted', 'backward' and 'irrational'.[14] Not without resonance to the Confucian strictures against irrational beliefs, modern writers explained reproduction as a bodily mechanism detached from the cosmological order: 'Pregnancy is the result of sexual intercourse. The spermatozoa of the male are discharged into the vagina of the female, they then enter the uterus, unite with the egg which comes from the ovaries and develops into a foetus.'[15] No longer the result of *yin* and *yang* energies, the human was but the product of an egg and a sperm. Mankind became head of the family of viviparous animals: he was 'born by embryo' (*taisheng*), not 'born by bud' (*yasheng*) or 'born by egg' (*luansheng*). Viviparity implied complementarity, and the contribution of man and woman to the process of reproduction were thought to be equal. The gift of life, moreover, became a purely physiological mechanism over which the married couple could assert control.

Although the extent to which medical theories in late imperial China stressed the inner mechanisms of male and female bodies at the expense of cosmological forces still remains to be properly assessed,[16] biologizing explanations of conception in Republican China virtually banned references to external influences of the supernatural world and the cosmos. The focus upon the interior

14 Huang Shi, 'Guanyu chanyu de mixin yu fengsu' (About superstitions and customs on birth), *Funü zazhi*, 16, no. 10 (Oct. 1930), pp. 97–105; in newspapers, see for instance 'Shouyun zhi yuanli' (Principles of impregnation), *Xunhuan ribao*, 15 Oct. 1935, 4:1; 'Renshen xuzhi' (Basic knowledge of childbirth), *Wuhan ribao*, 2 Feb. 1935, 3:2.

15 Guo and Li, *Nüxing*, p. 46.

16 Charlotte Furth, 'Concepts of pregnancy, childbirth, and infancy in Ch'ing dynasty China', *Journal of Asian Studies*, 46, no. 1 (Feb. 1987), pp. 7–35.

of the body and the emphasis on individual control was evident in the proliferation of publications on human reproduction, often written under the guise of science. The physiology of the male ejaculation became a popular topic for debate,[17] and the number of spermatozoa contained in each ejaculation was a matter for speculation. One book entitled *Love in marriage* claimed that each discharge contained between 200 and 500 million spermatozoa, but the *Problem of birth control* only counted 2,200,000. In response to one puzzled reader's inquiry, the editors of *New Woman* insisted that the first figure was correct.[18] The fascination with quantification and measurement, from the size of the penis to the number of sperm, was very much part of an effort to naturalize human sexuality. No longer a mysterious essence, semen was a material substance that could be expressed in figures. The spell of numbers also promoted an economic vision of finiteness and control: if sperm was a finite substance, the individual should monitor its production and manage its consumption (more on masturbation and uncontrolled emissions in chapter 6). Finally, abstract figures linked individual bodies to an administrative entity called 'population', equated as the sum total of a number of equal individuals, half of whom produced semen in similar quantities. Counting was a levelling activity.

The trajectory of the sperm to the egg also became a tale of hazardous encounters, much like the passage from puberty to marriage was considered a tumultuous path beset with temptations: semen moved through the spermatic duct, ejaculated through the urethra, landed in the vagina, entered the cervical canal where it ran into a sticky fluid with which it 'travelled' (*youxing*) towards the uterus finally to ascend to the ovaries and fertilize the egg. Sperm was described in anthropocentric terms: it was 'lively' (*huopo*) and 'courageous' (*yonggan*); it was extremely agile and moved in 'groups' (*chengqun*) or 'independently' (*dandu*). After excessive intercourse, sperm became 'retarded' and 'at its last gasp' (*yanyanyixi*): in the case of fertiliza-

17 'Gaowan zahua' (Chats about testicles), *Dagongbao*, 20 March 1937, 3:11.
18 'Tongxin' (Letters from readers), *Xinnüxing*, 1, no. 4 (April 1926), p. 305.

tion, offspring would be similarly 'weak', 'malformed' or 'moronic'.[19] The struggle for existence, a widespread theme in twentieth-century China, seemed to start at the microscopic level. Among these millions of little tadpoles (*kedou*), only that one which was the most valiant and strong would be able to enter the egg. The egg, symbol of the passive woman waiting for the enterprising male, would only 'receive' one sperm: like the married couple, the egg 'refused' a second sperm. Once the sperm reached the cervix of the uterus, a fluid released during orgasm by the female brought 'untold pleasure to the spermatozoa, so that their movements become more vivacious'.[20] Two sperms received by the egg would lead to twins (see illustration 6), although *Questions about birth control* (1925) insinuated that copulation with two males in one night could cause a woman to give birth to a pair.[21] The life expectancy of semen was also a matter of debate: it stultified on exposure to air but was thought to survive for weeks inside the uterus. Fertilization became the symbolic representation of a 'civilized marriage'; the union of sperm and egg stood for the conjugal relationship between husband and wife.

Despite an insistence on the theoretical equality of men and women, negative representations of female sexuality remained widespread. The concept of telegony (*qianfu ganying*, 'impression of the previous husband'), which posited that progeny might inherit characteristics from a previous sexual partner, is a good example. Although the theory was invalidated in the 1890s by Cossar Ewart, the belief that a baby could share the physical characteristics of any man with whom its mother had previously had intercourse remained powerful in both popular culture and medical discourses. Highlighting both the dangers of female sexuality and the necessity of individual restraint, semen was said

19 Ding Fubao, 'Lun nanzi zongyu zhi hai' (About the evil of young men indulging in carnal desires), *Zhongxi yixuebao*, no. 21 (Feb. 1912), p. 2.
20 Cheng Hao, *Renlei de xingshenghuo* (The sexual life of mankind), Shanghai: Yadong shuju, 1934, pp. 38–40.
21 Cheng Hao, *Jiezhi shengyu wenti* (Questions about birth control), Shanghai: Yadong tushuguan, 1925, p. 35.

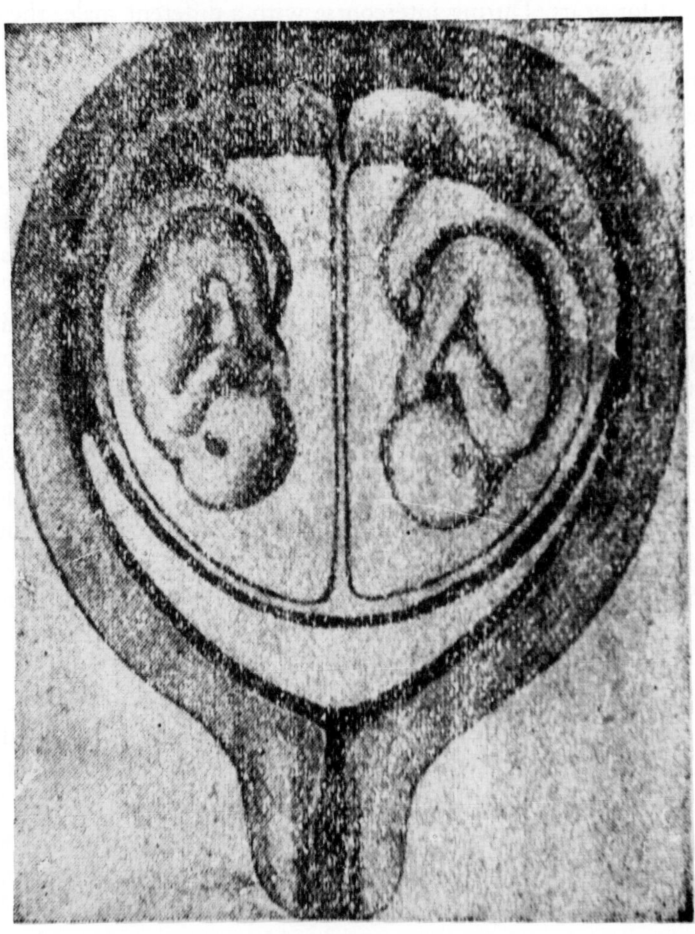

6. Twins. Wang Yang, *Shengyu guwen* (Advice on childbirth), Shanghai: Zhongyang shuju, 1933.

to dissolve into an impregnated woman's blood and to remain latent for years. During intercourse with a different male, these remnants would be reactivated and would enter the vagina through the bloodstream. A prostitute, for example, could carry the semen of numerous clients in her blood. 'Hence when a man wishes to marry, he should choose a virgin. Even if the couple are both of good quality, the quality of a previous partner may not have been good, and will influence the child', a widely circulated *Advice on childbirth* (1933) remarked.[22] The idea that offspring may inherit the physical characteristics of the mother's previous sexual partner remains relatively widespread to this day, including in parts of Europe. In Bristol, for instance, four out of a sample of twenty-five elderly women who had been schoolteachers still subscribed to the belief in 1973.[23] This example might serve to illustrate that there is not always much evidence for the existence of blank walls between 'East' and 'West', or for any well-defined gulf between 'modernity' and 'tradition'.

Strengthening the discursive link between sex and procreation, orgasm was generally discussed in the context of fertilization. Orgasm and the physical condition of both partners were seen to be central to conception: if the body was tired or infused with alcohol, the foetus would be retarded; a child born as the result of rape would be brutish. After copulation, the woman should lie down quietly so that the seed can be fully absorbed and reach the egg. Some writers regarded pleasure as peripheral to the biological act of conception. In Shen Junqi's mechanized version of the body, the vagina 'wriggled' (*rudong*) the better to absorb semen, but since spermatozoa were able to propel themselves, artificial insemination would be 'as effective' as copulation.[24] Other voices, on the contrary, suggested that the female orgasm fulfilled a physiological function which marked women as

22 Wang Yang, *Shengyu guwen* (Advice on childbirth), Shanghai: Zhongyang shuju, 1933, pp. 54–5.
23 Michael Banton, *Racial theories*, Cambridge University Press, 1987, p. 27.
24 Shen, *Jixie rensheng*, p. 634.

mediators of sexual harmony. Cheng Hao, a German-educated scientist with an interest in birth control, believed that the cervical canal of the uterus lowered itself as a result of orgasmic contractions, a privileged moment which allowed fertilization to take place.[25] According to Zhao Shifa, who was more interested in traditional medical theories, fertilization occurred during intercourse when man and woman experienced 'a kind of beautiful feeling and both essences would combine'.[26] Even when the female orgasm was seen as an indispensable part of reproduction, modernizing discourses claimed that the sexual desire of women was governed by a more passive physiology: when pleasure reached its height, the man's blood 'boiled', whereas that of the woman merely 'swelled'. Drawing on evolutionary theories which were so popular in Republican China, Miss Liu Yicang reported that women lacked the primeval impulse to discharge bodily fluids: they only occasionally pined for bodily contact. The intensity of the female sexual instinct, she claimed, was influenced by the periods and the cycle of the four seasons.[27] Constructed as a passive and weak instinct which was entirely dependent on male initiative and responsive to it, female sexual desire was subordinated to the duties of reproduction.

Unlike some of their European colleagues in the early twentieth century, medical explorers of human sexuality in China rarely emphasized the importance of the vagina. Freud and his followers relocated the female site of erotic life from the clitoris to the vagina, thereby reinforcing the construction of man and woman as two incommensurably different creatures.[28] Governed

25 Cheng, *Jiezhi shengyu*, p. 31.

26 Zhao Shifa, *Geren weishengxue* (Personal hygiene), Nanjing: Nanjing shudian, 1933, p. 186.

27 Liu Yicang, 'Nüzi xingyu zhi zhenxiang' (The true nature of female sexual desire) in *Xing de wenti* (The problem of sex), Shanghai: Xinghua shuju, 1933, pp. 30–6.

28 Thomas W. Laqueur, ' "Amor veneris, vel dulcedo appeletur" ' in Michel Feher, with Ramona Naddaff and Nadia Tazi (eds), *Fragments for a history of the human body*, vol. 3, New York: Zone Books, 1989, pp. 90–131.

by representations of conjugal harmony as a bounded union of opposites, the clitoris often continued to be represented as the female penis and the locus of female pleasure in early Republican China. The 'continuous friction of the penis on the clitoris' brought woman to orgasm, according to Cheng Hao.[29] In most of the literature on female sexuality, the vagina continued to be portrayed as a simple cavity through which most fluids had to pass: the ejaculation of sperm during intercourse as well as the expulsion of blood during menstruation took place in a vagina which was not granted an important part in the creation of pleasure.

If female anatomy and physiology were thought loosely to follow those of the man, however, women too could have an ejaculation. With the representation of the vagina as an interior penis, women too were expected by some observers to discharge a fluid similar to semen. 'During intercourse between a female and a male', Chai Fuyuan explained in his *ABC of sexology* (1928), 'the functions of her reproductive system are the same as his, and the bodily stimuli are also similar. The vaginal area opens, the lower ribs and the vagina widen, the uterus also slackens and is entirely prepared to respond to the movements of the male. Moreover it secretes a kind of fluid which is similar to the male ejaculation.'[30] The most controversial theory about female ejaculation was Zhang Jingsheng's 'third kind of fluid'. The first kind of fluid, he noticed, was the 'fragrant fluid' produced by the inner part of the clitoris. The second kind was secreted by the wall of the vagina and lubricated the organs during intercourse. Zhang's 'third kind of fluid' was produced by a gland at the entrance of the pubic path. The sexual functions of the woman were thought to be the same as those of the man, this fluid being discharged like a man's ejaculate: 'However, since the vagina is concealed inside the body, it is more difficult to stimulate it into an erection during normal intercourse in comparison to the penis.' This fluid could only be the result of

29 Cheng, *Jiezhi shengyu*, p. 31.
30 Chai, *Xingxue*, p. 42.

a heightened activity of the ovaries, which could take place when the woman was in a 'state of intoxication' and felt 'extreme satisfaction'. At this time, Zhang Jingsheng hypothesized, the ovary sent its egg into the womb. As the egg was stimulated by sexual activity, it was more easily fertilized and the child it produced would necessarily be 'robust and active'.[31] For Dr Zhang, 'the weakness of our country's race is due to various acquired factors, but the fact that the third kind of fluid is not sought during conception is an inborn reason. Because the majority of women in our country cannot release the third kind of fluid, the egg assumes a moronic and retarded shape. The sperm must undergo all sorts of tribulations in the vagina, and when it finally reaches the egg most of its original vitality has been eroded by acid fluids. The egg it encounters is also dejected and apathetic: no wonder that the foetus thus conceived will suffer from all kinds of abnormal weaknesses.'[32] Although Zhang Jingsheng's *Sex histories* were confiscated twice in the 1920s, his publications had a wide clandestine circulation.[33] They came under fierce criticism from other writers.[34] Zhang

31 Zhang Jingsheng, 'Di sanzhong shui yu luanqiu ji shengji de dian he youzhong de guanxi' (The third kind of fluid and the egg in their relationship to the current of vitality and eugenics), *Xinwenhua*, 1, no. 2 (Feb. 1927), pp. 23–48.

32 Zhang, 'Di sanzhong shui', pp. 33–4.

33 Ch'en, *China and the West*, p. 388.

34 Zhou Jianren, 'Xingjiaoyu yundong de weiji' (The crisis of the movement for sexual education), *Xinnüxing*, 2, no. 2 (Feb. 1927), pp. 135–9. Zhang Jingsheng's *Sex histories* were confiscated twice in the 1920s in Hangzhou and in Shanghai, translated into Japanese in 1951 but still forbidden in Taiwan in the 1960s. See Zhang Jingsheng, '*Xingshi zhi shi*' (The history of *Sex histories*), *Xinwenhua*, 1, no. 1 (Jan. 1927), pp. 125–6; for biographical information on Zhang, see Luo Dunwei, 'Wusi renwu zongheng tan: Zhang Jingsheng' (Free talks about Zhang Jingsheng, a figure of the May Fourth Movement), *Changliu*, 7, no. 6 (1953); Chen Jingzhi, 'Zhang Jingsheng lao er bu si' (Immortal Zhang Jingsheng), *Changliu*, 27, no. 3 (1963); Xiao Yaotian, 'Wo tan Zhang Jingsheng' (About Zhang Jingsheng), *Dacheng*, no. 10 (1974); Wu Wenwei, 'Zhong Xi xingxue liang boshi: Zhang Jingsheng yu Jin Sai' (Two doctors of Eastern and Western sexology: Zhang Jingsheng and Kingsley), *Zhongwai zazhi*, 30, no. 4 (1981); an extract of his

Xichen, leader of the publishing house Kaiming shudian and prolific author on the problem of women, compared them to 'pornographic' novels like the *Jinpingmei* and the *Rouputuan*.[35] Zhou Jianren, the science-editor of the prestigious Commercial Press, also contended with Zhang Jingsheng over definitions of 'science' and 'pornography'.[36] Despite these competing voices in Republican China, very similar cultural representations appeared in different modernizing discourses on sexuality. Even sophisticated accounts of the morphology and physiology of fertilization by eminent scientists like Fei Hongnian were justified as a contribution to the 'preservation of the race'.[37] Spanning a variety of discursive registers, from the provocative work of the sex revolutionary Zhang Jingsheng to the university texts of the academic scientist Fei Hongnian, married couples and the species were linked through the use of new knowledge which was spread under the cover of science.

THE PREGNANT WOMB

Traditional medical theories often represented birth as a polluting experience. The concept of foetal poison, which emerged in the sixteenth and seventeenth centuries, explained that neonatal illnesses and smallpox were caused by polluted maternal blood during pregnancy.[38] Notions of pollution also dominated new

---

autobiography was published as Zhang Jingsheng, 'Zhang Jingsheng zizhuan, 1–4' (The autobiography of Zhang Jingsheng, chapters 1 to 4), *Dacheng*, nos 19–22 (1975).

35 Zhang Xichen, '*Xinnüxing* yu xing de yanjiu' (*New Woman* and research on sex), *Xinnüxing*, 2, no. 3 (March 1927), pp. 237–41.

36 Yang Guanxiong, *Xingjiaoyu fa* (Method of sex education), Shanghai: Liming shuju, 1930, p. 123.

37 Fei Hongnian, *Shengwu de qiyuan* (The morphology and physiology of fertilization), Shanghai: Shangwu yinshuguan, 1926.

38 Charlotte Furth, 'From birth to birth: The growing body in Chinese medicine', paper presented at the Conference on Childhood in Premodern China, University of Virginia, May 1990, pp. 6–10.

knowledge about pregnancy and childbirth in Republican China. Pregnancy was portrayed as a pathological crisis, a period of disease and death in which women suffered from a physiological deterioration. Discarding traditional notions of internal imbalance and depletion of blood, new medical theories described pregnancy as a disease. The body changed, the womb expanded; the breasts became swollen with milk, the skin stretched and the nipples changed colour: milk could seep out even before lactation began. Compressed by the uterus, the bladder became rapidly filled with urine; the rectum was also trapped, leading to frequent constipation and retention of waste matter. Squeezed between urine and excrement, the placenta exerted an unbearable pressure on the waist and the thighs. Excess amounts of bodily fluids accumulated in the 'lower limbs' (*xiazhi*) and the 'lower stomach' (*xiafu*), while deoxygenated blood turned venules and veins blue, 'meandering over the legs like earthworms'. The sexual organs were tumescent: the mucous parts increased in size and turned purple, and vaginal discharges became more abundant. Conceptualized as being diseased, the pregnant woman was represented as a bag of filth ready for purgation. She became ugly, according to an *Essentials of obstetrics* (1920) printed in the Medical Series of the Commercial Press: 'Pale or sallow, even the most beautiful woman will wither at once.'[39] Her face became 'coarse'. Yellow or brown stains marred her face, neck and chest; purple varicose veins furrowed breasts and belly like a plough through the virgin soil (illustration 7). Pregnancy left indelible marks on the body: wrinkles, scars and birth-marks were 'never to disappear'. Respiration became difficult. The whole organism became a repository of pain: toothache, backache, headache, stomach-ache, all parts of the body were visited by the throes of gestation. Blood ascended to the brain, impairing mental control. Contact with the outside world became blurred: the senses of the pregnant woman lost their keenness and became obstructed (*zhang'ai*), leaving her prey to

39 Yao Changxu, *Taichan xuzhi* (Essentials of obstetrics), Shanghai: Shangwu yinshuguan, 1929 (1st edn 1920), p. 17.

a deregulated body which vomited food in the morning, oozed blood and suppurated through its orifices. Only 'delivery' (*fenmian*) would end the ascendancy of hidden forces, restoring to the woman a degree of autonomy for her womb.

Extremely graphic illustrations of open wombs in gynaecological and obstetric publications enhanced the medicalization of pregnancy and its representation as a potential disorder (illustration 11). Their visual impact was reinforced by the angle of the illustrations, as the gaze of the reader could explore the deeper recesses of hitherto uncharted parts of the body: human reproduction had become a public domain. Illustrations showed how organs developed inside the uterus of the pregnant woman. The placenta was made of a spongy, dark-red substance; the surface situated towards the uterus had deep grooves irrigated by blood, whereas the surface towards the embryo was smooth. It formed a screen, an intermediate substance (*zhongjianwu*) uniting mother and child in a single body. The embryo floated in the amniotic fluid, or 'sheep's liquid' (*yangshui*), a fluid which turned increasingly turbid with bodily detritus rejected by the foetus; this liquid had 'a bad smell similar to dish-water', according to an *Elementary knowledge of female hygiene* (1935).[40] The umbilical cord represented the 'passageway' (*tonglu*) of the body, infusing new blood into the foetus and exporting it back to the placenta through two separate channels.[41] Portrayed as a pathological and destabilizing event, gestation subjected women to an accumulation of unclean substances and an invasion of new life.

THE BODY WITHIN: THE FOETUS IN GESTATION

Ernst Haeckel's theory of recapitulation became a compelling explanation for biological evolution in early Republican China and its influence extended to embryology, anthropology, psychology, and even criminology, as the preceding chapter has

40 Su, *Funü*, p. 14.

41 Qu Shaoheng, 'Guanyu taipan ji qidai zhi tanhua' (About the placenta and the umbilical cord), *Shenbao*, 16 July 1934, 6:21.

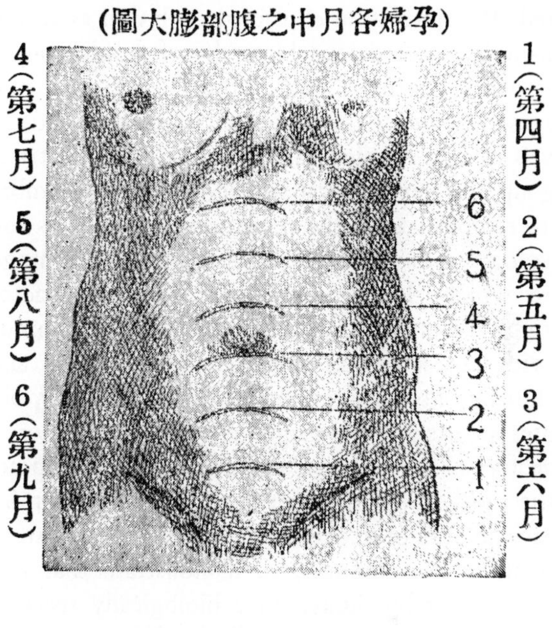

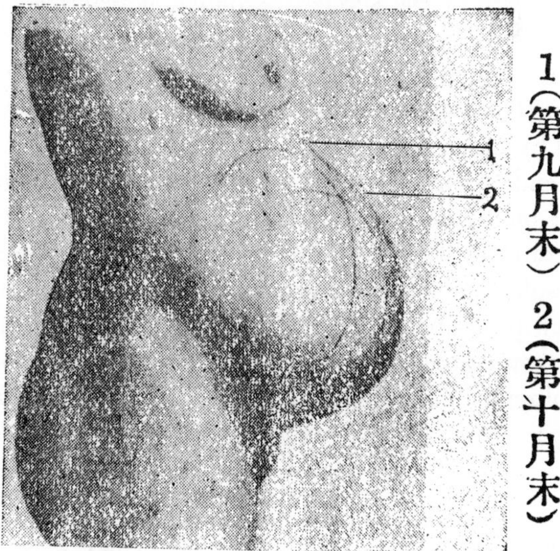

7. Different stage of pregnancy. Wang Yang, *Shengyu guwen* (Advice on childbirth), Shanghai: Zhongyang shuju, 1993.

highlighted. Recapitulation explained evolution as an inevitable ascent through a preordained hierarchy of development stages, and embryological growth was thought to pass through the earlier stages of evolution, starting with the amoeba and ascending to the levels of fish, reptile and finally mammal (illustration 12). Climbing up the genealogical ladder, the human embryo was thought to recapitulate all the transitional states of its ancestors. If embryology was believed to recapitulate cosmogony in an empire which closely linked microcosm to macrocosm,[42] modernizing discourses linked the foetus to a community of descent with characteristics inherited from remote ancestors. As Gui Zhiliang, a practising gynaecologist in Beijing, observed, the foetuses of early miscarriages resembled a pig or an ape, 'while the foetus has not yet acquired a human appearance'.[43] One of the most powerful theories of the early twentieth century, it gave an aura of scientific authenticity to a cluster of core beliefs. First, it was thought to demonstrate that individual bodies were inexorably linked to a biologically specific group called the 'race', and each individual's development recapitulated the life-history of the species. Secondly, it described evolution as a progressive and purposeful phenomenon, since every organism was thought to develop in a meaningful way towards maturity. Thirdly, it claimed that social hierarchies were preordained by nature, since a number of people, notably children, women and 'savages', would never evolve through the higher stages of biological development. Finally, it was thought that these hierarchies were irremediable, since they were imagined to be the result of biological determinants fixed at birth. In a secular age which proclaimed its belief in science, the theory of recapitulation lent support to racial mythologies and provided an epistemological foundation for claims about social order. Even in Europe, where it came under attack during the first decade

42 Norman J. Girardot, *Myth and meaning in early Taoism: The theme of chaos (hundun)*, Berkeley: University of California Press, 1983, p. 137.

43 Gui Zhiliang, *Nüren zhi yisheng* (A woman's life), Beijing: Zhengzhong shuju, 1936, p. 11.

of the twentieth century, it remained a widespread theoretical concept, used in such respected works as the *Textbook of Embryology* (1914).[44] Recapitulation offered a unified vision of mankind in which each creature was assigned a position. It was at once a message of hope – the 'race' was 'transformed forwards' (*jinhua*, the literal meaning of evolution) – and an anchor in times of change, since 'savages' and women were guaranteed never to attain the heights of civilization.

If woman was a man not fully evolved, according to some evolutionary theories, the reason for sex differentiation had to be found inside the embryo itself. Written in classical Chinese and published by small publishing houses which could hardly compete with powerful companies like the Commercial Press, traditional manuals of midwifery pointed at the position of the embryo in the womb, the relative temperature of the sperm and the phase of the moon on the day of impregnation.[45] These ideas were virulently attacked by modernizing writers in Republican China. In his *Misinterpretations in everyday biology* (1928), self-proclaimed natural scientist Liu Piji appealed to the chromosomal theory and the 'Western scientist Winiwarte' (*sic*) to discard traditional cosmologies which linked the development of the embryo to a higher metaphysical order.[46] Liu Piji also

44 E.W. MacBride, *Textbook of embryology*, London: Macmillan, 1914, vol. 1, pp. 20–5.

45 Chen Hu'an, *Taichan mishu* (The secrets of childbirth), Shanghai: Huiwentang xinji shuju, 1923 (Qing publication).

46 Hans von Winiwarter was an embryologist based at the University of Liège in the 1890s; he had little to do with the chromosomal theory which was first postulated by W.S. Sutton and T. Boveri at the beginning of the twentieth century. C.E. McClung did initial research on sex determination by chromosomes, the detailed study of which was carried further by N. Stevens and E.B. Wilson in 1905. Winiwarter's main interest was in mammalian ovogenesis in rabbits. How an obscure embryologist came to incarnate the chromosomal revolution for a popularizer of science living on the other side of the planet remains one of the lasting mysteries of 'Occidentalism'. Hans von Winiwarter, *Recherches sur l'ovogenèse de l'ovaire des mammifères (lapin et homme)*, Liège: Vaillant-Carmanne, 1900.

invoked a number of Chinese medical works which stressed the internalist perspective of procreation. He compared the chromosomal theory with the work of Chu Cheng (479–501), the alleged author of a treatise that was widely circulated in Ming and Qing times: 'When blood first reaches sperm, a male will be born; when sperm first reaches blood, a female will be born.' The famous sixteenth-century naturalist Li Shizhen, Liu Piji further underlined, had also emphasized the role of semen and blood in the process of reproduction. In portraying Chu Cheng and Li Shizhen as 'precursors' of 'modernity' who were only slightly 'less precise' than 'Winiwarte', Liu Piji insisted on the importance of locating the mechanisms of sexual differentiation within the bodies of partners rather than in the larger natural order: 'This interpretation entirely destroys the view that birth depends on destiny! The existence of man and woman is actually a matter of sperm. The birth of a girl or a boy is entirely dependent upon the bodies of the parents: it has absolutely nothing to do with destiny.'[47] The conjugal couple, represented as a union of opposites by modernizing voices like Liu Piji, was given an enhanced responsibility over the production of healthy offspring in which scientific knowledge spread by the new print culture played a fundamental role.

Even among embryologists in Europe, traditional notions of sex determination persisted well into the twentieth century. Although the popular belief in the spatial determinism of the womb, for instance, had been criticized by Patrick Geddes and John Arthur Thomson in 1889,[48] a certain Ernest Rumley Dawson published a book in 1909 entitled *The secret of sex: The discovery of a new law of nature*. Ernest Dawson claimed that the position of the embryo in the uterus determined the sex of a child, and his book included chapters on 'forecasting and pre-

47 Liu Piji, *Renjian wujie de shengwu* (Misinterpretations in everyday biology), Shanghai: Shangwu yinshuguan, 1928, pp. 85–7.
48 Patrick Geddes and John Arthur Thomson, *The evolution of sex*, London: Scott, 1889.

dicting the sex of the unborn child and on the determination or production of either sex at will'.[49] Dawson's approach was denounced shortly after the publication of his work,[50] but his book was introduced into China to cover in the cloak of science popular ideas about sex determination. Conspicuous advertisements flaunting a translation of Ernest Dawson's book by Luo Guangdao appeared in the summer of 1921 in several newspapers, to be attacked in turn by Chinese human biologists like Chen Jianshan.[51] Other dubious medical theories which claimed to have discovered the mechanism of sex determination were also quickly appropriated by unscrupulous commercial writers in Republican China. Wang Jungang, in a detailed piece of research on sex determination published by the Girl's Press, listed some of these theories: 'Maconnet', for instance, had proved that the sex of the embryo was entirely determined by the egg and was independent of sperm; 'Gedde' (*sic*) and 'Thompson' (*sic*) had written that well-nourished females often gave birth to females; 'Hosacker-Sadler' had statistically established that if the husband was older than the wife, the comparative birth-rate was 113 male versus 100 female infants; 'Schoner' had demonstrated that each ovary had three eggs, two of which were of the same sex: the left ovary statistically produced 63.82% females, the right exactly 63.77% males.[52] Some of these medical theories, often truncated and taken out of context, were not without resonances to traditional medical theories in China. If, for instance, some modernizing voices claimed that the European scientist 'Weill' had demonstrated that the sex of the embryo depended on the outcome of a battle between egg and sperm,

49 E.R. Dawson, *The secret of sex: The discovery of a new law of nature*, New York: Cochrane, 1909, preface.

50 Leonard Doncaster, *The determination of sex*, Cambridge University Press, 1912.

51 Chen Jianshan, 'Yichuan yu cixiong' (Heredity and sex determination), *Jiaoyu zazhi*, 15, no. 2 (Feb. 1923), pp. 21141–62.

52 Wang Jungang, *Xing de jueding* (The determination of sex), Shanghai: Nüzi shudian, 1933.

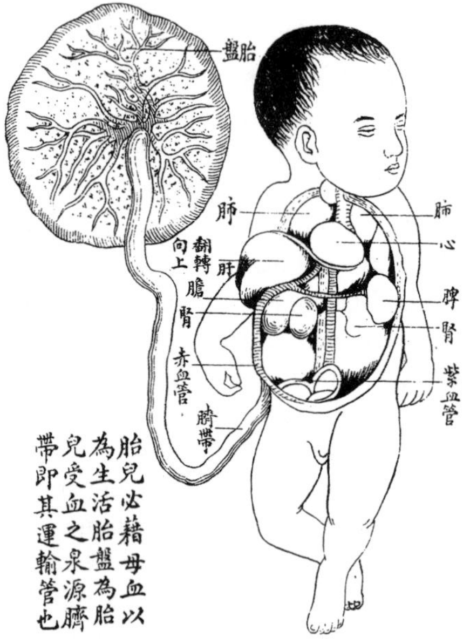

8, 9, 10. Illustrations of the foetus and the placenta first appeared in an anatomical treatise published by a foreign physician in Canton in 1850. The drawings were executed by Chinese artists and printed separately according to local custom during the 1880s and 1890s (illustration 8, from Benjamin Hobson and Chen Xiutang, *Quanti xinlun* [Outline of anatomy and physiology], 1850). The stylistic portrayal of a foetus attached to a placenta outside the womb became more common during the 1920s, and the drawing was reproduced with slight alterations in a 1932 medical compendium (illustration 9, from Gu Mingsheng, *Zhongxi hezuan fuke daquanshu* [Great compendium of Chinese and Western gynaecology], Shanghai: Dadong shuju, 1932). The same illustration can be found to this day in popular almanacs in Hong Kong (illustration 10, from *Yongjingtang* [Chinese almanac], Hong Kong: Wing King Tong, 1986). The history of this drawing shows how cultural representations could shift from high to low culture over the course of a century. First shared among a specialized group of scholar-intellectuals at the end of the Qing, circulated by the print culture of the coastal regions in Republican China, it became an integral part of popular culture in Hong Kong.

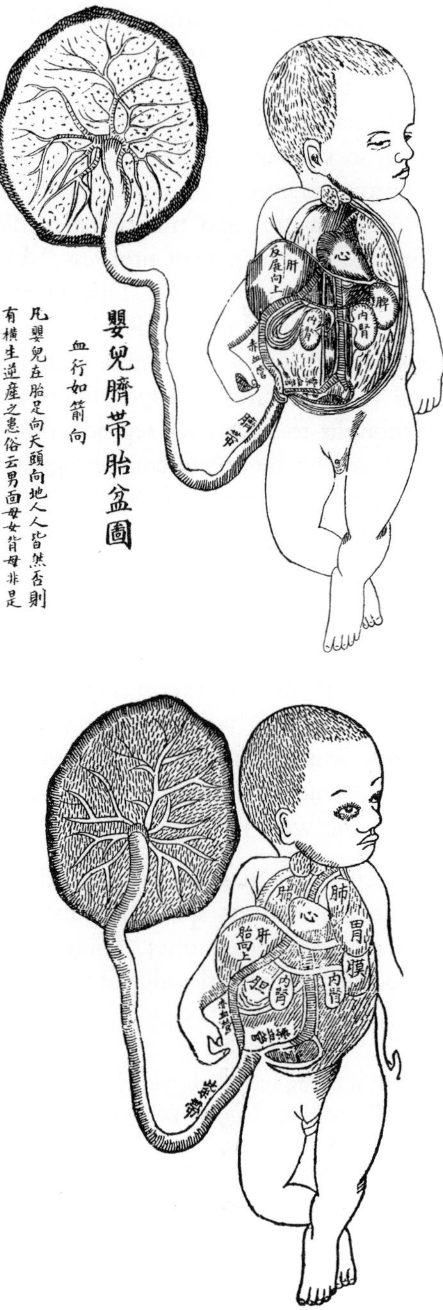
嬰兒臍帯胎盆圖
血行如箭向
凡嬰兒在胎足向天頭向地人人皆然否則
有横生逆産之患俗云男面母女背母非是
心
肝
反展向上
脾
内腎
肺
心
胃
肝
胎向上
膜
内腎
内腎

Zhu Zhensheng, author and editor of a number of works on traditional Chinese medicine, explained that the birth of a boy was the result of the original vitality of the father's sperm.[53] Human sexuality had become a cultural domain in which different versions of social reality competed with each other. In this social confrontation, references to science symbolically expressed an allegiance to modernity, and traditional medicine was identified as a banner of the enemies of progress.[54] Even in so-called 'traditional' theories, however, the focus was often on the inner workings of individual bodies. References to cosmological and demonological influences had almost entirely disappeared, a clear indication of the increased responsibilities which married couples were thought to have over reproduction. Readers were thoroughly confused by the many competing theories available, and wrote to specialized periodicals for further enlightenment. One example said:

> 'Dear Sir, many books on sex explain conception in different ways. Some say that intercourse within one to four days after menstruation produces a girl, within four to eight days a boy. Others claim that if the male sperm is ejaculated into the right side of the womb, a boy will be born, whereas the left side produces a girl. Some write that conception has to take place fifteen days after menstruation. I would be most grateful if you could tell me who is right and who is wrong.'[55]

Although the chromosomal theory assigned sex differences at random, a number of writers speculated about the proportion of male births *vis-à-vis* female ones. Some assigned a greater responsibility to the man with the idea of parental impregnation.

53 Chen Zejiang, 'Tai cheng nannü zhi yuanyin' (The reason for sex determination) in Zhu Zhensheng, *Qiuyun yu biyun* (Birth control), Shanghai: Xingfu shuju, 1933, pp. 12–14.
54 Ralph C. Croizier, *Traditional medicine in modern China: Science, nationalism, and the tension of cultural change*, Cambridge, MA: Harvard University Press, 1968.
55 'Tongxun' (Letters from readers), *Xinwenhua*, 1, no. 1 (Jan. 1927), p. 46.

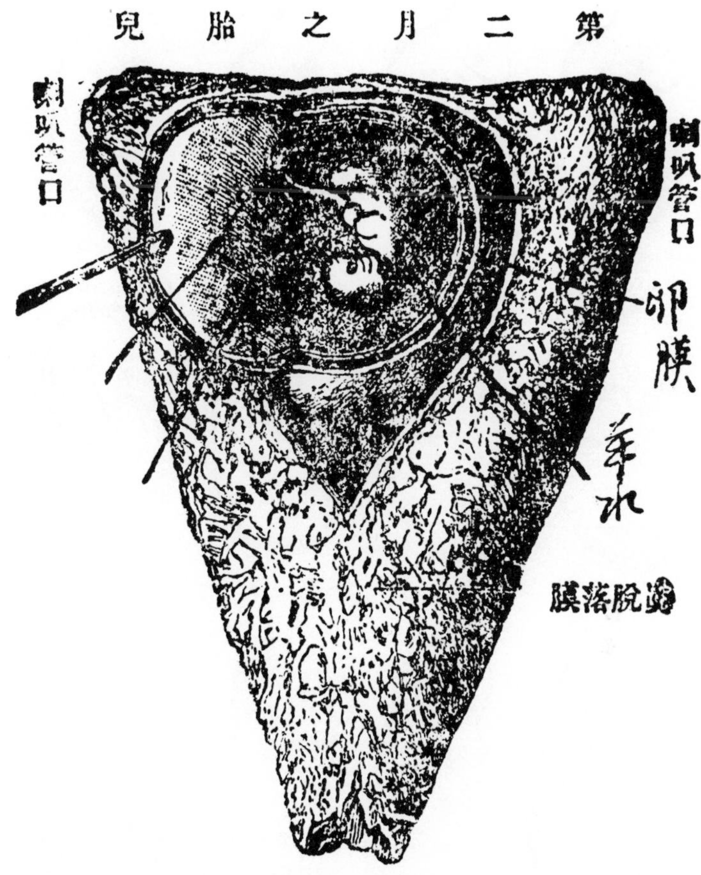

11. A pregnant womb. Yao Changxu, *Taichan xuzhi* (Essentials of obstetrics), Shanghai: Shangwu yinshuguan, 1929 (1st edn 1920).

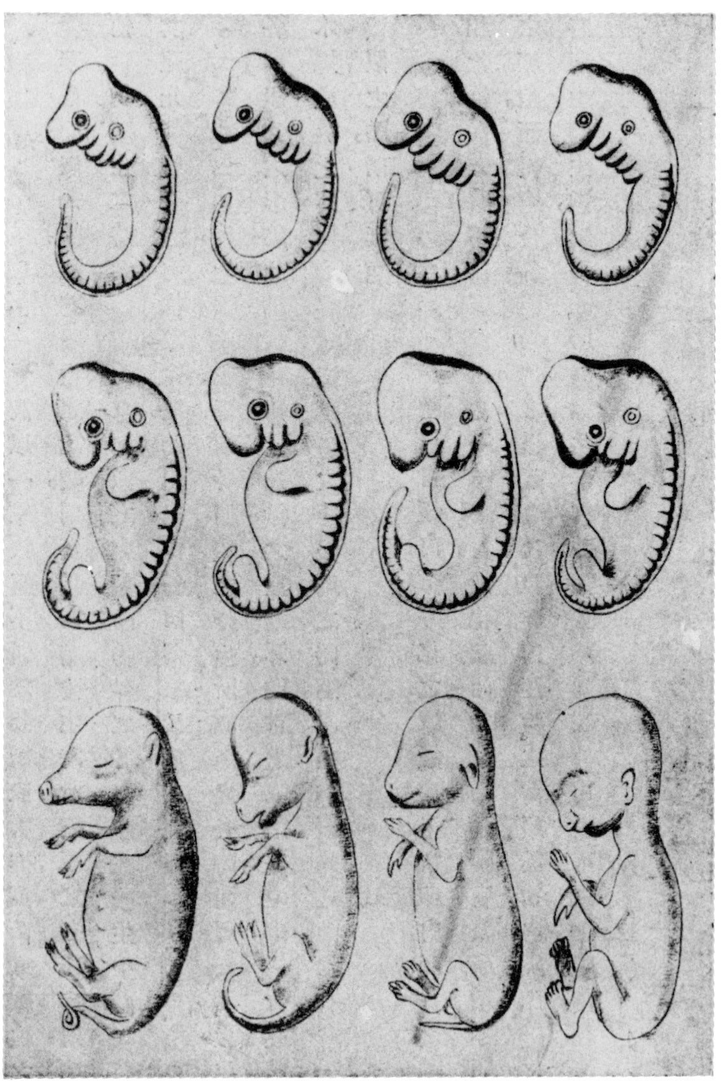

12. The theory of recapitulation illustrated: this picture was thought to reveal the similarities in foetal development of four different organisms (pig, cow, rabbit and human, from left to right) at three particular stages of growth, arranged from top to bottom. At the top of the facing page the nine stages of recapitulation through which the human foetus was thought to pass are detailed. Wang Shoucheng, *Gongmin shengwuxue* (A textbook of civic biology), Shanghai: Shangwu yinshuguan, 1928 (1st edn 1924).

THE DIFFERENT STAGES OF RECAPITULATION

First phase	The embryo is structurally similar to that of a worm, with no head, no central nervous system and no fully formed limbs.
Second phase	A cartilaginous skeletal rod called the notochord appears, and the embryo enters the stage of the slug.
Third phase	The two ventricles of the heart and the kidneys appear: the embryo transits through the stage of the fish.
Fourth phase	The limbs appear, and the foetus resembles a frog.
Fifth phase	Another ventricle leads to the reptile stage.
Sixth phase	The foetus is covered with hair and resembles a monkey; it has a long tail which will disappear before birth.
Seventh phase	The big toe appears at a right angle to the four other toes, exactly as in the anthropoid ape.
Eighth phase	The human features are completed.
Ninth phase	The human foetus is completely formed and ready for birth.

The first copulation would do no more than fertilize the female, wrote Chen Laoxin in the highly regarded journal *New Woman*: after fertilization, it would imprint the physical features of the father on the foetus.[56] New methods of choosing the sex of offspring, invoking the authority of science, were also regularly announced in daily newspapers.[57] The *Worker's Daily*, to take but one example, proudly described in 1935 how female spermatozoa survived much better than their male counterparts in the acid environment of the vagina, an advantage which would be greatly reduced by washing the female parts with sodium bicarbonate.[58] Images of female vulnerability and male physicality, widespread in Republican China, pervaded accounts of the influence of diet on the differential birth-rate of female and male children. In *Man may live two hundred years*, for instance, Gu Shi explained how the consumption of meat led to higher rates of male infants, since men were 'sturdier' and more 'physical' than women. Even in times of famine and hardship, natural selection

56 Chen Laoxin, 'Guanyu *Xingyu yu xing'ai*' (About *Sexual desire and sexual love*), *Xinnüxing*, 2, no. 2 (Feb. 1927), pp. 207–9.

57 For instance 'Yong dianliu jueding sheng nan sheng nü wenti' (Resolving the question of the sex of the embryo with the use of electric currents), *Guangming ribao*, 31 Aug. 1934, 4:1.

58 'Yu nan yu nü de rengong renshenfa' (Artificial pregnancy and a method to choose the sex of the child), *Gongshang ribao*, 11 July 1935, 4:1.

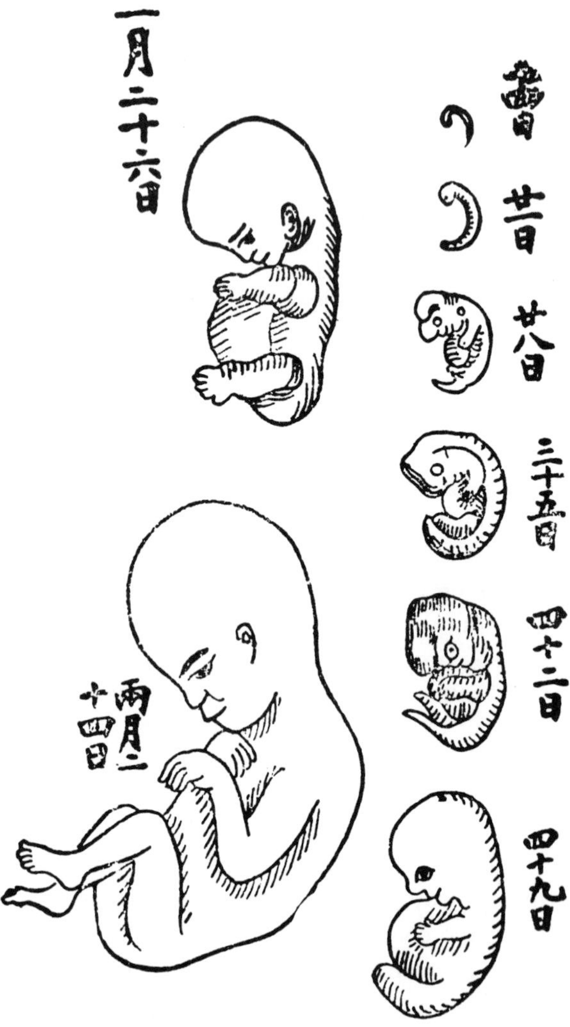

13. The different stages of foetal development. Yao Changxu, *Taichan xuzhi* (Essentials of obstetrics), Shanghai: Shangwu yinshuguan, 1929 (1st edn 1920).

somehow favoured male children, who needed less 'capital' (*ziben*) compared to the 'weaker' sex.[59] Gender representations of female passivity even characterized the work of sex revolutionary Zhang Jingsheng, who put it in elegantly constructed clauses reminiscent of classical Chinese:

> 'Civilized women produce more girls, barbarians produce more males. City people have more girls, country people more boys. With good harvests and mild weather more girls are born, in times of famine and war more males are born. In the plains and deltas people have more girls, in the highlands and mountains people have more boys. In retrospect, the production of male or female children depends on the diet and physical exercise of the parents.'[60]

THE LORE OF PRENATAL EDUCATION

In imperial China, the body was rarely imagined as a closed system living isolated from the environment, and foetal development was thought to be influenced by emotions and food. *Taijiao*, or prenatal education, was a set of practices based on the belief that external factors could influence the moral and physical characteristics of the foetus. Emotional or physical impressions from the outside world, it was held, were imprinted upon the child in the womb, and the mother was the medium through which baleful influences would make their way to the foetus. Strange stories about external impressions on the foetus abound in Chinese literature of the late imperial period, as Ann Waltner has suggested.[61] Although evidence for its importance in Ming and Qing medical discourse is contradictory,[62] prenatal

59 Gu, *Rensheng*, p. 123.

60 'Tongxun' (Letters from readers), *Xinwenhua*, 1, no. 1 (Jan. 1927), p. 46; see also 'Zhang Jingsheng de qilun sheng nan sheng nü juezhu yu fumu de jingli' (Zhang Jingsheng's strange claim that sex of the embryo depends on parents' vigour), *Xingzhou ribao*, 25 May 1936, 5:17.

61 Ann Waltner, *Getting an heir: Adoption and the construction of kinship in late imperial China*, Honolulu: University of Hawaii Press, 1990, pp. 37–43.

62 'Prenatal education' (*taijiao*) was not especially emphasized in the eighteenth

education was reinvented as a 'tradition' in Republican China by modernizing élites who assigned primary responsibility on women for the production of healthy offspring. Denounced as a 'superstition' by some,[63] a number of articles in the *Women's Journal* praised it as 'new prenatal education'.[64] Notions of prenatal education were compatible with some core themes of modernizing discourses, in particular because they emphasized that embryonic growth could be controlled, a departure from more fatalistic expectations which had already come under attack during the late imperial period.[65] They enhanced the status of the woman and identified her as an important mediator of marital harmony, thought to have a beneficial influence on the growth of the foetus.[66] Moreover, notions of prenatal education frequently invoked the 'future of the race' and the physical condition of next generations, establishing a link between the health of the foetus and the demographic strength of the

century, according to Charlotte Furth, 'Concepts of pregnancy', pp. 14–5; the idea of maternal impression (*ganshou muqi*), however, was important in sixteenth-century paediatric literature before it disappeared in the seventeenth century, according to Xiong Bingzhen, 'Chuantong Zhongguo yijie dui changcheng yu fayu xianxiang de taolun' (Debates about growth and development in traditional Chinese medicine), *Guoli Taiwan shifan daxue lishi xuebao*, no. 20 (July 1992), pp. 27–40.

63 For instance Chen Jianshan, *Taijiao* (Prenatal education), Shanghai: Shangwu yinshuguan, 1926; see also Huang Shi, 'Shenma shi taijiao' (What is prenatal education), *Funü zazhi*, 17, no. 11 (Nov. 1930), pp. 19–28.

64 Wang Chuanying (tr.), 'Xin taijiao' (New prenatal education), *Funü zazhi*, 4, no. 1–2 (Jan.–Feb. 1918); see also Xishen (tr.), 'Renshenzhong zhi jingshen ganying' (Spiritual impressions during pregnancy), *Funü zazhi*, 2, no. 10 (Oct. 1916), pp. 13–15.

65 Cynthia Brokaw, *The ledgers of merit and demerit: Social change and moral order in late imperial China*, Princeton University Press, 1991; Paolo Santangelo, 'Destiny and retribution in late imperial China', *East and West*, 42, nos 2–4 (Dec. 1992), pp. 377–442.

66 Zhu Wenyin, 'Taijiao yu youshengxue' (Prenatal education and eugenics), *Funü zazhi*, 17, no. 8 (Aug. 1931), pp. 11–19.

nation.[67] The embryo, the mother, the married couple and the nation were thus related in a biological bond and a common social responsibility. The uterine space, over which the mother was given responsibility, became a domain of public interest in which the state could claim a right to interfere. In one of the earliest debates on prenatal education, for instance, Kang Youwei envisaged that pregnant women would be supervised by qualified doctors in a prenatal education hospital (*taijiaoyuan*); in an effort to 'ameliorate the race': physically disabled and mentally deficient adults would be sterilized.[68]

Notions of prenatal education can be found in a great number of books on sexual hygiene, obstetrics and women's health in Republican China. An *Essentials of obstetrics*, first published in 1920 and running into its sixth reprint less than a decade later, sternly advised against any kind of emotion which would disturb the peace of mind of the pregnant woman. Any distressing news should be concealed, especially rumours of monstrous births, which might leave a lasting imprint upon the embryo. Vulgar songs and cheap novels were also said to have an impact upon the character of the foetus. High literature and refined music, on the contrary, would form a noble-minded baby. If the mother were suddenly scared, this would shock her foetus into a state of permanent epilepsy.[69] Although in China these prescriptions were generally absent from scientific publications like *The origin of sex of man* (1927) by Fei Hongnian, a professor at the Beijing Agricultural University,[70] even respectable scientists in parts of Europe were fascinated with questions of maternal influence on the foetus. Walter Heape, a reputed biologist and Fellow of the

67 Song Jiazhao, *Taijiao* (Prenatal education), Shanghai: Zhonghua shuju, 1914, p. 1; Song Mingzhi, *Taijiao* (Prenatal education), Shanghai: Zhonghua shuju, 1914, p. 5.

68 On Kang Youwei's racial thought, see Dikötter, *The discourse of race*, pp. 89–93 and 168.

69 Yao Changxu, *Taichan xuzhi* (Essentials of obstetrics), Shanghai: Shangwu yinshuguan, 1929 (1st edn 1920).

70 Fei Hongnian, *Renlei xingyuan lun* (The origin of sex in man), Shanghai: Shangwu yinshuguan, 1927.

Royal Society of Great Britain, suggested in his book entitled *Sex antagonism* (1913) that the metabolism of the mother could be affected by strong impressions, and that this stimulus was conveyed to the ovum or zygote by way of food; alternatively, he observed that the receptive power of the nervous tissue could be responsible for impressions on the foetus.[71] Similar debates took place in the pages of the *British Medical Journal* and the *Spectator*, a non-specialist journal of opinion, during the same period. The notion of maternal impression promoted 'the mind' as a powerful entity, a physical organ which increased in strength with the advance of 'civilization', and assigned greater responsibility for the health of offspring on pregnant women.

If an emphasis on diet as a foundation of health can be found in virtually all medical literature in Republican China, some popular obstetric guides continued to weave a network of correlations between macrocosm and microcosm through the assignment of symbolic meanings to food. The consumption of sparrow brain, for instance, would result in nyctalopia (night blindness), called 'sparrow's blindness' (*qiaomangyan*); rabbit meat naturally led to a harelip, according to a traditional *Questions and answers about obstetric problems* (1937), one of the few books printed by the new publishing houses which still used traditional concepts of vital energy (*qi*), blood (*xue*) and *yin* and *yang*.[72] Within more popular discursive registers, some booklets on childbirth also underlined analogies of sound and form, especially with ginger, thought to resemble a human finger and to cause the birth of a baby possessing an excessive number of fingers.[73] Ingestion of raw ginger (*shengjiang*) could also lead to the foetus being 'born dead and stiff' (*shengjiang*): did not the root of ginger resemble the numb corpse of a disinterred ghost, its limbs distorted in a devilish twist, the body disfigured by the entrails of the soil, reaching out its sterile flowers in despair? Following

71 Walter Heape, *Sex antagonism*, London: Constable, 1913, pp. 132–67.
72 Cai Luxian, *Taichan kebing wenda* (Questions and answers about obstetric problems), Shanghai: Huadong shuju, 1937, pp. 9–11.
73 Yao, *Taichan xuzhi*, p. 22.

the protein theory of semen (see chapter 6), modern manuals for pregnant women also continued to allude to the risk of eclampsia (*zixian*), or epileptiform seizures caused by *yin* deficiency and *yang* domination after excessive consumption of food rich in proteins.

Personal hygiene and bodily cleanliness, most modernizing writers were eager to emphasize, was a much more important key to health. Plenty of fresh air should be inhaled, and rooms were to be ventilated. Bolstered by popular ideas of *qi* ('gas', 'breath', 'odour' or 'air'), the atmosphere itself was thought to be prone to infection, spontaneously generated and spread in disease-engendering miasmas and effluvia;[74] foul effusions carried

74 Spontaneous generation was still a respectable topic for debate in Europe in the first decade of the twentieth century, and it was also an issue of some concern in China. In 1933, a participant at the Canton Exhibition exhibited the results of his research on heterogenesis: he claimed to have established that agar, a gelatinous substance obtained from seaweed, combined with the yolk of a chicken egg, could generate several small organisms, mainly bacteria and ticks. His findings attracted the attention of leading newspapers in Hong Kong and Shanghai, but were questioned by the scientific community. The South-West Commission on Educational Reform organized a Supervisory Committee for the Testing of the Theory of Spontaneous Generation, which invited him to repeat his experiences under scientific control. This committee, as well as the Department of Biology of the Sun Yatsen University, discovered the fraudulent methods of the doctor, and exposed his findings in several scientific journals (see Zhu Xi, *Women de zuzong* (Our forefathers), Shanghai: Wenhua shenghuo chubanshe, 1940, pp. 27–32; see also *Xiancun shengwu ziran fashengshuo zhi piping wenlu* (Documents criticizing the theory of spontaneous generation), Canton: Zhongshan daxue shengwuxi, 1933). Notions of spontaneous generation, in resonance with Buddhist beliefs in metempsychosis and Confucian conceptions of *yin* and *yang*, appealed to the traditional theory of 'birth by transformation' (*huashengshuo*); see Zhu Xi, 'Huashengshuo de jinhua' (The evolution of generation theories), *Ziran kexue*, 4, no. 4 (1933); Hu Xiansu, 'Huashengshuo yu shengming zhi qiyuan' (The origins of generation theories and destiny), *Kexue*, 12, no. 5 (May 1927), pp. 71–583; R. Hoeppli and Chiang I-hung, 'The doctrine of spontaneous generation of parasites in old-style Chinese and Western medicine: A comparative study', *Peking Natural History Bulletin*, no. 19 (1950). Hu Dunfu (1886–1978), founder of the private Datong University in 1922, based his theory of spontaneous generation on parallels derived from chemistry: water,

decayed organic matter. Although these conceptions were superseded by the germ theory of contamination in Republican China, notions of disease breeding in dark, murky and humid places continued to hold sway on modern minds. Sunbeams, one textbook on *Physiology and hygiene* (1927) written for middle schools and in its thirteenth edition explained, would destroy germs lurking in dank corners, whereas ventilation would drive infectious particles from the room.[75] Denouncing a popular taboo, Gu Shoubai, a German-educated anthropologist who wrote a number of textbooks on human biology for the Commercial Press, thought that health depended on exposure to solar rays.[76] Ideally, a house should face south, in accordance with

---

under certain circumstances, generated inorganic substances that could grow and multiply. The division and formation of the nucleus, a phenomenon directly responsible for cellular multiplication, had already been reproduced artificially with the help of electric currents: 'It is true that on the strength of experiments made with microbes, Pasteur claimed (with Virchow against Pouchet) that the spontaneous generation of life is impossible. But these experiences only prove that under certain conditions certain microorganisms do not reproduce themselves. They do not prove the absolute impossibility of spontaneous generation in the world. I do not see why life could not be brought about one day in a properly conducted experiment. The old vital theories are turned on their head, and the new ones spread [. . .] The great question is whether in suitable matter, life can be brought about by the influence of physical and chemical laws, as crystals are born in water. So far this has not been observed, but I believe it will be one day. I consider the attribution of life to the intervention of a Creator as being absolutely devoid of scientific foundation. I consider speculation about the transport of life germs through space to be useless, as the sowing of our planet leaves unanswered questions concerning the origin of life. I believe that life came directly and immediately out of matter on our earth when the matter had become suitable. Life then flourished in many forms by gradual evolution. I go so far as to deny that there is any essential difference between animate matter and inanimate matter.' Hu Dunfu, 'Shengsi zhi xin fenjie' (The new border between life and death), *Dongfang zazhi*, 9, no. 12, vol. 10, no. 3 (June-September 1913).

75 Wang Jianshan, *Shenglixue ji weishengxue* (Physiology and hygiene), Shanghai: Shangwu yinshuguan, 1927 (1st edn 1914), pp. 248–50.

76 Gu Shoubai, *Qihou yu jiankang* (Climate and health), Shanghai: Shangwu yinshuguan, 1924.

the rules of geomancy (*fengshui*); health guides advised against the western and northern directions. The bed should be placed in the middle of the room. Ancient-style wooden beds were described as inconvenient, as one could only enter them from one side.

Modernizing childbirth manuals enjoined on the pregnant woman to avoid strenuous activities such as working in the fields, lifting heavy bags of rice, carrying buckets of water on a shoulder-pole or riding on a horse-drawn cart. In a country afflicted by wars, famines and frequent natural disasters, the irony of such prescriptions is self-evident, and yet another indication that modernity was only meant for the new social formations in the coastal cities. Cheap obstetric manuals, on the other hand, continued to emphasize the benefits of work for pregnant women: the *Dashengpian*, a traditional handbook widely used in late imperial China and still printed by a Buddhist society in the 1930s, claimed that physical activity contributed to the circulation of blood and vital energy.[77] Obstetric manuals marketed by the powerful new publishing houses, on the other hand, underlined that excessive activity drained the nervous system, represented as a circuit with finite quantities of electric energy (more on this in chapter 6). Governed by representations of female vulnerability, diffusing new cultural models of behaviour, they advised the expectant mother to be careful when climbing the stairs and when travelling by train or in a rickshaw. Physical exercise was not allowed, although walking and taking deep-breathing exercises on clear days could be beneficial. The fashionable high-heeled shoes, status symbols of the urban middle class which were singled out by medical literature, were to be temporarily forsaken, as falls often led to premature birth. Bathing would keep the body clean and stimulate the circulation of blood; once fortnightly for fifteen to twenty minutes was sufficient, as longer periods were believed to lead to 'cerebral anaemia', considered to be another medical consequence of female

77 *Dashengpian* (Obstetrics), Shanghai: Foxue shuju, 1934 (orig. 1715), p. 15.

fragility.[78] New normative discourses of hygiene, based on notions of self-discipline and the regulation of bodily fluids, were even explained in daily newspapers.[79] Disinfection, or 'elimination of poisons' (*xiaodu*), was claimed to kill disease, and soap was recognized as having preventive virtues. The emphasis on soap was part of new cultural notions of cleanliness based on a clearer delineation of bodily boundaries: it would cleanse the surface of the body, dissolve dirt and kill germs. In the mechanical model of bodily representations, pores had to be opened and the skin had to breathe, otherwise carbon dioxide would get trapped and asphyxiate the body. In conformity with the medicalization of childbirth and its representation as a pathological process, it was advised to clean the room with a disinfectant and to sterilize any object coming into contact with the vagina.

If childbirth was represented as a pathological process, female sexuality was identified with danger. Sexual abstinence during pregnancy was recommended in the name of maternal and child health. Medical opinion considered that sexual intercourse during the last months could lead to miscarriage (*liuchan*) or premature delivery (*zaochan*). Excessive sexual arousal would dislodge the child or damage its shape; penetration could wound the womb and cause uterine contractions that destroyed the foetus. Only a few isolated voices were willing to reconsider the ban on intercourse during pregnancy in the name of conjugal harmony: 'In the past, some extremists and one-sided thinkers [. . .] used to advocate total abstinence during pregnancy. Such a request, however, imposes an unnecessary stress upon the continuation of normal marital relations between the couple, and therefore it is unreasonable and inappropriate.'[80] The author of *The happy*

78 Su, *Nüxing*, p. 13.
79 For instance Shen Jian'an, 'Renshenshi weishengfa' (Hygienic rules during pregnancy), *Shenbao*, 15 April 1934, 6:21; 'Chanfu weisheng' (Hygiene during parturition), *Dagongbao*, 24 April 1934, 3:11.
80 Wang, *Qingchun*, p. 99.

family (1931) also described the refusal to allow for 'physiological needs' to be satisfied during pregnancy as a threat to marital harmony.[81] Generally, however, admonitions against intercourse during the last months of pregnancy, which corresponded to reproductive concerns about female fertility, foetal growth and sexual hygiene, dominated most gynaecological and obstetric texts. Handwritten pamphlets distributed in Shanghai by the Ministry of Education in the 1930s for 'popular enlightenment' even banned intercourse for three months before and three months after the birth of a child.[82] Despite the paradoxes, contradictions and ambiguities which characterized these medical discourses in Republican China, all of them approached the individual through the prism of sexuality, from the uterine space of the woman to the private space of the conjugal couple. Sexuality emerged as an effective means of gaining control over the unborn child, the individual and the very species itself.

81 Liu Wang Liming, *Kuaile jiating* (The happy family), Shanghai: Shangwu yinshuguan, 1931, pp. 22–3.
82 Weisheng jiaoyubu (eds), *Chanfu baojian xuzhi* (Basic knowledge of health for lying-in women), Shanghai: Zhonghua pingmin jiaoyu cujinhui, no date, no pagination, 1930s.

4

'FOUR HUNDRED MILLION SIBLINGS': THE REGULATION OF 'POPULATION'

If the authority and prestige of Confucian knowledge rapidly declined after the fall of the last dynasty in 1911, a growing number of scholars increasingly invoked scientific categories of analysis in their search for national wealth and power. The biological category of 'race' and the administrative category of 'population' were heralded by modernizing élites as objects worthy of systematic investigation. Interest in the species was intimately linked to political ends, in particular to the growth of the state and the strengthening of the nation. If the empire's prosperity was previously defined in terms of grain or silver, 'population' was now valued as the main source of social and economic wealth, a force of great potential which should be properly measured and managed by the state. Considered to be a quantifiable entity with parameters such as 'size' and 'growth', it was also an anonymous mass, the sum total of individual bodies biologically joined together by ties of blood: 'population' became a universalizing concept which transcended lineage, class or region. Unlike a discourse of 'all under heaven' and 'common people' as during the empire, 'population' was a finite entity with a fecundity, health and hygiene that should be investigated for the benefit of the state.

The control of human reproduction in particular was seen as a key to the achievement of wealth and power. In order to control the 'population' for the requirements of the state, it seemed natural to analyse the age of marriage, sexual behaviour, coital frequency, rates of reproduction, numbers of births, the incidence of infanticide and other questions not previously considered to be of major importance. Discourses of sexuality and reproduction were the most powerful strategy in which individuals and population were united through the use of new knowledge. The supervision of life expectancy, of the relation between births and deaths, of the growth, density, distribution and structure of the population became the task of 'demography' (*renkouxue*, 'the science of population'), and its biological improvement became the concern of 'eugenics' (*youshengxue*, 'the science of superior birth'). Quantity and quality became the two aspects of the regulation of births and the administration of sexuality in modern China. Although the shift from metaphysics to science in debates about demographic strength took place between 1895 and 1927, a period dominated by cultural interaction with foreign discursive repertoires, the emergence of demographic thought can partly be traced back to the late imperial period.

THE EMERGENCE OF 'POPULATION'

Official assertions that the country had to be populated in order to be rich, and proclamations of the government's care for its subjects were common in imperial China: to govern was to populate. However, a specific interest in population numbers and reproductive rates was relatively new in the Qing dynasty. Although the history of demographic thought in China is a field which remains to be investigated, it seems reasonable to hypothesize that a concern with the sexual economy of individuals and a finite conception of 'population' as an object in its own right appeared among a small number of scholar-officials. Xu Guangqi (Paul Xu, 1562–1633), for instance, developed a theory of birthrates (*shengren zhi lü*) at the beginning of the seventeenth century. A leading Christian convert who collaborated with Matteo Ricci (1552–1610), Xu Guangqi explained his theory in a treatise on agriculture written in 1604: 'The law of birth of men is that generally they double every thirty years.'[1] During the same period, the man of letters Feng Menglong (1574–1646) metaphorically alluded in a tale to the

1 Xu Guangqi, *Nongzheng quanshu jiaozhu* (Complete book on agricultural management with annotations), Shanghai: Guji chubanshe, 1979, p. 90.

problem of unlimited growth: 'If each couple gives birth to a boy and a girl, population will never increase and we can subsist permanently. If a couple gives birth to two boys and two girls, population will double with each generation and will increase forever: on what could they be fed?'[2] Hong Liangji (1746–1809), a scholar interested in evidential research and statecraft scholarship (*jingshi*), was also alarmed by the soaring population growth around the end of the eighteenth century.[3] He developed a theory of overpopulation in a short essay published in 1793, five years before Thomas Malthus' *Essay on the principle of population*. Hong Liangji compared the unlimited increase in the population with the limited increase of the means of subsistence, and found too a correlation between demographic growth and economic decline. He proposed intervention by government to relieve people from the hardships of overpopulation: the state should encourage full cultivation of available land, reclamation of wasteland, a reduction in taxes, prohibition of luxury, equalization of wealth, and the opening of more granaries.[4] Although the available evidence remains fragmentary, it seems plausible that a number of scholar-officials in the seventeenth and eighteenth centuries had started to envisage 'the population' as a distinct category which should be quantified and administered.

The 'peril of overpopulation' (*renman zhi huan*) emerged as a cause for concern in the course of the nineteenth century. Tang Peng (1801–44), a scholar-official from Hunan province, devoted

2 Wang Shihe, 'Feng Menglong yu jihua shengyu' (Feng Menglong and birth control), *Renkouxue*, 1985, no. 4, p. 54.
3 On Hong Liangji, see Zhang Yinlin, 'Hong Liangji ji qi renkoulun' (Hong Liangji and his population theory), *Dongfang zazhi*, 23, no. 2 (January 1926), pp. 69–73, a summary of which appeared in C.F. Lung, 'A note on Hung Liang-chi, the Chinese Malthus', *Tien-hsia Monthly*, 1 (1935), pp. 248–50; see also Susan Mann Jones, 'Hung Liang-chi (1746–1809): The perception and articulation of political problems in late eighteenth-century China', Ph.D. dissertation, Stanford University, 1972.
4 Hong Liangji, 'Zhi ping pian' (On peace) in *Hong Beijiang shiwenji* (Poems and writings of Hong Liangji), Taibei: Shijie shuju, 1964, vol. 1, pp. 33–4.

much attention to the problem of vagrancy in his *Fu Qiuzi*, and considered overpopulation to be one of the causes of the empire's decline.[5] Xu Naiji (1777–1839), a high official in Beijing who opposed the prohibition of opium, suggested that in view of the demographic pressure, it was unnecessary to feel concerned for opium addicts, described as 'vagrants, lazy, without ambition or old'.[6] Starting with Gong Zizhen (1792–1841), a growing number of prominent scholars commented on the alarming increase in population,[7] although most conservative scholars continued to believe that the country should be densely populated in order to achieve wealth and power. Xu Zi (1801–62), for instance, blamed economic decline on the circulation of silver money, explicitly denying the existence of demographic pressure.[8] Even some scholar-officials interested in foreign affairs like Bao Shichen (1775–1855) haughtily dismissed the idea of overpopulation: 'The land under heaven is proportionate to the number of people that should be raised under heaven. If the number of people increases, production will also increase. Numbers are the foundation of wealth. How could it be reversed and lead to poverty?'[9] Traditional arguments in favour of an increase in the number of the emperor's subjects conceived of man as a producer, and more people were thought to produce more food to feed more people. It was in opposition to these orthodox ideas that some voices expressed concern about the economic effects of demographic growth.

These voices were sometimes articulate in the privacy of

5 Tang Peng, 'Yi pin' (To cure poverty) in *Fu Qiuzi* (Works of Tang Peng), Changsha: Yuelu shushe, 1987, pp. 313–19.
6 Qi Sihe (ed.), *Huang Juezi zoushu – Xu Naiji zouyi: hekan* (Combined publication of the memorials of Huang Juezi and Xu Naiji), Beijing: Zhonghua shuju, 1959, pp. 216–19.
7 Wu Shenyuan, '"Renman zhi huan": jindai Zhongguo renkou sixiang de "redian"' (The peril of overpopulation: a 'hot point' in modern Chinese demographic thought), *Renkouxue*, 1987, no. 3, pp. 92–3.
8 Xu Zi, *Weihuizhai wenji* (Collected writings of Xu Zi), Taibei: Wenhai chubanshe, 1970, p. 28.
9 Bao Shichen, 'Gengzhen zazhu er' (Notes on agriculture), *Qimin sishu* (Works on economy), 1888, *juan* 26, p. 2a.

personal diaries. In his journal kept during the turbulent years of the Taiping rebellion (1850–64), Wang Shiduo (1802–89), preceptor of the Imperial Academy and adviser to the governor of Hubei province, even outlined a theory of state power based on the limitation of births and the regulation of individual sexuality. He observed that 'there are too many people (there are too many women, hence there are too many people); because there are too many people, they are poor (there is not enough land to support them).' He calculated that the population doubled every thirty years, 'hence for every single person in the first year of this dynasty [1644], there are now 128 people.' Reclamation of land had reached its limits, and natural resources were exhausted:

> The calamity of overpopulation is such that even the summits of mountains have been planted with millet, the islets of rivers have been used for rice paddies. Virgin forests have been penetrated in Sichuan, groves of bamboo have been opened up in Guizhou, and still there is not enough land to support the people: all the resources of heaven and earth have been exhausted.

In a gruesome anticipation of twentieth-century totalitarian utopias, Wang believed that female children should be drowned, taxes should be imposed on the female population to implement a thorough infanticide policy, all female children born of poor parents should be drowned, sons that were physically abnormal or did not have handsome features should be drowned, temples, nunneries, 'institutes for virgin women' and 'halls of chastity' should be constructed in large numbers, people should be encouraged to become monks or nuns or to remain unmarried, and women with one existent child should be legally compelled to take abortifacient drugs.[10] The more explicit expression of a

10 Wang Shiduo, *Wang Huiweng yibing riji* (Diary of Wang Shiduo), Taibei: Wenhai chubanshe, 1967; Frank Dikötter, 'The limits of benevolence: Wang Shiduo (1802–1889) and population control', *Bulletin of the School of Oriental and African Studies*, 55, no. 1 (Feb. 1992), pp. 110–15.

concern which would surface periodically in the writings of other nineteenth-century scholars, Wang Shiduo focused on the regulation of reproductive behaviour for the sake of state power. From a concern within individual families over the continuation of the lineage, human sexuality and reproduction emerged as a public domain linked to the strength of the nation.

The interest in the mechanisms of human sexuality and reproduction culminated in the movement for political reform in the last decade of the nineteenth century, which openly sought to challenge imperial institutions and orthodox ideology. Selectively appropriating normative notions from foreign discursive repertoires, actively syncretizing indigenous trends of thought which have flourished since the seventeenth century, many prominent reformers proclaimed that the wealth and power of the nation were based on the physical strength of the population. Yan Fu (1853–1921) advocated a ban on early marriage, referring to the reproduction rate of the lower strata of society: 'Children feed on coarse food and live in filthy places; they are not properly bred, growing up amid disease and distress: the body becomes weak and the mind turns muddled. When they grow up, lust appears but intelligence stays dormant; they are anxious to take a wife, thereby spreading the wrong seed [*zhong*, 'race'] generation after generation.'[11] In Yan Fu's texts, the focus of the discourse was no longer on ethical values or on an order of virtue. The emphasis was on the control of human reproduction, the disciplining of individual behaviour for the sake of the nation. Human sexuality appeared as an object of inquiry, a target of intervention, the link between individual destinies and the fortunes of the modern state. In a utopian vision which derived more from indigenous scholarly trends than from foreign thought systems, the reformer and philosopher Kang Youwei proposed that selected women be impregnated in medical institutions for the propagation of the species. The diet

11 Yan Fu, 'Baozhong yuyi' (Afterthoughts on the preservation of the race) in *Yan Fu ji* (Collected works of Yan Fu), Beijing: Zhonghua shuju, 1986, p. 87.

and clothing of these women would be determined by medical authorities, and pregnant mothers would be allowed to have sexual intercourse with mechanical robots only. Nurses would take care of the delivery, census officers would record new births, doctors would eliminate inferior babies, and the population office would name the successfully selected infants who would be placed in special institutions.[12] For Kang Youwei and his successors, the disciplining of individual sexual conduct and the regulation of the population's reproduction were seen as the key to wealth and power. Represented in evolutionist terms of national survival and struggle for existence, political power was no longer considered to be the result of public virtue or individual morality: demographic strength was the only criterion by which the expansion or destruction of the state could be measured. In political discourse, practical knowledge about national populations superseded moral theory concerning the emperor's subjects.

Thomas Malthus's population principles were introduced in China by a foreign missionary in 1880,[13] but remained unnoticed until the reformers endowed them with meaning by effectively linking new knowledge to political power in 1898. Even in the first decade of the twentieth century, in which neo-Confucian knowledge still represented power and prestige, appeals in favour of the regulation of births remained relatively rare.[14] Zhang Zongyuan, writing in a prominent journal pub-

12 See part 6, chapters 2 and 3 of Kang Youwei, *Datongshu* (One World), Beijing: Guji chubanshe, 1956; partial translation in Laurence G. Thompson, *Ta t'ung shu: The one world philosophy of K'ang Yu-wei*, London: Geo. Allen and Unwin, 1958.

13 Wang Shengduo, 'Maersaisi renkoulun zai Zhongguo de liuchuan he lunzheng' (The spread and debate on the population theory of Malthus in China), *Shehui kexue yanjiu*, no. 6 (Nov. 1986), p. 17.

14 'Lun Zhongguo zhi luan youyu renkou zhi zhonggua' (A large population causes political unrest in China), *Dongfang zazhi*, 1, no. 6 (June 1904), pp. 115–20; 'Lun Zhongguo zhi luan yu renkou zhi guanxi' (The relationship between overpopulation and political unrest), *Dongfang zazhi*, 4, no. 7 (July 1907), pp. 129–32.

lished by the Commercial Press, noticed that wealthy families had less children than commoners: 'Statistically, the families called wealthy have a rather low rate of growth, precisely because wealth is often the result of ability and intelligence, and the intelligent are able to control their sexual desires. If the children of dissipated people were also to enjoy the kind of lifes lived by the wealthy, they would not be able to restrain themselves, so how could growth be limited? This is why intelligent people should be allowed to enjoy the results of their self-control, whereas common people should be encouraged to practise self-restraint: only then will wealth increase and growth decrease.'[15] Individual restraint and social discipline would become core themes of modernizing discourses after the disintegration of neo-Confucian knowledge in 1911.

EUGENICS AND RACIAL HYGIENE

Sexual desire, conceptualized as an impulsive and instinctual urge, was increasingly targeted as a domain for state intervention and public control in Republican China. Introduced by the liberal professions of the civilization of the coast, medical sciences such as human biology, physiology and genetics provided a scientific legitimacy for the notion of self-discipline, first outlined by the reformers of the late imperial period. Individual desire, it was claimed, had to be disciplined, evil habits had to be eliminated, and couples were to regulate their sexual behaviour strictly to help bring about the revival of the nation. The survival of the social group, represented in biologizing terms of 'race', was thought to be founded on a sense of self-discipline and restraint: 'To strengthen the country, one first has to strengthen the race; to strengthen the race, one first has to improve sex education.'[16] The regulation of desire came to be considered as the

15 Zhang Zongyuan, 'Lun gujin shengjijie zhi jingzheng' (About competition over the means of livelihood in past and present), *Dongfang zazhi*, 3, no. 9 (Oct. 1906).

16 Wang, *Qingchun*, p. 1; see also Du Zuozhou, 'Xingyu jiaoyu' (Sex education), *Zhonghua jiaoyujie*, 15, no. 12 (June 1926), pp. 1–8.

very basis for racial regeneration, and Yun Daiying (1895–1931), an early Communist Party member and editor of the periodical *Young China*, put it in unambiguous terms: 'The existence of the individual is but a means to transmit the race.'[17] For the academic scientist Xue Deyu, an editor of books on natural sciences in a publishing house in the capital Nanjing, the purpose of sex was 'the reproduction of the race'.[18]

Representations of racial degeneration further strengthened the discursive link between sex and procreation. Civilization, according to some observers, had blotted out the natural laws of selection, and 'unfit' people proliferated on the edges of society. Pan Gongzhan (1895–1975), a notorious journalist and publisher, director of the Bureau of Social Affairs and the Bureau of Education in the municipality of Shanghai before serving the government as vice-minister of information between 1939 and 1941, was one of the first to take an active interest in 'the science of sex'. For this influential public figure, the physical degeneration and the moral dissolution of the 'race' were the twin dangers of 'modern civilization'.[19] In a period of 'moral decline', other sex educators clamoured for chastity before marriage, eugenic criteria in the choice of a marriage partner, the prevention of hereditary diseases and the elimination of deviant practices. Heredity, descent, sexual hygiene and race became the core themes of medical and eugenic discourses. The family would regulate the procreative functions of the social subject for the sake of the nation. Discipline supplanted love in the rules which governed conjugal alliances, claimed Zhou Jianren, a respected expert on biology: 'Eugenic principles should guide love. Many people believe that love is difficult to direct; in the West, people say that love is blind, which means that Amor, the spirit of

17 Yun Daiying, 'Lun shehuizhuyi' (About socialism), *Shaonian Zhongguo* (Young China), 2, no. 5 (Oct. 1922), pp. 1–6.
18 Xue Deyu, *Shengwu de mudi shi baozhong* (The goal of organisms is the preservation of the race), Shanghai: Xinya shuju, 1933, p. 53.
19 Pan Gongzhan, 'Liangxing jiaoyu' (Education for both sexes), *Jiaoyu zazhi*, 12, nos 10 to 12 (Nov. 1920 to Jan. 1921).

love, blindly shoots his arrows, but in reality, things are quite different.'[20] Instead of conferring rights to individual expression, as a conception of 'sexuality' entailed in Europe, a discourse of desire demanded that the social subject subordinate his drives to the needs of a higher collectivity.

If the social subject could be taught the disciplines of the body, the menaces of heredity should be averted by the intervention of the state. In their racialization of the nation, discourses of eugenics most clearly endowed the state with a responsibility in the production of a healthy population. Proponents of eugenics claimed that breeding principles such as assortative mating and artificial selection could prevent further degeneration. 'Positive eugenics', a term first coined by Francis Galton (1822–1911), whose portrait quickly became an emblem of modernity in many textbooks on human biology (illustration 14), would ensure that individuals with above-average abilities would breed at a higher rate than ordinary people. 'Negative eugenics' would restrict the reproduction of inferior people; those having subnormal abilities would have to be physically prevented from perpetuating their infirmities. Mainline eugenists assumed that intellectual capacity and behavioural traits were inherited and could not be significantly enhanced by education. Those defined as being of the lowest intelligence became the main target of eugenic discourses, which campaigned for their segregation or sterilization. Although eugenics never achieved a significant degree of institutional organization in Republican China, notions of race improvement were widespread and pervasive in civil society.[21] It was actively supported by members of the professional classes, in particular intellectuals, university teachers, sociologists and biologists, and cut across most political positions, from the fascist core of the

20 Zhou Jianren, 'Shanzhongxue de lilun yu shishi' (The theory of eugenics and its implementation), *Dongfang zazhi*, 18, no. 2 (Jan. 1921), pp. 63–4.
21 Frank Dikötter, 'Eugenics in Republican China', *Republican China*, 15, no. 1 (Nov. 1989), pp. 1–18; Frank Dikötter, *The discourse of race in modern China*, London: C. Hurst/Stanford University Press, 1992, chapter 6.

14. Francis Galton, father of eugenics and emblem of modernity. Wang Qishu, *Jinshi shengwuxue* (Modern biology), Shanghai: Shangwu yinshuguan, 1925.

Guomindang to the communist theories of Chen Duxiu. The latter published an article on Malthusianism advocating population control,[22] and privately underlined that 'racial selection

22 Chen Duxiu, 'Maersaisi renkoulun yu Zhongguo renkou wenti' (The demographic theory of Malthus and the population problem in China) in Chen Duxiu, *Chen Duxiu wenzhang xuanbian* (Selected writings of Chen Duxiu), Beijing: Sanlian shudian, pp. 505–6.

should be implemented and inferior elements (*elie fenzi*) forbidden to marry' in order to arrest the intellectual and physical degeneration of the country.[23]

Although modernizing élites were instrumental in putting forward eugenic views, theories of race improvement circulated among a much wider audience in China. Cheap textbooks on heredity and genetics explained to the public the dangers of racial degeneration (illustration 15). Primers, self-study manuals, cheap pamphlets and 'ABC' introductions to mainline eugenics were published throughout the 1920s. Hereditary principles, endowing sex with a biological responsibility for future generations, were thought to highlight further the need for social discipline. Mendelian laws were spread by popular journalists and commercial writers to underline how genetic factors determined the endowment of an individual. Student magazines urged university students to undertake eugenic research for the sake of advancing the 'race', the state, and the individual.[24] In the 1930s, eugenic discourses became increasingly common in medical circles, 'degeneration' and 'racial hygiene' being the catchwords of the day. Official marriage guides encouraged 'superior' people to marry for the regeneration of the 'race',[25] since 'inferior' and 'weak' characteristics were transmitted through sexual congress; a popular guide for women published by the Commercial Press described hereditary diseases as the 'germs of race betterment' which threatened the 'race' with degeneration and final extinction (*zhongzu zimie*).[26] Medical journals initiated the study of 'racial biology'. For instance, Dr Jin Zizhi explained in his widely read book *Racial hygiene* how the future of the nation

23 Chen Duxiu, 'Chen Duxiu da Mo Fuqing' (Reply of Chen Duxiu to Mo Fuqing) in Chen Duxiu, *Chen Duxiu shuxin ji* (Collected correspondence of Chen Duxiu), Beijing: Xinhua chubanshe, 1987, p. 51.
24 Wu Zhenzi, 'Women wei shenma yao yanjiu youshengxue' (Why we should study eugenics), *Xuesheng zazhi*, 15, no. 9 (Sept. 1928), pp. 31–6.
25 See for instance Ma Chonggan, *Jiehun zhidao* (Marriage guide), Shanghai: Qinfen shuju, 1931, pp. 11–12.
26 Zhang Jixiu, *Funü zhuance* (Special handbook for women), Shanghai: Shangwu yinshuguan, 1937, pp. 52–61.

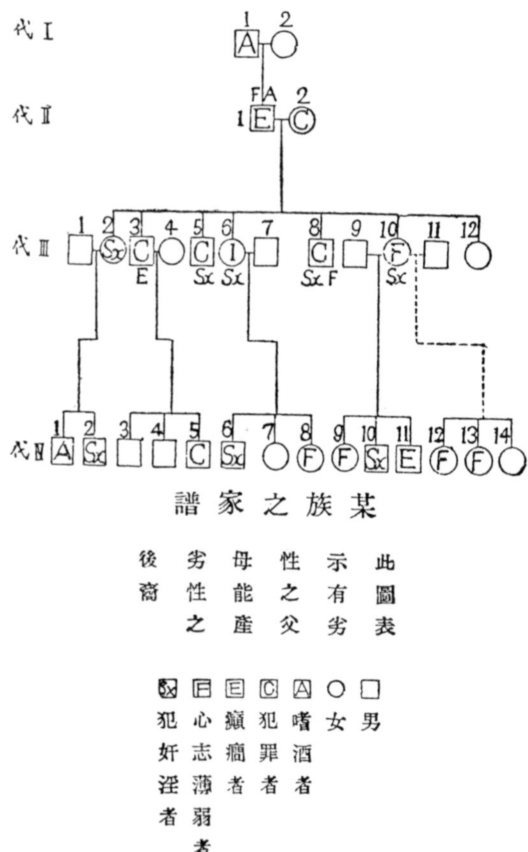

15. Graph illustrating how 'inferior characteristics', including alcoholism, criminality, epilepsy and adultery, can be transmitted genetically to the next generation. Wang Shoucheng, *Gongmin shengwuxue* (A textbook of civic biology), Shanghai: Shangwu yinshuguan, 1928 (1st edn 1924).

was dependent on the physical condition of its population.[27] Professor Yi Jiayue, a highly respected member of the academic community, made the forceful statement that 'if we want to strengthen the race, there is no time to waste. We should first implement a eugenic program. Strictly speaking, we should not just forbid the sexually diseased, the morons and the insane to marry. For those who abuse the sexual instinct and create a menace to future generations, there can only be one appropriate law of restraint: castration!'[28]

Collective reproductive strategies were considered to be the solution to racial degeneration. Handbooks and self-study booklets on heredity, genetics and biology often included a chapter on the need to eliminate 'inferior' characteristics. As Wang Shoucheng put it in a *Textbook of civic biology* (1924), which was approved by the Ministry of Education for use in middle schools, 'the choice of an unfit partner harms society and the future of the race. To establish a strong country, it is necessary to have strong citizens. To have strong and healthy citizens, one cannot but implement eugenics. Eugenics eliminates inferior elements and fosters people who are strong and healthy in body and mind.'[29] By the mid-1930s, medical debates on race improvement even reached the daily newspapers. One Hong Kong daily heralded as imminent the breeding of 'scientific babies' by eugenic methods,[30] the *Central Daily* devoted two pages to the 'Question of race improvement',[31] and the *New*

27 Jin Zizhi, *Minzu weisheng* (Racial hygiene), Shanghai: Shangwu yinshuguan, 1930.

28 Yi Jiayue, 'Zhongguo de xingyu jiaoyu wenti' (The problem of sex education in China), *Jiaoyu zazhi*, 15, no. 8 (Aug. 1923), p. 22160.

29 Wang Shoucheng, *Gongmin shengwuxue* (A textbook of civic biology), Shanghai: Shangwu yinshuguan, 1928 (1st edn 1924), p. 52.

30 'Renzhong gailiang xiansheng jiang you kexue yinghai chuxian' (First signs of race improvement: Imminent appearance of scientific babies), *Xianggang gongshang ribao*, 18 Jan. 1935.

31 'Minzu gaizao wenti' (The problem of race reform), *Zhongyang ribao*, 20 Aug. 1935.

China Times introduced heredity and eugenics to its readers.[32] Similar developments took place in the West, as has been documented in the enormous secondary literature produced in recent years.[33] In the USA, moreover, a number of states actually passed eugenic sterilization laws and limited marriage selection.[34] In Germany, the Nazi regime translated its racial ideology into official policy by systematically persecuting Jews, Gypsies, mentally and physically handicapped people, and homosexuals.[35] Contrary to these developments, eugenics in Republican China never achieved legislative expression.

THE REGULATION OF BIRTHS

A proliferation of publications in the 1920s and '30s conceptualized 'the population' as a fundamental category for economic and political analysis, a discursive practice sustained by study societies and institutions exclusively dedicated to demography, such as the Institute of Census Research. Population specialists attempted to quantify the population in censuses, statistics, charts, diagrams and mathematical models. Their classifications, moreover, constructed boundaries between the 'national' population and 'foreign' populations, contributing to the racialization of the nation as if it were a distinct biological group. The hydraulic metaphor, which used a vocabulary of 'population flow' and 'population pressure' (*renkou yali*), also fostered repre-

32 'Yichuan yu yousheng' (Heredity and eugenics), *Shishi xinbao*, 11 Jan. 1935.

33 P.J. Pauly, 'Review article: The eugenics industry – Growth or restructuring?', *The Journal of the History of Biology*, 26, no. 1 (Spring 1993), pp. 131–45; Mark Adams, *The wellborn science: Eugenics in Germany, France, Brazil and Russia*, Oxford University Press, 1990.

34 D.J. Kevles, *In the name of eugenics: Genetics and the use of human heredity*, New York: Alfred Knopf, 1985.

35 Michael Burleigh and Wolfgang Wippermann, *The racial state: Germany 1933–1945*, Cambridge University Press, 1991; Robert N. Proctor, *Racial hygiene: Medicine under the Nazis*, Cambridge, MA: Harvard University Press, 1988; Paul J. Weindling, *Health, race and German politics between national unification and Nazism, 1870–1945*, Cambridge University Press, 1989.

sentations of human beings as a homogeneous entity which could be measured and regulated. More important was the comparison of society to a body, an organism, a biological entity requiring administration and control. Demographic discourses mapped the population in terms of state of health, patterns of disease, diet and habitation. Public health, as we see in the next chapter, became a concern of the state. The nation became an organic tissue and its vitality needed medical supervision. Individual bodies were related to the national body in representations derived from pathological terminology: man was condemned as a 'diseased particle' or praised as a 'valid element'. Bodies became economic units with specific values (*jiazhi*): 'If the value of an individual is weak, the collective strength will be below par. When collective strength is below par, the individual cannot survive either,' according to *The Chinese population problem* (1930) written by the demographer Xu Shilian.[36] Medical concern over the regulation of reproductive strategies was also clearly expressed in discussions about birth control.

The official ideology of the Guomindang, based on Sun Yatsen's Three Principles of the People, was opposed to the limitation of births. As an exponent of Jiang Kaishek's regime put it, 'To solve the population problem, the economy must be developed and wealth fairly distributed, so that each person may have enough to eat and all may live and procreate happily and peacefully; one should definitely not advocate the limitation of births, which is committing race suicide.'[37] Even within official circles, however, contradictory voices emerged, and Chen Changheng, a committee member of the Legislative Yuan, identified the limitation of births as a key policy in *The Three People's Principles and population policies* (1930).[38] The notion that the strict regula-

36 Xu Shilian, *Zhongguo renkou wenti* (The Chinese population problem), Shanghai: Shangwu yinshuguan, 1930, p. 7.
37 Li Meishi, 'Sanminzhuyi de renkoulun' (The Three Principles of the People and demographic theory), *Xiandai Zhongguo zazhi*, 2, nos 1–2 (Aug. 1928).
38 Chen Changheng, *Sanminzhuyi yu renkou zhengce* (The Three Principles of the People and population policies), Shanghai: Shangwu yinshuguan, 1930, chapter 3.

tion of reproductive rates was a path to national power and racial strength was not only shared by most demographers,[39] but also by other sectors of the academic field. Although contraceptive methods in Republican China were adopted exclusively by the professional classes,[40] control over the conception of life became a heated topic of debate among intellectuals with the visit of Margaret Sanger in 1922.[41] A Birth Control League was finally organized in Shanghai in the beginning of the 1930s by Yan Fuqing (1882–1970) and a Eugenics Society mainly interested in contraception was established in Hong Kong in May 1936 under the direction of Nie Kesheng.[42] During the mid-1930s, the

39 The following are some of the most influential works which advocated birth control: Chen Da, *Renkou wenti* (Population problems), Shanghai: Shangwu yinshuguan, 1934; Chen Tianbiao, *Renkou wenti yanjiu* (Research on population problems), Shanghai: Liming shuju, 1930; Ke Xiangfeng, *Xiandai renkou wenti* (Modern population problems), Shanghai: Zhengzhong shuju, 1934; Sun Benwen, *Renkoulun ABC* (ABC of population theories), Shanghai: Shijie shuju, 1928; Wu Zelin and Ye Shaochun, *Shijie renkou wenti* (Problems of the world population), Shanghai: Shangwu yinshuguan, 1938; Xu Shilian, *Renkoulun gangyao* (Essentials of population theory), Shanghai: Zhonghua shuju, 1934.

40 In a survey of thirty-four educated urban women conducted in 1930, it was found that only three of them were in possession of information on birth control; see H.D. Lamson, 'Educated women and birth control in China', *China Medical Journal*, 44, no. 12 (Dec. 1930), pp. 1100–9.

41 Margaret Sanger, *My fight for birth control*, New York: Farra and Rinehart, 1931, and *Margaret Sanger: An autobiography*, New York: Norton, 1938, reprint by New York: Dover, 1971 (both autobiographies were ghost-written and should be treated with caution). The American crusader for birth control was asked by Hu Shi to address students at the Beijing National University. Students arranged to have notes of her talk transcribed, and a copy of Sanger's *Family limitation* was translated the same evening. A pamphlet of twenty-six pages was published in 1922, and other translations followed. See Margaret Sanger, *Shengyu jiezhifa*, Shanghai: Zhonghua jieyu yanjiushe, 1922; Margaret Sanger, *Nüzi yingyou de zhishi* (What every girl should know), tr. by Zhao Yuanren, Shanghai: Shangwu yinshuguan, 1931.

42 'Bengang yixuejie chouzu Xianggang youshenghui' (Medical circles in Hong Kong organize a Hong Kong Eugenics Society), *Xianggang gongshang ribao*, 21 May 1936, 3:3.

issue was eagerly taken up by the popular press, and contraceptive knowledge spread in vernacular newspapers.[43] Birth control was generally ignored by official publications and only rarely discussed in government circles, particularly since Sun Yatsen had favoured an unconditional increase of China's population. Concern with birth control rarely achieved real organizational expression.

Birth control was initially called 'limitation to the production of children' (*chan'er zhixian*), a mechanized representation which allowed the detailed portrayal of means to stop 'production'. Birth control pamphlets, best understood as a part of the marriage advice literature which flourished during the 1920s, listed all the methods available to the 'modern couple'. Some handbooks even prescribed how to make condoms out of animal guts: a fresh caecum should first be thoroughly washed, then soaked in water containing a thousandth part of mercuric chloride before being degreased in alcohol. Mechanical dilation and a rubber ring to seal off one end would make the condom ready for use.[44] The cervical cap, which was only invented at the turn of the century in Europe, was also recommended in the 1920s. Detailed descriptions of other methods of birth control, such as vaginal sponges, pessaries, inter-uterine devices, acidic powders and jellies were also circulated in the literature on birth control.

Proponents of reproductive control underlined the medical disadvantages of unrestricted procreation. The physical hardships of repeated pregnancies, the high maternal mortality rate, the lack of appropriate hygienic care during childbirth and improperly performed abortions were denounced by modernizing élites as the result of 'popular ignorance'. Birth control, a special issue of the *Women's Journal* claimed, would contribute to the 'regeneration of the race'.[45] Raising the spectre of a differential

43 Guo Taihua, 'Biyunfa lüeshu' (Brief discussion of birth control methods), *Shenbao*, 21 Sep. 1934, 5:20; 'Nüxing yingyou de yousheng zhishi' (Basic eugenics for women), *Shishi xinbao*, 16 Nov. 1934, 2:4.
44 Cheng, *Jieyu shengyu*, p. 99.
45 'Ying Sanger Furen' (Welcoming Miss Sanger), *Funü zazhi*, no. 6 (June 1922), p. 3.

birthrate between 'educated classes' and 'lower classes', on the other hand, some prominent voices opposed the spread of contraceptive knowledge. Pan Guangdan (1898–1967), the most notorious eugenist in China, predicted how hordes of inferior creatures would swamp the professional classes who practised birth control.[46] Gao Xisheng, the author of an *ABC of birth control* (1929), emphasized that 90 per cent of the children born of factory girls were 'mentally retarded' (*dineng*),[47] a dysgenic tendency which was thought to increase with the dissemination of contraceptive knowledge to the educated public. Pan Guangdan even expressed concern about the lack of fertility among the 'superior elements' of the 'race', and suggested implementing a 'birth release program' for the higher strata of society. Many members of the professional classes shared the belief that birth control would lead to the decimation and extinction of the more gifted 'stocks' in the population. Despite the very contradictory and competing voices that emerged in debates on the limitation of births, however, all of them represented human reproduction as the biological link between the individual and the population which needed to be regulated for the health of the species.

The Japanese invasion in 1937 plunged the country into a prolonged war that pushed population policies into the background. Pan Guangdan's views, however, were officially endorsed in the 1940s. The Committee for the Study of Population Policies, organized by the Ministry of Social Affairs in 1941, was the first official attempt to approach demographic issues systematically. It recommended the segregation of physically and mentally handicapped persons from the 'normal population' for what was called 'cultural advancement and racial rejuvenation'. As

46 On Pan Guangdan, see Frank Dikötter, *The discourse of race*, pp. 174–85; the following is based on Dikötter, 'Birth control and eugenics in Republican China', paper presented at the Contemporary China Institute, London, 11 Dec. 1990.
47 Gao Xisheng, *Chan'er zhixian ABC* (ABC of birth control), Shanghai: Shijie shuju, 1929.

people were considered to have unequal endowments, the report advocated a differential birthrate: 'Thus viewed', it said, 'some individuals may have children, others not.' The members of the committee encouraged the use of sterilization for the 'racial rejuvenation' of the country.[48] The administration of the sexual economy of the population had become a matter of state concern.

48 Chen Da, *Zhongguo renkou* (Population in China), Shanghai, 1946.

5

'CIVILIZATION IS SYPHILIZATION': THE CULTURAL MEANINGS OF 'DISEASE'

Controversies over population control and race improvement were closely related to discussions about public hygiene, venereal disease and prostitution in Republican China. The physical vigour and moral purity of the nation demanded the elimination of deviant practices. They were described as 'social problems' (*shehui wenti*), and the debates on sexual hygiene and venereal disease were indicative of social anxieties among the new professional élites of the urban centres. Thought to be a product of 'modern civilization', syphilis in particular conjured up images of urban decay and racial decline: sex could transmit diseases, infect the body of society and threaten future generations. Dispensaries for treating venereal disease, licensed houses to regulate prostitution, medical dossiers for the registration of infected individuals – in short, an entire disciplinary system was required in publications about sex. Through discourses on sex, modern-educated élites pushed for an increased intervention of the medical professions and the state in the sexual lives of citizens. The transformation of sex into a medical category denoting degeneracy, disease and contamination was also part of a broader shift in emphasis towards biology and the body as the foundation for prescriptions about social order. Medical rationalizations about human reproduction included an emphasis on 'diseases' as entities which had their own 'personality' consisting of signs and symptoms, with a cause, a clinical picture, a natural history, a prognosis and an appropriate treatment. Venereal diseases were assumed to be universal in form, progress and content, and numerical definitions were provided through the use of blood tests, radiographs and scans in specialized laboratories and clinics. Despite an increased emphasis on the obligation of the state to supervise the sexuality of its citizens, discourses about disease also contributed to the construction of personhood as a relatively autonomous and responsible category.

'THE BODY IS A BATTLEFIELD': HYGIENE AND THE CONCEPT OF DISEASE

Although the term 'hygiene' (*weisheng*) first appeared during the Song dynasty (960–1279), it achieved an unprecedented status of power and prestige only in the early twentieth century. Hygiene referred to a specialized field, a distinct discipline defined by a body of knowledge and a set of social practices based on medical science. Its status was enhanced by new social formations in the cities, which emphasized the scientific competence of new knowledge in order to further their own claims to professional autonomy. Medical professions in particular were instrumental in the development of new institutions, organizations, committees and periodicals, such as the *World of Hygiene* (*Weisheng shijie*, 1907), soon followed by the *Vernacular Journal of Hygiene* (*Weisheng baihuabao*, Shanghai, May 1908) and the *Journal of Medical Hygiene* (*Yixue weishengbao*, Canton, August 1908). The first professional organization to appear was the China National Hygiene Committee, established by students abroad in Japan in 1907. The spread of sub-disciplines in the 1920s and '30s like 'personal hygiene' (*geren weisheng*), 'public hygiene' (*gonggong weisheng*), 'social hygiene' (*shehui weisheng*) and 'racial hygiene' (*zhongzu weisheng*) indicated that this new branch of medicine was located at the intersection of the private and the public, straddled the boundary of the personal and the social, and linked the individual to the species.

New norms and attitudes towards bodily cleanliness were explained by a burgeoning number of family handbooks, manuals on hygiene and treatises on physiology. Under the guise of science, these popular booklets liberally dispensed advice and enunciated precepts on hygiene, housekeeping, proper clothing, diet and related matters. They were written in simple language and served as a guide to the new social formations of the coastal regions. Primary and secondary schools also became centres for the dissemination of new knowledge. Textbooks were printed for a new curriculum which included classes in hygiene, and teachers preached the physiology of health. A textbook used in primary schools for boys explained how 'rotting objects and filthy places breed a kind of microscopic insect called a germ. Germs are so small that the eye cannot see them. Light and tiny, they spread everywhere and get into the human body where they proliferate.'[1] Within the coastal citadels, public bathhouses, water distribution networks and sewage systems were gradually installed: 'public hygiene' as a social practice spread. With the creation of the Ministry of Health by the Guomindang in 1928, social regeneration and a strengthening of the nation became official slogans used in campaigns of public education, prominent for example during the New Life Movement (1934–7).[2]

With the framing of bacteria as agents of ill-health, a military terminology of 'assault', 'invasion of the organism' and 'bodily defences' started to pervade medical representations of disease in Republican China. An expression of the rise of the modern state, official organs became responsible for waging a war against disease with government money: in theory, at least, public hygiene became a prerogative of the state. From the collective campaigns for hygiene and sanitation under the Guomindang in the 1930s to mass ideological mobilization under the communists, disease was portrayed as the enemy within upon which fantasies of social decay and contamination could be projected. A textbook on human physiology for school children published in 1935 explained how individual hygiene would contribute to the fight against the enemy: 'Little friend, our country is now in the course of a life and death struggle, and if we wish to save it, we should first build up our bodies in a healthy way. Once we all have very healthy bodies, we can all apply our healthy

1 Léon Wieger, *Moralisme officiel des écoles, en 1920*, Hien-hien, 1921, original Chinese text, p. 168.

2 Ka-che Yip, 'Health and society in China: Public health education for the community, 1912–1937', *Social Science and Medicine*, no. 16 (1982), pp. 1197–1205.

minds to various tasks and go and fight with our enemy in order to achieve our goal of saving the country!'[3] The body itself was seen as a battlefield (*zhanchang*) where bacteria crossed swords with antibodies.[4] 'From birth to death, not a single day in man's life is without a struggle with microbes. The body is a battlefield.'[5] On the skin, between the teeth and in the eyes the enemy lay in wait, ready to strike. Nails were a favourite hide-out for germs, according to Huang Zifang, head of the Beijing Bureau of Hygiene: they should be cut short.[6] Concepts of hygiene encoded ideas about social distinction, much as the enlightened bourgeoisie had demarcated itself from the aristocracy in France before the Revolution. Long nails, once a symbol of social prestige prominently displayed by the mandarin, were now replaced by the short nails of the urbanite who was attached to the new values of 'modernity'. The virtues of austerity, physical strength and moral force were contrasted to the degenerate habits of evanescent scholars. Reminiscent of Yan Yuan (1635–1704), who derided the 'effeminate' bodies of Confucian scholars and extolled the virtues of physical exercise,[7] modernizing élites thought that bodily discipline and hygiene would regenerate the country. 'The aborigines of Africa do not pay attention to hygiene, and have no future. The red race of America does not pay attention to hygiene and declines further every day. The whites make population surveys, compile statistics on the causes of disease, make thorough investigations of the reasons of death, and examine the number of new births.

3 Shen Zhijian, *Women de shenti* (Our body), Shanghai: Xin Zhongguo shuju, 1935, p. 67.

4 'Renjun zhanzheng' (The struggle between bacteria and man), *Dagongbao*, 15 Dec. 1936, 3:11.

5 Yu Fengbin, *Weisheng conghua* (Chats on hygiene), Shanghai: Shangwu yinshuguan, 1927, vol. 3, pp. 1–2.

6 Huang Zifang, *Weisheng changshi wenda* (Elementary questions and answers about hygiene), Shanghai: Shangwu yinshuguan, 1937, pp. 24–5.

7 Frank Dikötter, 'Body, discipline and modernity in late imperial China', paper presented at the Annual Conference of the Association for Asian Studies, Boston, 24–26 March 1994.

All contribute to the science of public hygiene. We cannot but use every ounce of our energy to combat the evils of our race', wrote Professor Yu Fengbin (1881–1930) of St Johns College, Shanghai, president of the prestigious China Medical Association from 1920 to 1922.[8] Sexual hygiene in particular became a widespread topic of debate.

'THE POISON OF THE PLUM': VENEREAL DISEASE

Grounded in the new sciences of genetics and reproductive biology, the sexualization of syphilis was closely linked to a number of social anxieties expressed by the new professional élites of the urban centres in early Republican China. Unregulated sex was no longer seen as an ethical question only, but as a biological threat to the health of the individual, the family and the population. A macabre procession of genetic mutants, hereditary syphilitics and the mentally retarded shuffled through the pages of medical literature, and writings on sex conjured up visions of a bedraggled humanity with contaminated mothers and infected babies on the verge of racial extinction. Individual responsibility, social morality and biological purity became intimately intertwined in discourses which called for the regulation, administration and policing of sex.

Although some of the cultural values and social attitudes behind medical responses to venereal disease could be traced back to the imperial period, epidemiological knowledge had remained generally unfocused until the end of the Qing. As in Europe up to the end of the nineteenth century, non-venereal means of transmission were emphasized, although it was recognized that social proximity and sexual promiscuity encouraged the spread of the disease. Medical literature under the Tang dynasty (618–907) indicated the existence of types of venereal diseases, in particular certain forms of what would now be called gonorrhoea. Some texts provided detailed descriptions of chronic ulcers

8 Yu Fengbin, *Geren weisheng pian* (Personal hygiene), Shanghai: Shangwu yinshuguan, 1931 (1st edn 1917), p. 11.

of the genitals, stricture of the urethra and symptoms indicating gonorrhoeal arthritis. None of these infections, however, was recognized as being transmitted exclusively by sexual intercourse. Called 'strangury' (*linzhuo*), the symptoms of gonorrhoea were thought to be limited to pain in the penis during urination and viscid discharges from the urethra. According to traditional medical theories, it was a benign disease due to an accumulation of wetness-heat (*shire*) in the bladder.

Syphilis is thought to have appeared only at the beginning of the sixteenth century through contact with Europeans. In a medical survey of the ravages caused by a skin-disease in Canton, Yu Bian noted syphilitic chancres and prescribed sarsaparilla and mercury for relief. A more detailed account of venereal disease, entitled *Secret account of plum sores* (*Meichuang bilu*), was published in 1632 by Chen Sicheng. Most sources of this period referred to the disease as 'Cantonese sores' (*guangchuang*) or 'plum-blossom sores' (*yangmeichuang*), a term which evoked the resemblance of the chancre to a plum-blossom. Syphilis was not seen as an infection characterized by latent periods. With the natural disappearance of the initial chancre, it was generally thought of as being cured. Only with the introduction of new knowledge at the end of the nineteenth century was the pathology of syphilitic infection highlighted. By framing it as a contagious disease caused by a spirochete transmitted through sexual intercourse, syphilis was demonstrated to cause systemic dangers such as cardiovascular ailments, partial paralysis and mental disorders. With the differentiation of syphilis into stages by the French venerologist Philippe Ricord in the 1830s, various illnesses which had previously been unrelated were proved to be the result of venereal infection.[9] The syphilitic chancre, called 'hard chancre' (*yingxiagan* or *yingxing xiagan*), was differentiated from the chancroid, or genital ulcer called 'soft chancre' (*ruanxiagan* or *ruanxing xiagan*), a common infection in parts of China. Syphilis and gonorrhoea had hitherto not been strictly demarcated, and the specificity of both diseases was emphasized

9 Claude Quétel, *The history of syphilis*, London: Polity Press, 1990, p. 149.

in modernizing medical circles. With a new focus on the gonococcus as a bacterial organism responsible for infection, gonorrhoea was shown to lead to a variety of severe ailments such as dermatitis and arthritis.

The problem of venereal disease in Republican China can hardly be understated,[10] although its precise incidence remains a matter of conjecture. Measures for investigation into the sources of infection were only implemented after 1949, and few hospitals or health departments collected venereal statistics. Although reliable data on the incidence and prevalence of venereal diseases are not as yet available, the introduction of serological tests during the 1920s in the better-equipped hospitals allowed some medical missionaries to reveal the extent of infection.[11] James Maxwell was the first to establish how severe venereal diseases were in China.[12] Later surveys provided more detailed data, such as Lennox's study in 1923, based on 35,000 hospital cases which found that 8.4% of in-patients and 6.1% of out-patients

10 For an overview, see Frank Dikötter, 'The cultural history of sexually transmitted diseases in modern China', *Genitourinary Medicine*, 69, (Oct. 1993), pp. 341–45.

11 For contemporary reports, see Harry Sutherland Gear, 'The incidence of venereal diseases in hospital patients in China', *China Medical Journal*, 49, no. 10 (Oct. 1935), pp. 1122–35; L.F. Heimburger, 'The incidence of syphilis at the Shantung Christian University dispensary', *China Medical Journal*, 41, no. 6 (June 1927), pp. 541–50; Daniel G. Lai and Suchen Wang Lai, 'Incidence of syphilis among Chinese civilian patients in Swatow district', *China Medical Journal*, 43, no. 1 (Jan. 1929), pp. 22–7; Daniel G. Lai and Suchen Wang Lai, 'Incidence of syphilis among the Chinese soldiers at Swatow', *China Medical Journal*, 43, no. 8 (Aug. 1929), pp. 557–67; T.H. Wang, James Y. Shen and C.C. Chung, 'An inquiry into the prevalence of syphilis in Nanking', *China Medical Journal*, 51, no. 6 (June 1937), pp. 983–8. Christian Henriot has summarized the findings of these foreign missionary doctors and their disciples in 'Medicine, VD and prostitution in pre-revolutionary China', *Social History of Medicine*, 5, no. 1 (April 1992), pp. 95–120; how generalizations about 'Chinese society' and the 'medical discourse in China' can be made on the basis of a dozen articles written by foreigners remains unclear.

12 J.L. Maxwell, 'Some notes on syphilis among the Chinese', *China Medical Journal*, 27, no. 6 (Dec. 1913), pp. 379–86.

were suffering from syphilis. This represented three times the average in the United States.[13] Although the different statistical methods used by physicians do not allow for any meaningful comparisons, other figures based on hospital statistics also indicate that the incidence of syphilis was very high during the period between the two World Wars, and typically ranged between 20 and 25% of all patients.[14] Estimates for the general population have ranged from 5% to as high as 50 or 60%.[15] A contemporary observer estimated the total number of those infected with syphilis at 20 million on the eve of the Second World War, a conservative figure which should probably be increased by half again.[16]

More directly relevant to the cultural historian, however, are the attitudes to venereal disease shaped by modernizing discourses on sex. New medical knowledge spurred a growing number of social reformers and professional physicians into action. Treatises on the medical pathology of syphilis, handbooks on venereal disease and booklets on sex education proliferated. The gruesome consequences of venereal disease for the individual, the family and the 'race' were spelled out in harrowing detail by popular writers. The sexualization of syphilis allowed modernizing writers to express both moral and medical concerns: sin and sickness became closely related in discourses which stressed the sexual agency of responsible individuals. The existence of venereal infection, generically called 'sex diseases' or 'sexual maladies' (*xingbing*), highlighted the perils of sex and the corruption of the flesh. Syphilis, or 'plum poison', was 'received', 'transmitted' by a 'carrier' on the market of venereal trade, the

13 W.G. Lennox, 'Neurosyphilis among Chinese', *China Medical Journal*, 37, no. 8 (Aug. 1923), pp. 663–71.

14 E.C. Faust, 'Social diseases in China', *Social Pathology*, 1, no. 6 (June 1925), pp. 274–7.

15 L.T. Wu, 'Problem of venereal diseases in China', *China Medical Journal*, 41, no. 1 (Jan. 1927), pp. 28–36.

16 C.N. Frazier, 'The prevention and control of syphilis', *China Medical Journal*, 51, no. 9 (Sept. 1937), pp. 1043–6.

morbid gift for which the customer did not pay. Representations of social degeneration flourished with the rise of the idea of 'race' in an era of rabid nationalism. Syphilis was interpreted as a cause of 'racial decline':[17] the idea of degeneracy, encompassed in the powerful myth of hereditary syphilis, was debunked in Europe in the aftermath of the First World War,[18] but a combination of nationalist rhetoric and social hygiene contributed to the perpetuation of such notions in China well into the 1940s. Eugenists added hereditary syphilitics to the list of 'unfit elements' who should be banned from marrying.

Pollution was thought to be of a foreign origin. Much as syphilis was construed as a foreign disease during the epidemic of the late fifteenth century ('French pox' for the English, 'Neapolitan disease' for the French), syphilis was described by nationalist writers as a Western import. A variation on the theme of the Golden Age, a timeless utopia which was thought to have reigned in China before the first Opium War (1839–42), it allowed the ultimate blame to be fastened upon an entity called 'the West'. Cultural representations of syphilis gave expression to the idea that China had been colonized by the dual force of foreign capital and fatal disease. Imperialists 'violated' the country's territorial integrity, and germs 'encroached' (*qinfan*) upon the urethra. Depicted as an alien evil which insinuated itself through the most intimate parts of the body, images of syphilis also reinforced negative representations of foreign sexuality: writers rarely failed to mention that the ports frequented by foreign sailors were the places most severely affected by the

17 Jianmeng, 'Meidu shi zhongzu shuaitui de yuanyin' (Syphilis is the cause of racial decline), *Dongfang zazhi*, 19, no. 7 (April 1922), pp. 85–6; Jianmeng, 'Minzu zhi shuaitui' (The decline of the race), *Dongfang zazhi*, 18, no. 21 (Nov. 1921), pp. 1–3; Hu Zhengxiang, 'Meidu' (Syphilis), *Kexue*, 5, no. 2 (Feb. 1920), pp. 177–96.

18 On the importance of hereditary syphilis in nineteenth-century medical literature in France, see Alain Corbin, 'L'hérédosyphilis ou l'impossible rédemption. Contribution à l'histoire de l'hérédité morbide' in *Le temps, le désir et l'horreur*, Paris: Aubier, 1991, pp. 141–70.

disease. Syphilis became the first version of the bacteriological warfare myth: engineered by imperialists, it had been spread by soldiers as an instrument of death. The conceptual link between nationalism and sexuality, expressed most clearly by representations of an uncontrolled and 'foreign' sexuality, was as widespread in Republican China as it was in Europe.[19]

Syphilis was a time-based notion, charted as a sequence of 'stages', a normative approach which implied an inexorable 'process'. The symptoms of syphilis remained hidden, and the long latent periods which could extend for as long as several decades highlighted the devious character of the disease. Venereal infections, particularly syphilis, were 'slow' or 'chronic' (*manxing*) diseases: a teleological view of inevitable development towards total infection led to the description of germs as 'insidious', 'tenacious' or 'stubborn' (*wangu*). The military vocabulary and anthropocentric epithets combined to instil the idea of a strategy of assault on the human organism by germs: the 'cleverest' germs lay in wait on the towels in public toilets and 'chose' weak spots into which they 'marched'.[20]

New spatial notions were also conveyed by representations of disease. Infection 'spread' throughout the body as it 'spread' throughout society. Bacteria 'invaded' it through the reproductive system and, multiplying, finally crippled the entire organism; syphilis 'spread' through the internal organs and the spinal cord. The syphilitic became a social symbol of degeneration and corruption, and medical demonology dwelt on the physical decay of the contaminated individual. Descriptions insisted on the grisly aspects of suppurating lesions, which were frequent on skins and scalp and impaired the muscular function: they were said to attack the nasal and adjacent bones and destroy the jaw, a physical disintegration which was the consequence of

19 G.L. Mosse, *Nationalism and sexuality: Respectability and abnormal sexuality in modern Europe*, New York: Howard Fertig, 1985; Andrew Parker, Mary Russo, Doris Sommer and Patricia Yaeger (eds), *Nationalisms and sexualities*, London: Routledge, 1989.
20 Cheng, *Jieyu shengyu*, p. 89.

a lack of self-discipline. Morbid representations of bodily decay further underlined how the nose, symbol of the self, started to rot away in the third stage of syphilis, giving the victim a 'hideous appearance' (*chouren*). Bodily disintegration became a signifier of the dangers of sexual pollution and transgression, and symbolized the fragility and vulnerability of human existence.

Syphilis was a disease of 'modernity', a symbol of the decline of civilization thought to be confined to the great metropoles of the coast. As in Russia before the Revolution,[21] medical writers defended the moral integrity of peasant life and interpreted contamination as a sign of the moral dereliction of city-dwellers. The countryside was a repository for hope and purity, the peasant a symbol of probity and moral innocence. Women and children were equally represented as the innocent victims of modernity. The husband brought the disease home to his wife and children, introducing the germs from public spheres of pleasure to the private sphere of domesticity. The discovery in Europe during the last decades of the nineteenth century of venereal insontium, also termed infections of the innocent, had a particular impact in modern China. Venereal disease was viewed as a poison brought home by sinful husbands and threatening to engulf the entire family. Only the man was endowed with a powerful sexual drive that sought an outlet beyond the sphere of domesticity: he was portrayed as a sexual agent capable of transgression, and the sexuality of woman was reduced to a 'maternal instinct' which found expression in reproduction alone: women remained 'passive victims' of 'male excesses'. Tales of horror underlined the nefarious effects of syphilis upon pregnancy. After corruption of the seed, 'some are born mute, some are born blind, some are born deaf, others have their skin peeled off, and some have all kind of monstrous features.'[22] Opthalmia neonatorum, or blindness at birth caused by the passage of the infant through an infected birth canal,

21 Laura Engelstein, *The keys to happiness: Sex and the search for modernity in fin-de-siècle Russia*, Ithaca: Cornell University Press, 1992, pp. 165–213.
22 Cheng, *Jieyu shengyu*, p. 92.

became the quintessential image of the carnal scourge that fell upon the innocent members of society. Fears of easy contagion also multiplied, and the threat of venereal disease being passed on by non-venereal means occasionally surfaced in popular accounts of syphilis. In an early communist handbook written before the takeover in 1949, it was stated that while venereal diseases were caused by intercourse with prostitutes, they could also be transmitted by handshakes and shared toilet articles.[23]

The employment of women actors, increased social mobility, and the free advertising of prostitution in vernacular daily newspapers since the collapse of the empire were commonly blamed for the expansion of the sex trade in Republican China. If the student, the husband and the soldier were accused of going to brothels, the prostitute was also targeted as a source of contamination. The topic of prostitution in twentieth-century China has been treated in detail elsewhere, particularly in the work of Gail Hershatter, and there is no need to cover this ground again.[24] Commercial sex was reviled as a social evil

23 Chen Shu, *Xingbing changshi* (Elementary knowledge of venereal diseases), Harbin: Guanghua shudian, 1948.

24 Gail Hershatter's excellent studies of prostitution in modern China are based on archival material, literary documents, guidebooks to brothels and other printed sources; see Gail Hershatter, 'Courtisans and streetwalkers: The changing discourses on Shanghai prostitution, 1890–1949', *Journal of the History of Sexuality*, 3, no. 2 (1992), pp. 245–69; 'The hierarchy of Shanghai prostitution, 1919–1949', *Modern China*, 15, no. 4 (1989), pp. 463–97; 'Prostitution and the market in women in early twentieth-century Shanghai' in Rubie S. Watson and Patricia B. Ebrey (eds), *Marriage and inequality in Chinese society*, Berkeley: University of California Press, 1991, pp. 256–85; 'Regulating sex in Shanghai: The reform of prostitution in 1920 and 1951' in Frederic Wakeman and Yeh Wen-hsin (eds), *Shanghai sojourners*, Berkeley: Center for Chinese Studies, 1992, pp. 145–86 ; 'Sex work and social order: Prostitutes, their families, and the state in twentieth-century Shanghai', paper presented at the Conference on Family Process and Political Process in China, Taibei, 3–5 Jan. 1992. See also Jean Duval, *A study of prostitution in Shanghai at the end of the Qing dynasty as it appears in the 'Shanghai novels'*, Paris: VERLCA, 1972; Sue Gronewold, *Beautiful merchandise: Prostitution in China 1860–1936*, New York: Harrington Park Press, 1986.

which spread disease and decay, and prostitution was increasingly medicalized in modernizing discourses. Prostitutes were considered 'culture farms' (*yangchengsuo*) for disease: 'The majority of the most common venereal diseases like syphilis and gonorrhoea are contracted when visiting prostitutes. After having been contaminated by this type of sexual disease, besides the harm inflicted to one's own body, one will also infect one's wife and genetically transmit the disease to one's children. The infection of offspring affects the health of the nation and the future of the race.'[25] In the view of Wu Liande (1879–1960), a scholar of international repute, adolescents should be taught the 'significance of nocturnal emissions, the real results of masturbation and the dangers of illicit sexual intercourse, as well as the compensations of continence'.[26] Like many other academic scientists and clinically-oriented physicians, he proposed the compulsory notification and treatment of patients, clinics and special laboratories for the treatment and investigation of venereal diseases, health education, and the 'scientific control' of brothels.

As the quintessence of female sexual deviancy, and the very embodiment of a stigmatized disease, the prostitute was a criminal. The work of forensic anthropologists was influential in Republican China, especially that of Cesare Lombroso, who explained crime as a hereditary feature which could be isolated and identified by anthropometry. For Lombroso, the habitual criminal was a biological degenerate, a throwback to a more primitive level on the ladder of evolution. With the theory of recapitulation, which represented women, children and 'savages' as less evolved creatures, the Lombrosian approach was eager to detect criminal features in women, a theory that had some success with a number of authors in Republican China. For Bao Zuxuan, author of a booklet on *The problem of prostitution* (1935), the prostitute should be regarded as the female equivalent of the

25 Fan, *Qingnian weisheng*, p. 44.
26 Wu Lien-teh, 'The prevention of sexual diseases', *The China Critic*, 16 April 1931, pp. 367–8.

male criminal.[27] Prostitution was interpreted both as the result of heredity and as the product of an unwholesome environment. Crime was the child of vice: illegitimate by birth and raised in the shadow of debauchery, the product of carnal trade could only grow into a criminal.

Commercial interest in the new cultural domain of sexually transmitted diseases was widespread, and the most common treatment was sublimate of mercury. Preparations with arsphenamine, such as salvarsan or '606', made rapid inroads during the early 1900s, but they did not replace older methods; even neosalvarsan, or '914', only gradually took the place of mercury. Most new drugs, however, were confined to the urban centres and remained beyond the means of the lower classes. For instance, silver nitrate for the treatment of blindness among infants was rarely available even in the 1930s.[28] The high cost of medical treatment and the unwillingness to follow it for long periods made people turn to quack doctors and traditional physicians.[29] Advertisements for medicines to combat sexually transmitted diseases were seen by readers of mass circulation newspapers in China from the early twentieth century onwards.[30] The 'Modern Medical Supplements' printed in newspapers were often no more than disguised advertisements for quack medicines to treat diseases, as contemporary observers such as Lin Yutang remarked: 'The quack advertisements, by their constant exaggerations and alarmist statements over every variety of known sexual disease, are doing untold psychological harm to the men

27 Bao Zuxuan, *Changji wenti* (The problem of prostitution), Shanghai: Nüzi shudian, 1935, pp. 62–68.

28 H.S. Gear, 'The incidence of venereal diseases in hospital patients in China', *China Medical Journal*, 49, no. 10 (Oct. 1935), pp. 1122–35.

29 L.F. Heimburger, 'The incidence of syphilis at the Shantung Christian University dispensary', *China Medical Journal* (June 1927), 41, no. 6, pp. 541–50.

30 Huang Kewu, 'Cong *Shenbao* yiyao guanggao kan minchu Shanghai de yiliao wenhua yu shehui shenghuo, 1912–1926' (Medical culture and social life in the early Republican era as seen through the medical advertisements of the *Shenbao*, 1912–1926), *Zhongyang yanjiuyuan jindaishi yanjiusuo jikan*, 17, no. 2 (Dec. 1988), 141–94.

and women of China. The very fact that every day the terms "nocturnal emission", "self-abuse", "impotence", "syphilis", "gonorrhoea", etc. confront the eyes of the reader in articles written by quack doctors in these "medical supplements" creates at least a dismal picture of normal sexual functions in the mind of its readers. To make the situation worse, it is a fact that the same *Shun Pao* is carrying on different days not one, but four such "medical supplements" and "health supplements", run by different groups of doctors with different medicines to sell.'[31] In Harbin, a city in the north of China with a population of 300,000, there were 200 self-proclaimed 'hospitals' which derived their main income from injecting patients with salvarsan or substitute solutions, as was noticed with alarm in 1927.[32] The rampant spread of quack medicine in the field of sexually transmitted diseases is common to many modern societies,[33] and Chinese and Western doctors alike relentlessly attacked charlatans and self-styled clinics. The need for new medical science to be accepted by the public and to achieve professional integrity, the competition over the shifting allegiance of certain sectors of the public, the emergence of new social norms of behaviour, and the spread of general education are some of the underlying reasons for the fear of quack medicine in modernizing nations.

The sexualization of syphilis and the medicalization of sexuality itself also considerably enhanced the status and role of the new medical professions after the disintegration of the imperial system in 1911. Posing as the guardians of public health and national vitality, they clamoured for individual self-regulation and for increased state intervention under the guise of medical advice. Sex became both a cultural and a medical domain which was harnessed by the modernizing élites for social promotion and

31 Lin Yutang, *History of the press and public opinion in China*, Oxford University Press, 1937, p. 143.

32 Wu Lien-teh, 'Problem of venereal diseases in China', *China Medical Journal*, 41, no. 1 (Jan. 1927), p. 34.

33 See Roy Porter, *Health for sale: Quackery in England, 1660–1850*, Manchester University Press, 1989.

professional autonomy in the early years of the Republic. Yet despite the widespread debates about syphilis, no network of prophylactic institutes and dispensaries was ever elaborated, and official efforts in public education remained minimal. Police regulations required that all women in brothels be periodically inspected, but no programme to reduce and regulate prostitution was set up until 1928. Although the National Medical Association made a statement in March 1922 on the threat of venereal disease and the need for public information, no consistent policies to combat syphilis were adopted by independent organizations.[34] Official measures remained limited even after the unification of the country by the Nationalist government between 1927 and 1937. A Ministry of Health was created in 1928, but public health authorities lacked the financial resources and the political will to combat sexually transmitted diseases effectively.

'A FILTHY HABIT': THE INVERTED HOMOSEXUAL

As a threat to the sexual bond within the conjugal family, uncontrolled male desire became the main target of debates about commercial sex. Social order was also thought to be threatened by another type of extramarital sexuality, namely sodomy. Prostitution and sodomy represented the two extreme forms of non-procreative sex which needed to be eliminated for the sake of the family and the nation. As transgressions against the closely guarded boundaries between the private and the public, the sexually infertile and the socially barren, both forms of behaviour were considered 'social evils' that took place outside the legitimate domain of conjugal sexuality and domestic love. The construction of sodomy as a category of sexual deviance, however, was already in place well before the selective introduction of new knowledge from foreign countries. In the eighteenth and nineteenth centuries, official intolerance and legal condemnation helped to end the high visibility of sodomy and pederasty which

34 W.W. Peter, 'Fighting venereal disease openly', *China Medical Journal*, 35, no. 1 (Jan. 1924), pp. 1–29.

had prevailed in parts of China.[35] Specific laws for the prosecution of rape between men were added to the Qing code in 1740 with minor amendments in 1819 and 1852. Although these laws seem to have been designed primarily to stop the widespread prostitution and forced procurement of male children, they were also targeted at more isolated cases of male sexual violence. The Qing legal records provide many cases of convictions which involved sodomy, and a great number of these led to execution or deportation. Judicial hostility to sodomy and male sexual violence, however, was part of a more general effort by Qing officials to combat all forms of extramarital sexuality and to enforce male and female chastity. Although this aspect of legal history still needs to be thoroughly investigated, it seems that the Qing code made no distinction between homosexual and heterosexual extramarital intercourse, which suggests that the main purpose of promulgating these laws was to protect marriage and limit sexuality to a marital context. The Qing law against rape, moreover, did not take gender into account but relied instead on the age of the victim and the degree of violence inflicted.[36] The Qing authorities thus draw a line between procreative and nonprocreative acts: sex, in other words, was never dissociated from procreation.

If very similar discourses condemning sodomy existed in seventeenth- and eighteenth-century Europe, a distinction between 'heterosexuality' and 'homosexuality' as different modes of sexual preference became increasingly widespread during the late nineteenth and early twentieth centuries in medical and psychiatric literature. The term 'homosexual' only appeared in German, English and French in the 1890s, an indication that

35 M.P. Lau and M.L. Ng, 'Homosexuality in Chinese culture', *Culture, Medicine, and Psychiatry*, 13, no. 4 (Dec. 1989), pp. 465–88; Xiaomingxiong, *Zhongguo tongxingai shilu*, Hong Kong, 1984, and, more important, Giovanni Vitiello, ' "The dragon's embrace": Ming and Qing homoerotic tales from *The Cut Sleeve*', *T'oung Pao*, 78, nos 4–5 (1992), pp. 341–72.

36 M.J. Meijer, 'Homosexual offenses in Ch'ing law', *T'oung Pao*, 71 (1985), pp. 109–33, and Vivien W. Ng, 'Ideology and sexuality: Rape laws in Qing China', *Journal of Asian Studies*, 46, no. 1 (Feb. 1987), pp. 57–70.

desire was not only interpreted as a means to the ultimate goal of procreation, but also as an end in itself. No longer described as a number of prohibited sexual acts which were nonprocreative, sexual discourses started to focus on a particular type of person: homosexuality was individualized by focusing on the person. Social concern with sexual preferences instead of sexual acts also led to the appearance of sharper identities, including the medical and psychological categorization of 'the homosexual' as a distinct type of personality.[37] While sexual variations were previously explained as innocent errors or cultivated vices which deviated from a 'natural' sexual impulse to heterogenital intercourse, the emphasis on sexual preferences gradually led to the recognition of the potential equality of heterosexual and homosexual desires. Although the dissolution of the idea of heterogenitality as a natural need and the recognition of a plurality of individual desires was a very gradual and uneven cultural development in Europe, no similar tendency took place in China. On the contrary, medical science was selectively appropriated by modernizing élites in Republican China to consolidate the widespread distinction between procreative and nonprocreative sexual acts. The concept of 'sexuality' never made a significant impact, and even the term 'heterosexuality' (*yixingai*), remains to this day a highly specialized medical term which is rarely used. Instead of conceptualizing 'homosexuality' as a sexual preference distinct from 'heterosexuality', it continued to be interpreted as a nonprocreative act which should be condemned as a form of extramarital sexuality.

Termed *tongxinglian* or *tongxingai* ('same-sex love'), homosexuality was widely interpreted as a temporary aberration, a mental disease or an 'inversion'. Despite widespread exposure to foreign medical literature on 'homosexuality' as an organic pathology or a perverted preference, sodomy continued to be portrayed as an act of social transgression which was acquired like a bad habit. The army, the school and the prison were new

37 For an introduction, see Jeffrey Weeks, *Sex, politics and society: The regulation of sexuality since 1800*, London: Longman, 1989, pp. 96–121.

social spaces where it was thought to develop. Like 'germs', sodomy could spread rapidly to 'contaminate' the social 'organism'. The evil was twofold: medically, it led to a pathological state of debilitation and exhaustion, and socially, it was claimed to corrupt innocent youth. Sodomy among young males was not seen as the premature manifestation of a pathological inclination and a fundamentally warped sexuality, but more as a stage of development towards the 'normal' expression of sexual desire. It was regarded as acceptable behaviour specific to certain situations. Gui Zhiliang, a practising gynaecologist, thought that love between people of the same sex was an inevitable stage on the path towards marriage: 'Homosexuality is a kind of intermediate or preparatory stage to heterosexuality; it is necessary for people to go through it.' The 'normally' developed person would 'transit' (*guodu*) through homosexuality, but some would 'get blocked' (*zu'ai*) or 'bogged down' (*tingzhi*) in what was described as a form of 'abnormal homosexuality' (*bu putong de tongxing lian'ai*). Only a small minority of adolescents were thought to display an innate proclivity towards homosexual intercourse: as with genetic morons, it was impossible to 'correct' them.[38] If homosexual tendencies were allowed to develop into an 'addiction' (*xingpi*), it would not even be possible for the 'victim' to be 'rescued' through marriage. The homosexual was thought to have strayed from the right 'path' (*tujing*), entered 'wrong ways' (*xietu*), turned his back on 'normal' (*zheng*) intercourse, 'inverted' or 'turned upside down' (*diandao*) the natural order, and developed 'abnormal' desires (*xingyu biantai*).[39] By calling homosexuality a 'diseased state' (*bingtai*) or a 'metamorphosis' (*biantai*), it was implied that a 'normal' heterosexual instinct was originally present even in 'abnormal' bodies. Instead of a radically different type of sexual preference, it was portrayed as a 'bad habit' which led to a waste of precious semen. The possibility of an exclusive desire for the same sex was never envisaged. Similar to masturbation, adolescent homosexuality

38 Gui, *Nüren zhi yisheng*, pp. 63–6.
39 Wang, *Qingchun*, p. 114.

was represented as a socially acquired vice which discipline should overcome for the sake of the self, the married couple and the nation.

The concept of 'inversion' contributed to keep sexuality firmly linked to procreation: in its representation of the homosexual as a female trapped in a male body, heterogenitality continued to be viewed as a natural need. Although the medical literature on sexuality in Republican China granted relatively little attention to homosexuality, a few writers drew on embryology and endocrinology to explain it as the product of an inverted biological development. Insisting that all desire was by nature heterosexual, reducing masculinity and femininity to an expression of sexuality, most biologizing theories represented 'the homosexual' as the very opposite of 'manliness'. Effeminate, frail and evanescent, the image of the homosexual as a female mind in a male body was central to Cheng Hao's *The sexual life of mankind* (1934), a book which even included a list of the biological reversals which were thought to characterize male and female homosexuals (see accompanying table).

Represented as a topological inversion of male homosexuality, female homosexuality was rarely discussed in Republican China, a discursive silence which can probably be ascribed to the overwhelming concern with regulating male extramarital sexuality. Women, moreover, were gendered as an essential category endowed with a passive instinct for reproduction, and were rarely thought to be capable of autonomous desires. When young women and old harpies, as chapter 2 shows, were granted the power to incite male desire, their active female sexuality was thought to be dangerous to men. Female desire for the same sex was not only a threat to the male monopoly over sexual agency, it also undermined the concept of heterosexuality as a natural drive towards reproduction in women. More importantly perhaps, a lack of concern for female homosexuality indicates that sodomy was condemned as an occasional nonprocreative sexual act which threatened married harmony rather than as a sexual preference which was fundamentally different from heterosexuality. Even the 'sex revolutionary' Zhang Jingsheng attributed sodomy to a

CHENG HAO'S LIST OF THE PRESUMED BIOLOGICAL REVERSALS IN MALE AND FEMALE HOMOSEXUALS[40]

	MAN	WOMAN
Skeleton	Resembles mostly that of a girl, particularly the pelvis	Similar in size and strength to that of a man; the pelvis is not very broad and has a small gradient, the spine is long and thin, the middle is not curved
Skin	Soft and warm	
Limbs	Relatively small	
Pace	The step is short and slow, like that of a girl	Similar to men
Voice	High-pitched	Gruff like men, structure of the larynx similar to men, weak laryngal nodes
Chest	Developed like that of a girl, to the point of secreting milk in the mammary glands	Flat, barely developed
Facial hair	None	Can sometimes grow thickly like a man's
Character	Likes girls' games, activities and clothes	Generally like a man, the exact opposite of the male homosexual
Emotions	Used to saying sweet expressions of love, bashful in presence of other men	
Sex drive	Very feeble in relation to women, to the point of impotence; can develop abnormal impulses when in presence of the same sex	Cold towards men, sensitive to the same sex

40 Cheng, *Xingshenghuo*, pp. 133–4.

temporary aberration which could also take place between a male and a female: 'One can say that the slackness of the vagina indirectly encourages the fondness for sodomy. However the anus is the faecal passage and is dirty. Moreover since there is neither vigorous activity nor electrical functioning, it ordinarily does not constitute a rival to the vagina. Therefore I should like to urge all of my gentlemen readers to note that through giving full consideration and research to the vagina not only can one bring about a perfection and completeness of intercourse between the sexes, but one can also exterminate the evil habit of sodomy, a habit which is abnormal, dirty, meaningless, inhuman, and not even indulged in by the birds and beasts.'[41]

Ignoring the possibility of exclusive homosexuality, solidly linking sex to procreation, the conception of heterogenitality as a natural desire was also conducive to silence about sexual variations. In Europe, the publication of *Psychopathia Sexualis* in 1886 brought instant fame to Richard von Krafft-Ebing. An inventory of case studies of so-called 'sexual perversions', his work was based on concepts of genetic predisposition current in his time. The psychiatrization of perverse pleasures, according to Michel Foucault's history of sexuality, became vital in the detailed description and regulation of individual life. The impressive repertoires of anomalies, perversions and deformed sexualities constructed by psychiatrists and sex researchers in Europe envisaged the social subject as a site of individualized desires, and expressed the possibility that pleasure could be an end in itself. Such a possibility was not envisaged by modernizing élites in China. If Cheng Hao's *The sexual life of mankind*, published in 1934, was one of the few texts to explore different aspects of human sexuality, including fetishism, urophilia, voyeurism, exhibitionism, masochism, sadism, frottage and necrophilia,[42] most of the literature in Republican China remained entirely independent from the sexological inquiries into 'perversions' which became widespread in European medical circles. Sexual

41 Chang, *Sex histories*, pp. 90–1, heavily altered translation.
42 Cheng Hao, *Renlei*, p. 126.

variations were not seen as an expression of human diversity which needed to be catalogued and investigated, but rather as a mark of the uncivilized 'other'. Yi Jiayue, for instance, remarked that politicians in France were eager to debate natural rights and 'humanism', although 'bestiality' was on full display in the red light districts of Paris, where prostitutes even copulated with dogs.[43] Zhu Yunying's *History of man's sexual life*, which appeared in 1936, equally revolved around prurient discussions of the presumed sex life of 'primitive' peoples, as opposed to the 'civilized races' of China and the West, and was mainly inspired by Western works like Fehlinger's *Sexual life of primitive peoples* and Bäsche's *Liebesleben der Natur. Eine Entwicklungsgeschichte der Liebe*. Reminiscent of the ritualistic court records of the mores of remote peoples in imperial China, his account was detached from actual sexual practices and remained confined to lengthy descriptions of customs such as clothing and dancing.[44] New divisions and classifications of

43 Yi Jiayue, 'Zhongguo de xingyu jiaoyu wenti' (The problem of sex education in China), *Jiaoyu zazhi*, 15, no. 8 (Aug. 1923), pp. 22151 and 22161; Yi based his observations on Zhuang Qi, *Zhanhou Ouyou jianwenji* (Record of a journey to Europe after the war), Shanghai: Shangwu yinshuguan, 1926, p. 235. Zhuang had not been able to witness this occurence personally, since the only dog trained to perform on stage had died. Alain Corbin, *Les filles de noces. Misère sexuelle et prostitution aux XIXe–XXe siècles*, Paris: Aubier, 1978, pp. 182–9, notes the use of Great Danes for this purpose in Paris.

44 Zhu Yunying, *Renlei xingshenghuo shi* (The history of man's sexual life), Shanghai: Zhengzhong shuju, 1936. Hoping to instil nationalist sentiments of 'shame' and 'humiliation' in their readers, some writers highlighted that indigenous customs like footbinding were treated with contempt in foreign sexological catalogues. Cheng Hao reported how a German called 'Strotz' had compiled a book on 'Pretty Girls of All Races' at the end of the nineteenth century. The Chinese girl with bound feet from this collection looked 'shameful', according to Cheng, 'just like pictures of nudes of savage races'. Cheng Hao, *Jiezhi shengyu wenti* (Questions about birth control), Shanghai: Yadong tushuguan, 1925, p. 62; Cheng, who had studied in Germany, probably referred to Carl Heinrich Stratz (1858–1924), *Die Rassenschönheit des Weibes*, Stuttgart: Ferdinand Enke, 1901, a lavishly illustrated book which was reprinted many times. Illustration 35 (p. 83) showed a drawing of a naked Chinese girl – 'not a particularly pretty specimen', Stratz observed, but an 'interesting' one with crippled feet.

desires, new catalogues of pleasures elaborated by sexologists in the beginning of the twentieth century undermined the idea that only one universal drive existed. Where a multiplication of 'sexualities' occurred in European sexology, particularly in the work of Freud and his followers, modernizing élites in China on the contrary reduced all sexual practices to the expression of one 'natural' desire for heterogenitality. Instead of attributing social prejudice and official hostility towards homosexuals in twentieth-century China to an 'importation of Western intolerance' – a simplistic and naive interpretation put forward by Bret Hinsch[45] – the strong conceptual link between sex and reproduction was precisely what impeded the recognition that 'homosexuality' was more than a nonprocreative act. The criminal code in China, to this day, does not have a specific law recognizing or prohibiting homosexuality: similar to masturbation or chicken pox, it is interpreted as an acquired aberration or a temporary disease which should be eliminated.

45 Bret Hinsch, *Passions of the cut sleeve: The male homosexual tradition in China*, Berkeley: University of California Press, 1990, p. 163.

6

THE CULTURAL CONSTRUCTION OF 'YOUTH'

THE EMERGENCE OF 'YOUTH'

If biologizing discourses in Republican China ascribed new meanings to the categories of 'manhood' and 'womanhood', the invention of 'youth' as a social category was also important. 'Youth' or 'adolescence' is a historically contingent concept defined in different ways by different cultures.[1] Boundaries between 'childhood' and 'youth' have often been blurred, and young people were not always thought to belong to a separate age of life with specific psychological characteristics. No strict legal or ritual boundary existed between children and adolescents in late imperial China, and they were classified as non-adults together with old and infirm people.[2] The term *qingnian* ('youth') was restricted to males aged sixteen to thirty; it excluded girls, who were expected to marry as soon as they reached sexual maturity. During the late Qing, the term *qingnian* was increasingly used to describe young males from rich households.[3]

1 Philippe Ariès, *Centuries of childhood: A social history of family life*, New York: Vintage, 1962; Harry Hendrick, *Images of youth: Age, class, and the male youth problem, 1880–1920*, Oxford: Clarendon Press, 1990; for a critique of Ariès, see Michael Mitterauer, *A history of youth*, London: Blackwell, 1992.

2 Derk Bodde, 'Age, youth and infirmity in the law of Ch'ing China', in Jerome A. Cohen, R. Randle Edwards and Fu-mei Chang Chen (eds), *Essays on China's legal tradition*, Princeton University Press, 1980, pp. 137–69; see also Ann Waltner, 'The moral status of the child in late imperial China: Childhood in ritual and in law', *Social Research*, 53, no. 4 (winter 1986), pp. 667–87.

3 Marion J. Levy, *The family revolution in modern China*, New York: Atheneum, 1949, pp. 84–6.

A reflection of the rapid rise in social status and political power of young people, 'youth' became a widespread category of analysis in the wake of the New Culture Movement. The scope of 'youth' was universalized to encompass young women as well as young workers of the industrial sector,[4] and distinct physiological and psychological features were now thought to characterize the 'adolescent' stage. Emotional turbulence, mental imbalance and accelerated physical growth were described as 'natural' processes of change. Couched in biomedical terms of 'impulses', 'instincts' and 'energy', the young person was portrayed as a bundle of passions that needed to be properly disciplined and guided through education.

'Youth' was also turned into a powerful symbol of regeneration, vitality and commitment to modernity: it was invented as standing for reason, progress and science. New professional groups in the urban centres, in particular the radical intellectuals and modernizing scientists, increasingly focused on 'oppressed youth' and 'oppressed women' as the two social groups which should be liberated from the bonds of Confucianism. Represented as the custodians of racial health, young people were claimed to have a right to develop freely and contribute to the building of the nation. 'Adolescence' became part of a programme of racial health. Based on the popular theory of recapitulation, 'youth' was seen as the birth of the individual, a turbulent stage of development marked by biological changes which would transform the young person into a mature adult. A 'period' (*shidai*) on the path to maturity, it was compared to the nation in an 'epoch' (*shidai*) on the way to a better future.[5]

4 New attitudes towards childhood, the emergence of the 'child' as a category of person, and the individualization of the child in China are important historical issues which remain to be analyzed; see Jon L. Saari, *Legacies of childhood: Growing up Chinese in a time of crisis, 1890–1920*, Cambridge, MA: Harvard University Press, 1990.

5 On a new mode of consciousness centred around the notion of 'period' or 'epoch' (*shidai*), see Sun Lung-kee, 'Out of the wilderness: Chinese intellectual odysseys from the "May Fourth" to the "Thirties"', Ph.D. thesis, Stanford University, 1985, p. 9. See also Leo Ou-fan Lee, 'In search of

In his 'Call to Youth' of 1915, Chen Duxiu compared adolescence to 'early spring, like the rising sun, like trees and grass in bud, like the newly sharpened blade. It is the most valuable period of life. The function of youth in society is the same as that of a fresh and vital cell in a human body. In the process of metabolism, the old and the rotten are incessantly eliminated to be replaced by the fresh and living.' In the 'process of natural selection', youth would revitalize the social body by eliminating the 'poisonous germs' of tradition.[6]

If modernizing discourses created what they described, the emergence of a category of adolescence also reflected shifts in the social field. The discursive invention of 'youth' as a separate stage in the life-cycle was largely derivative of social and economic reconfigurations in the cities of the coast. A rising number of unmarried appeared among young people of all classes, a trend sustained by imbalances in the sex ratio in parts of the new occupational sector. Opportunities for economic independence gradually spread, and this applied to temporary migrants in the new industries of the coast, young army recruits and young professional people in the offices of Shanghai. The new educational system offered young students better chances of social mobility. A lengthened period of formal training generally increased the cultural distance between young people and their parents, with a tendency for weakened control over arranged marriages by the extended family. Young people of both sexes rapidly acquired a new outlook through formal education and extracurricular reading. The publishing industry thrived on the mass production of self-study series for young readers; called *congshu*, these booklets used a limited vocabulary and vernacular language to ensure the widest possible circulation. Magazines

---

modernity: Some reflections on a new mode of consciousness in twentieth-century Chinese history and literature' in Paul A. Cohen and Merle Goldman (eds), *Ideas across cultures: Essays on Chinese thought in honor of Benjamin I. Schwartz*, Cambridge, MA: Harvard University Press, 1990, pp. 109–12.

6 Chow Tse-tsung, *The May Fourth Movement*, Cambridge, MA: Harvard University Press, 1960, pp. 45–6.

and periodicals catering to this new readership – such as the *New youth (Xinqingnian)*, founded by Chen Duxiu in 1915, and the *Chinese youth (Zhongguo qingnian)* founded by Yun Daiying in 1923 – proliferated during this period. Young people also started to embrace social and political activities, and student demonstrations became a powerful driving force of change, from 4 May 1919 to 4 June 1989. The May Fourth Movement in particular was an intellectual revolution in which students played a vital role. Youth as a social and political issue was so important that the Communist Party set up a Youth League in the 1920s, while the Guomindang established a Youth Department. After the communist victory in 1949, every Fourth of May became a Youth Day.

The problematization of 'youth' into a 'social issue' spurred the growth of a body of specialized knowledge, particularly in the new fields of social science, psychology and human biology. Medical science in particular became important in defining the specificity of adolescence. By tracing strict biological boundaries between 'childhood', 'adolescence' and 'adulthood', by focusing on the internal mechanisms of youthful bodies, scientists universalized and naturalized the social category of 'youth'. Biology gave a meaning, a status and a direction to social debates about the youth problem. It was thought that the fragile adolescent should be warned of the grave moral dangers of modernity, and the need for discipline, guidance and education was proclaimed. An enormous amount of didactic literature for young readers, closely linked to the social anxieties of professional élites, was published in Republican China. Self-study books on sexual hygiene, textbooks on adolescent physiology and pamphlets on the evils of masturbation flourished, and notions of social responsibility and individual restraint spread to most cultural levels. Ageism and the stereotyping of youth, in China as in most other secular nations of the twentieth century, became a widespread discriminatory practice supported by scientific theories, a legal system and state institutions. Normative discourses, however, not only attempted to assert control over young people, but also created them as relatively independent persons. In imperial

China, young people had no particular moral status and did not form a legal class of their own. Biologizing discourses, on the other hand, recognized the young as moral persons, legal individuals and psychological beings. Texts produced, reproduced and maintained 'the adolescent' as a category of person.

ENDOCRINOLOGY AND THE HORMONES OF FEMININITY AND MASCULINITY

Traditional medical theories considered the circulation of bodily fluids at the onset of puberty to be important,[7] but biologizing discourses about adolescent bodies only gained widespread scientific legitimacy in China following advances in endocrinology in Europe at the beginning of the twentieth century.[8] Underlining the shared nature of both genders, modernizing writers appealed to medical science to represent the child as a neuter body which was only transformed by sexual differentiation at puberty. Before hormonal secretions produced a biological boundary (*fen*) between male and female bodies, the child was thought to be undifferentiated. 'If the sex glands do not produce hormones, we cannot distinguish boys from girls,' claimed a popular *Life of the human body* published in 1931.[9] The girl resembled the boy before the chemical messengers conveyed their mandate of change: 'During childhood there is no difference whatever between girls and boys.'[10] The girl was thought to be slightly

7 Some medical writers in China even denied that endocrinology was a 'Western' science and claimed that the the hormonal theory was first mentioned in the classics; see, for instance, Yun Tieqiao, *Shengli xinyu* (New language of physiology), Shanghai: published by the author, 1928, pp. 20 ff.

8 Nelly Oudshoorn, 'Endocrinologists and the conceptualization of sex', *Journal of the History of Biology*, 23, no. 2 (fall 1990), 163–87; and Nelly Oudshoorn, 'On measuring sex hormones: The role of biological assays in sexualizing chemical substances', *Bulletin of the History of Medicine*, 64, no. 2 (summer 1990), pp. 243–61.

9 Hu Zhenyuan, *Renti de shenghuo* (Life of the human body), Shanghai: Shijie shuju, 1931, pp. 116–17.

10 Chai Fuyuan, *Xingxue ABC* (ABC of sexology), Shanghai: Shijie shuju, 1928, p. 43.

'boyish', to display a sort of 'male temperament' (*nanxing qizhi*). Castrated boys, on the other hand, were said to be 'girlish' with their high-pitched voices: 'The eunuchs in our country [. . .] are simply the same as girls, [. . .] their bones are more fragile, the facial hair is sparse, the fat tissues increase and the voice becomes shriller.'[11] The boy who failed to develop into a man was considered a 'neuter male' (*zhongxing nanzi*), an intermediate type who symbolized the permeable nature of gender boundaries. The precise location of hormonal glands, part of a mechanized vision of the human body, also highlighted how tenuous the boundary between male and female was: removal of the thyroid gland, for instance, led to the atrophy of female sexual organs, and of the pineal gland to precocious sexual growth in the male.

Like a precision instrument, the body was a collection of interlocked components, and the hormones were said to determine the character of young people. For Zhuang Weizhong, a practising doctor, hormones in the testicles were necessary for the development of 'the air of a man' (*zhangfu qi*), whereas hormones in the ovaries caused 'the air of a woman' (*nüzi qi*).[12] Not so much ordained by Heaven, social roles were thought to be prescribed by a biological mandate: glandular secretions transformed the androgynous girl into a nubile woman. The marks of femininity were claimed to be imprinted on her body, and most texts dwelt at length on the accumulation of fat tissues, the increase in size of the buttocks, the broadening of the pelvis and the emergence of the breasts. It was thought a set number of psychological features inevitably accompanied these physiological changes. The young girl became 'gentle and soft', 'bashful' and 'sentimental'.[13] According to the sexologist Chai Fuyuan, one of a legion of self-proclaimed sex educators who wrote on

11 Chen, *Renti de yanjiu*, p. 221.

12 Zhuang Weizhong, *Jiankangshu wenda* (Questions and answers on the art of health), Shanghai: Dahua shuju, 1934, p. 139.

13 Wang Yang, 'Renlei faqingqi zhi xing de tezheng' (The sexual characteristics of humans during the heat period) in *Xing de wenti* (The problem of sex), Shanghai: Xinghua shuju, 1933, pp. 36–48.

medicine without a licence, the uterus secreted a fluid which circulated throughout the body in the blood. This secretion was responsible for pleasure during vaginal intercourse, for the appearance of secondary sexual characteristics during puberty, and for 'nourishing the body and strengthening the mind'.[14] The face, he went on, 'easily blushes, which is why the girl is often bashful, lowers her head and stares at the floor. During this period, vanity and a sense of shame are pronounced, while the sexual impulse also develops.'[15] For the sex revolutionary Zhang Jingsheng, bashfulness was even considered to be the result of natural selection, since it normally attracted the male to the female.[16] Fan Shouyuan, a municipal senator and director of the Worker's Hospital in Shanghai, also observed in his *Guide to youth hygiene* that increased blood circulation during puberty made the young woman blush.[17] Even a sophisticated university textbook, first published in 1944 and reprinted in Taiwan as late as 1961, stated that the appearance of secondary sexual characteristics was responsible for the female's 'tender feelings and bashful attitude'.[18] Gendered as an essential category endowed with a passive instinct to obedience, girls were thought to be naturally destined to fulfil a submissive role in the sphere of domesticity.

If proper deportment was thought to be dictated by biology, irrational behaviour, lack of self-control and mental instability were at the same time interpreted as the natural consequences of hormonal turbulence. 'This sort of emotionalism is closely related to the changes which take place in the internal organs. Since the organisation of the internal organs – such as the ovaries, the uterus, the breasts, etc – is more complex in girls than in boys, external stimuli easily bring about vast and com-

14 Chai, *Xingxue*, pp. 42–3.
15 Chai, *Xingxue*, p. 44.
16 Chang, *Sex histories*, p. 35.
17 Fan Shouyuan, *Qingnian weisheng jianghua* (Guide to youth hygiene), Shanghai: Zhengzhong shuju, 1947, p. 43.
18 Zheng Zuoxin, *Putong shengwuxue* (General biology), Taibei: Zhengzhong shuju, 1961 (1st edn 1944), p. 246.

plex internal reactions.'[19] As with humoural theories in imperial times, in which specific organs were thought to govern different moods, modernizing writers in China tried to establish a correlation between physiological changes and psychological states. The lungs were transformed under the influence of moods: they choked with grief, burst with rage and contracted with fear. Digestion was eased by bursts of joy but impeded by anger. Adrenalin ('a sort of hormone') best illustrated how women lived under the grip of nature: in extreme anger, it entered the bloodstream, raised blood pressure, increased the rate of the heartbeat and caused the organism to gather strength. The biological step from androgynous child to fertile female also seemed to involve some degeneration, since the nerves generally weakened, physical strength withered away, and there was a decline in imagination and judgement. Puberty even brought the female a step closer to the animal, a phenomenon which justified increased social control: 'Difficult problems and mental work should be avoided', wrote the female authors of a popular *Mirror of health for women*. 'Also, novels and other reading material which stir up passions should be forbidden, or mental decline will set in without hope of recovery.'[20]

Anxiety about the dangers presented by urban degeneration and fear of the uncontrolled sexuality of the poor was reflected in discourses about sexual precocity. According to the observations of two female doctors of the Zhejiang Hospital, degenerate slums containing people of dubious character could prompt the hormones of the city girl into precocious activity.[21] Newspapers, aimed at a more popular readership, also reported that loose girls became pregnant at the age of five, highlighting how a depraved environment could stimulate their hormones into dangerous precocity.[22]

19 Zhu Yunping, *Xingjiaoyu gailun* (Outline of sex education), Shanghai: Shijie shuju, 1941, p. 60.
20 Guo and Li, *Nüxing*, pp. 33–4.
21 Guo and Li, *Nüxing*, pp. 24–5.
22 'Yixue xin faxian wuling nütong huaiyun' (New medical discovery of pregnant young girl of five years), *Xianggang gongshang*, 23 Oct. 1935, 4: 2.

In an age marked by the construction of nationalist identities, the onset of puberty in girls was also claimed to change from nation to nation: 'It is different for girls from different countries, and in our country, in general, the prevailing age is about sixteen years and seven months.'[23] Female puberty, it was said, started earlier in the regions located under the 'red path' (*chidao*), as the equator was known. Governed by nature more than by culture, African girls had a type of blood which swelled earlier to burst into a menstrual flow between the age of ten and twelve. The hormonal cycle was chilled in the frigid zones, where menstruation would start only around the age of eighteen. Women from the far north had their periods only during the summer; ovulation ceased when the winter set in, drawing mankind back into barrenness and gloom. Theories of humours and environmental determinism accorded well with racial categorizations, current from the end of the nineteenth century onwards. The 'Jewish race', for instance, was thought to reach puberty relatively earlier than the 'Arab race', and the 'four races' in Hungary were said to do so at different ages.[24]

Hormones also set in motion the transformation of the boy into a man. The prolix theories on male puberty churned out in Republican China show how important social thinkers considered the regulation of male adolescent sexuality, which was imagined to be the matrix of manliness, fatherhood and citizenship. Sexuality became the prism through which adolescent identities were constructed. A sex handbook printed in Hong Kong expressed it in unambiguous terms: 'All the aspirations, skills and intelligence of a person are contained in his testicles. If they are strong, his talent will be great; if they are weak, it will be feeble.'[25] For Zhang Dianjie, writing in 1922, a kind of 'primal fluid' (*yuanye*) circulating throughout the body fostered pubertal growth. It irrigated the brain, giving rise to 'vivid

23 Hu Dingan, *Shengyu changshi* (Common knowledge about childbirth), Shanghai: Dadong shuju, 1933, p. 2.
24 Guo and Li, *Nüxing*, pp. 24–5.
25 *Nannü*, p. 3.

thought', a 'bright outlook' and 'lofty ambitions'. During this period of change, the weight of the brain could increase fourfold, whereas the capacity of the lungs increased by as much as twenty times. The second type of fluid identified by Zhang was seminal. Retained in the testicles, it was the 'savings fund' which nourished life. Economic metaphors were used to emphasize the finite nature of semen, which Zhang could only urge his young readers to 'cherish as if it were sacred': 'Semen is the lifeline of mankind. It normally condenses in the kidney, which is why physicians call the kidney the gateway of vitality. The life expectancy of mankind depends entirely on the rise and fall of semen. Semen is to the life of man what oil is to the lamp and what water is to the fish: the lamp will fade when the oil runs out, the fish will die without water; life can obviously not be preserved if semen is dissipated.'[26] Zhang Dianjie, like other writers in the early Republic, appealed to both evolutionary biology and traditional medical terms in his *Essentials of hygiene for youth* (1922) which stressed the importance of the kidney and the role of semen. In traditional medical terms, the kidney stored the *yuanye* ('primal fluid') which nourished the viscera, the bones and the brain. It shared in the economy of bodily fluids and was responsible for reproduction. Unlike Zhang Dianjie, however, few modernizing writers were willing to invoke traditional theories which had lost much of their status since the fall of the empire. Zhou Jianren, the science editor of the Commercial Press in Shanghai and a popularizer of human biology and the life sciences, rejected older medical theories of 'primal fluids' in favour of more modern terms: 'The testicles produce spermatozoa and semen. These life-giving secretions directly enter the blood stream, insufflating courage and maturity into the boy. [. . .] These secretions are continuously released during the period of maturation, and receive greater stimulation as the result of a full and healthy love life.'[27]

26 Zhang Dianjie, *Qingnian weisheng bidu* (Essentials of hygiene for youth), Shanghai: Wenming shuju, 1922, pp. 10–17.
27 Wang, *Qingchun*, p. 104.

The protein theory of semen, popular throughout the Republican period, was also strikingly reminiscent of traditional medical representations of the male body. Similar to notions of seminal retention advocated in ancient sex handbooks, in which semen was supposed to ascend via the spinal column to nourish the brain, medical science was invoked to stress that seminal secretions contained numerous small protein particles which were released into the bloodstream by the testicles. These proteins were thought to build up the nervous system: 'The male's semen is secreted by the testicles; it is a sticky white fluid [. . .] which contains a great quantity of proteins and phosphates. The bright white radiance which can be observed under the microscope is called spermin; it is a chemical reagent for the stimulation and the fortification of the brain and the nerves. Hence all three substances – spermin, proteins and phosphates – supply nourishment and movement to our brains.'[28] The protein theory firmly located the mechanisms of adolescent development inside the individual body, a departure from more customary explanations which gave greater importance to the role of the environment or the cosmos. By constituting the person as a site of an autonomous bodily economy, it also gave strong support to notions of individual discipline and restraint. For Ding Fubao, as for so many others, prolonged abuse of the sexual function led to the decrease of life forces within the body and to great physical and mental harm. 'Semen is one of the nutrients of the organism, and the entire body suffers great harm when it is wasted, leading to various serious diseases. Spermin, proteins and phosphates are the three ingredients of this essential nutrient which feeds the brain and the nerves.' Repeating the traditional medical belief that semen was a fluid condensed from blood, Ding also calculated that the body lost forty drops of blood for every drop of semen wasted.[29] Ding Fubao (1874–1952) was an expert in medical syncretism. Having studied under

28 *Nannü*, p. 28.
29 Ding Fubao, 'Lun nanzi zongyu zhi hai' (About the evil of young men indulging in carnal desires), *Zhongxi yixuebao*, no. 21 (Feb. 1912), pp. 1–2.

the conservative scholar Wang Xianqian, he became interested in new knowledge during the Reform Movement in 1898, taught mathematics and physiology at the Imperial University of Beijing and in 1906 began to publish medical books. After a short period of study in Japan in 1910, he returned to China and founded *Chinese and Western Medicine*, a syncretic journal which combined various medical approaches.[30] A less traditional background can be found in the career of Hu Dingan (1898–1965). The son of a practitioner of Chinese medicine, Hu spent four years in the late 1920s studying medicine in Germany and was a graduate of Zhejiang Medical College. He also served as an editor with the Commercial Press. His popular book, *Common knowledge about childbirth* (1933), also devoted much space to the protein theory.[31] Outside literary circles, advertisements for spermin as a tonic even appeared regularly in the daily press of Republican China.[32] Despite a plurality of voices, in other words, the protein theory appealed to a variety of social and cultural groups: no blank walls existed between 'traditional' and 'modern' medicine, and very different writers often found a common interest in the appropriation of new medical knowledge.

The protein theory was mobilized in representations of female passivity. Folk beliefs and medical rationalization converged in the construction of a system of social order in which an active sexual role was limited to the male. According to Wang Yang's *Advice on childbirth* (1933), the sexually active woman developed a kind of enzyme in the blood which killed sperm by dissolving the protein contents of the male ejaculation.[33] Virgins, on the other hand, were easily impregnated, since their blood contained no semen which would activate the lethal enzyme. Healthy growth in the female was said to depend on the invigorating effect of absorbing male secretions; the

30 Croizier, *Traditional medicine*, pp. 64–5.

31 Hu, *Shengyu*, p. 16.

32 For instance in the *Shenbao yuekan* of February 1935.

33 Wang Yang, *Shengyu guwen* (Advice on childbirth), Shanghai: Zhongyang shuju, 1933, p. 44.

deflowering of the virgin lead to physical and physiological changes induced by semen. The proteins contained in the male ejaculation stimulated the growth of the female reproductive and hormonal system. Even down-market sex handbooks like the *Secrets of the bedchamber* (1938) made good use of the protein theory in their insistence on female virginity: 'It is enough for a couple to copulate once and the semen of numerous men will mix in the blood of the girl. These male components will never be eliminated from the bloodstream, moreover they contain a kind of defensive enzyme. Hence many virgins are skinny and small before they get married, but after marriage, their bodies undergo many changes. It is unavoidable that her thyroid gland will develop after marriage: this is the sign that semen has entered her bloodstream.'[34] White milk became a new symbol of vivifying semen, and the protein theory appeared in the dietary rules prescribed for girls by popular guidebooks: consuming milk (which disappeared from China as a drink after the Song dynasty[35] to reappear in the Republic as the epitome of an enlightened diet) could be healthy for weak and anaemic girls, but virgins were advised to take care when it came to eating 'stinking cheese', since it would make their skin gradually darken.[36] Disorders such as painful menstrual periods, anaemia and chlorosis would 'naturally' disappear after marriage, claimed Zhu Zhenjiang, who punctuated his book with frequent references to 'Western scientists'.[37] Chlorosis, a form of anaemia also called 'greensickness' in English, was believed to be a serious disease in young women. Explained either as a disorder of the menstrual cycle which could be cured by marriage in medical

34 Xu Zheshen, *Xingfang mijue* (Secrets of the bedchamber), Shanghai: Xinxin shudian, 1938, pp. 4–5.
35 Françoise Sabban, 'Un savoir-faire oublié. Le travail du lait en Chine ancienne', *Zinbun (Memoirs of the Research Institute for Humanistic Studies)*, no. 21 (1987), pp. 31–65.
36 Ge Shaolong, *Nüzi weishengxue* (Science of hygiene for women), Shanghai: Youzheng shuju, 1918, p. 88.
37 Zhu Zhenjiang, *Rufang ji qita* (About breasts and other things), Shanghai: Kaiming shudian, 1933, p. 84.

theories in nineteenth-century Europe, or as a depletion of vital energy, it focused on female puberty as a potential source of deregulation.[38] Reminiscent of traditional medical theories of female weakness in China, in which a 'sallow complexion' (*weihuang*) in young women was sometimes attributed to an insufficiency of 'vital blood' and 'energy', 'chlorosis' (*weihuang-bing*) was a new 'scientific' label which conferred legitimacy on a widespread belief in female vulnerability.

The development of the glands during puberty was said to lead to pungent odours. Closely charting shifting thresholds of tolerance towards smells, medical texts in the Republican period underlined how noxious effluvia emanated from the private parts, offending the delicate olfactory senses of the new urban élites. The vagina emitted a fluid which was 'particularly malodorous',[39] the prostate produced a 'stinking fluid',[40] the uterus excreted a 'smelly secretion'.[41] Semen had a 'particular stink',[42] and even fresh blood was described as having a 'raw stench'.[43] The individual became responsible for the control of his bodily fluids, and lack of personal hygiene was denounced. The smell of accumulated smegma under the foreskin and stale secretions in the female genitalia were branded as symbols of bodily decay. The unpleasant smells associated with sex, moreover, were thought to indicate its base origins: distance from the private parts was deemed proper in an age of modernity. In animals, readers were reminded, the scent of musk had the power to attract the female, and in 'primitive races', the lower faculties were also kindled into activity by the smell emitted by sebaceous glands. Underarm odour (*yechou*), which was not given off before puberty, was considered particularly offensive in Westerners: closer to the beast, they had powerful sexual urges. Degrees of

38 Jean Starobinski, 'Sur la chlorose', *Romantisme*, no. 31 (1981), pp. 113–30.
39 Cheng, *Renlei*, p. 38.
40 *Nannü*, part 2, pp. 18–8.
41 Chai, *Xingxue*, p. 42.
42 Su Yizhen, *Funü shengyu lun* (About women bearing children), Shanghai: Zhonghua shuju, 1922, p. 10; also Gu, *Fangzhongyi*, p. 7.
43 Liu, *Shengwu nanti*, p. 14.

olfactory discrimination were also thought to reflect the existence of a natural hierarchy in mankind: 'Normally the sense of smell is keener in women than in men, in children than in adults, in savages than in civilized races, in animals than in human beings.'[44] Distancing oneself from bodily functions was a sign of 'civilization'; disgust with the flesh became an expression of the modern spirit.

Smells were also mobilized in the construction of national space, and the cultural management of odour contributed to the naturalization of national identities. Olfactory and racial frontiers were made to coincide, as specific odours were assigned to all the 'races' scientists believed they had identified. It was claimed that each 'race' had an easily recognizable scent. In a popular introduction to 'human races', Gu Shoubai wrote that blacks were recognizable due to their 'offensive smell'. Professor Gong Tingzhang claimed that even the slightest physical contact with the black man was enough for the olfactory organs to be repelled by his 'amazing stench'. Each race gave off its own peculiar odour: 'Africans have a smell of rotten meat one can detect from far away. Browns from America also have a specific odour.'[45] As Alain Corbin has demonstrated, similar discourses also existed in Europe. Dr Bérillon, for instance, achieved fame in France with his analysis of the body odour of the 'German race', called *foetor germanica*. Cabanès, on the other hand, described the stale smell of the 'English race', which he claimed permeated their bedrooms (some attributed this odour to the proximity of the English to algae and seaweed).[46] In nationalist China, the aversion of smells was epitomized in the discourse on armpit odours: the 'white race' and the 'yellow race' would always remain separate, some Chinese writers imagined, since the former were actually attracted to body odours which the latter abhorred.[47]

44 Chen, *Renti*, p. 195.
45 See Dikötter, *The discourse of race*, pp. 47–8, 89 and 142.
46 Alain Corbin, *The foul and the fragrant: Odor and the French social imagination*, Cambridge, MA: Harvard University Press, 1986, pp. 209–10.
47 Cheng, *Renlei*, p. 142.

Reminiscent of the historical anecdotes about the 'evil odour' of barbarians, notably that from the armpits which was commonly described as the 'fox's stench' (*huchou*), the relative absence of sweat-glands in the armpits came to be considered as a characteristic of racial superiority. The smell imputed to excessive secretions, moreover, was not the only difference thought to exist between the 'Chinese race' and 'foreign races': the Japanese-educated biologist Wang Qishu surmised that different hormones in other 'races' could affect the size of the reproductive organs and body height.[48]

A bond of union was thought to exist between the different erectile structures, notably the nose and the penis. Interest in naso-sexual medicine in Europe culminated around the turn of the century. Between 1900 and 1912, more than 200 papers were published on the relationship between the nose and the reproductive system; interest in the topic thereafter rapidly declined. Wilhelm Fliess, the German gynaecologist who studied the effect of the menstrual cycle on the nose in women, was perhaps the most notable student in this field.[49] If relatively little was published on the relationship between smell and sexual desire in Republican China,[50] traditional medicine sometimes underlined the effects of increased blood circulation during puberty on the nose. These ideas were perpetuated by modernizing élites, who were keen to stress the vulnerability of 'adolescents': in puberty, the face often turned red and the nose could suffer from bleeding.[51] Theories of rejuvenation and the prolongation of life, which were popular at all cultural levels in China, were also stimulated anew with the discovery of internal secretions in the 1890s in Europe. Dr Brown-Séquard's rejuvenating fluid, for instance, was based on injecting testicular extracts to restore

48 Wang Qishu, *Jinshi shengwuxue* (Modern biology), Shanghai: Shangwu yinshuguan, 1925, pp. 58–9.

49 D.M. Stoddart, *The scented ape: The biology and culture of human odour*, Cambridge University Press, 1990, p. 80.

50 Gu Shaoyi, 'Xiujue yu qingyu zhi guanxi' (The relationship between olfaction and desire), *Dongfang zazhi*, 15, no. 9 (Sep. 1918), pp. 99–104.

51 Chai, *Xingxue*, p. 26.

physical strength.[52] Acclaimed as a pentacle of rejuvenescence in Europe, the therapeutic use of organic liquids also became successful in China.[53]

'*MALADIE D'ÉPOQUE*': SEXUAL NEURASTHENIA

'Sexual depression' (*xing de kumen*) was a danger to youth. Between puberty and marriage, it was claimed, years of sexual agony and distress took their toll on the fragile adolescent, who could suffer from 'perversion' or 'neurosis' (*shenjingbing*). Tormented by carnal 'impulses', and a victim of instincts which attacked him unremittingly, youth was mired in sex. Of course, 'sexual depression' was a '*maladie d'époque*' (*shidaibing*), a sign of modernity. On the one hand, new moral codes were opposed to premarital sex and postponed the age of marriage, imposing even greater restrictions on anguished young men. On the other hand, life in the inner cities of the coastal metropoles could lure them into courses that would lead to their ruin: obscene literature and houses of ill-repute, it was argued, appealed strongly to a young man's lower instincts. In an impersonal urban world, the anonymous letter for publication became the voice of the sexually deprived. Letters to specialized periodicals, confessions in the agony columns of daily newspapers and inquiries to medical journals abounded, reported Jin Zhonghua (1907–68), editor of several periodicals that were popular with

52 Merriley Borell, 'Organotherapy, British physiology and the discovery of the internal secretions', *Journal of the History of Biology*, 9, no. 2 (fall 1976), pp. 235–68.

53 Zhang Xichen, 'Renshou erbaisui shuo' (The theory of man living two hundred years), *Dongfang zazhi*, 10, no. 10 (April 1914), pp. 1–4; Tianmin, 'Rensheng erbainian shuo' (The theory of man living two hundred years), *Xuesheng zazhi*, 2, no. 9 (Sep. 1915), pp. 296–306; Hu Yuzhi, 'Changsheng xinlun' (A new debate about the prolongation of life), *Dongfang zazhi*, 14, no. 7 (July 1917), pp. 109–13; 'Kexue de changshengshu' (The scientific technique of prolonging life), *Dongfang zazhi*, 18, no. 7 (July 1921), pp. 70–80; Peiyu, 'Yanshou xinshu' (A new technique for prolonging life), *Funü zazhi*, 7, no. 2 (Feb. 1922), pp. 37–42; Jin Ke'nan, 'Women keyi changsheng busi ma?' (Can we live eternally?), *Zhongyang ribao*, 5 and 12 Oct. 1934, 3: 2.

the young.[54] Estranged from their families and alienated from their teachers, youth was portrayed as the prisoner of solitude. Sex education, social reformers pleaded, offered a glimmer of hope to these lonely people: it would instil high ideals and healthy attitudes to combat the evils of modernity.

Neurasthenia in particular was a 'modern disease' which conveyed a certain prestige: only cultivated city-dwellers suffered the unbearable strain on the nervous system imposed by the delights of modern civilization. As a new nosological category, it was eagerly promoted in Republican China. The nerves had been conceptualized as a 'system' (*xitong*) since the beginning of the twentieth century, and it was thought that they could be shattered and become exhausted, particularly through the abuse of sex. Half a century after the death of George Beard, the appearance of whose *Sexual neurasthenia (nervous exhaustion): Its hygiene, causes, symptoms, and treatment, with a chapter on diet for the nervous* in 1884 had heralded a new area in the cultural construction of nervous disease, sexual neurasthenia aroused intense medical discussion in China.[55] Xie Yunshou dedicated an entire chapter to it in his *Guide to Venereal Diseases* (1933), and he distinguished three stages: (1) nervous weakness of the reproductive organs, manifested by nocturnal emissions and premature ejaculation, (2) nervous weakness of the spine, leading to impotence, and (3) nervous exhaustion of the spine and the brain, the ultimate stage which made the entire body collapse.[56] The private entrepreneur Wang Yugang, like some others, wrote,

54 Jin Zhonghua, *Qingnian yu shenghuo* (Youth and life), Shanghai: Kaiming shudian, 1933, pp. 151–2.

55 On George Beard, see Barbara Sicherman, 'The paradox of prudence: Mental health in the Gilded Age' in Andrew Scull (ed.), *Madhouses, mad-doctors, and madmen: The social history of psychiatry in the Victorian age*, Philadelphia: University of Pennsylvania Press, 1981, pp. 218–40, and Eric T. Carlson, 'George M. Beard and neurasthenia' in E.R. Wallace and C. Pressley (eds), *Essays in the history of psychiatry*, Columbia, SC: W.S. Hall Psychiatric Institute, 1980, pp. 50–7; F.G. Gosling, *Before Freud: Neurasthenia and the American medical community, 1870–1910*, Chicago: University of Illinois Press, 1987.

56 Xie, *Xingbing*, p. 103.

printed and himself distributed a pamphlet on the self-treatment of sexual neurasthenia, a tribute to the commercial success this type of literature enjoyed in Republican China.[57] Classical economic ideas about self-contained systems supported the representation of the human body as an organism with limited nervous energy. The nerves could be quickly exhausted under the heavy demands of civilized life. Like semen, nervous energy existed in finite quantities and should be dispensed with restraint. Similar to a machine, moreover, the body could easily be overworked: it needed 'rest'. One of the great dangers to vulnerable adolescent girls was 'overwork' (*guolao*). The advice given by a *Hygiene for Girls* (1918) was typical: 'It is dangerous to use the nervous function over an extended period of time. There are certain limits to its use and a certain time for rest should be respected [. . .] Uninterrupted mental effort can have unfortunate results; for instance, the brain could sink into total paralysis. Although this phenomenon is also frequent with boys, it is even more difficult to avoid with girls whose constitution is much more fragile. Hence excessive mental activities can lead to a rush of blood to the brain [. . .] Serious mental disease like neurasthenia can result from daily abuse.'[58] Neurasthenia was also a threat to the weaker nervous system of children. Hu Dingan, in his popular *Common knowledge about childbirth*, explained how it was wrong to terrorize small children with frightening words like 'tiger', 'foreigner' or 'ghost'.[59] Fear for the lack of control, angst for any excesses and a dislike for the public display of emotions as well as a growing anxiety over urban life as a site of 'degeneration' contributed to the popularity of 'neurasthenia' in Republican China. Fostered by gruesome representations of mental disease, 'youth' was defined in terms of a number of physiological dangers and threats. If nervous debility could cause the flower of youth to wither, masturbation would nip it in the bud.

57 Wang Yugang, *Xing shenjing shuairuo ziliao fa* (Self-treatment of sexual neurasthenia), published and distributed by the author, 1932.
58 Ge, *Nüzi*, pp. 22–3.
59 Hu, *Shengyu*, pp. 99–100.

'THE EVIL HABIT': MEDICAL DISCOURSES OF MASTURBATION

'To predict the rise or fall of the nation, one should look at the physique of the race; to assess the future of the state, it is enough to examine the bedclothes of our youth,' proclaimed Yi Jiayue, a sociologist who favoured an 'anti-masturbation movement' and a forum on 'Masturbation among Students and the Future of the Chinese Republic'.[60] Nationalist discourses introduced a polarity between a relatively independent individual, based on the idea of self-regulation, and the coercive intervention of civil society, justified in the name of the collective health of the nation. A conceptual link was established between the individual, the conjugal couple, the population as a whole and the state in which the power of the latter was founded upon the discipline of the former. Nowhere is this normative pressure more evident than in the medical debates on masturbation.

'Guard the body like a piece of jade; hold on to your aspirations as if they were gold' (*shou shen ru yu zhi zhi ru jin*) was a common saying in late imperial China, reflecting the neo-Confucian view of the body as a precious vessel which should be kept free from defilement. In seventeenth-century fiction, the economy of sperm became an important literary topic, based on a vocabulary of seminal capital (*benqian*), savings and spending in which frugality with money was compared to caution in the expenditure of semen.[61] In popular literature, mythical monsters sucked dry hapless youths in their search for vivifying semen.[62] The Buddhist term 'illegal ejaculation' (*feifa chujing*) and Daoist ideas about seminal retention and the nourishment of the brain also retained some credibility until the beginning of the twentieth century. Traditional terms and a more

60 Yi, 'Zhongguo', p. 22151.

61 Keith McMahon, *Causality and containment in seventeenth-century Chinese fiction*, Leiden: Brill, 1988, pp. 10, 84 and 103; Indira Satyendra, 'Metaphors of the body: The sexual economy of the *Chin P'ing Mei tz'u-hua*', *Chinese Literature*, 15 (1993), pp. 93–6.

62 Kristofer Schipper, *Le corps Taoïste*, Paris: Fayard, 1982, p. 205, n. 71.

fashionable vocabulary derived from medical science became intermingled in early Republican China, underlining the fatal consequences of sexual indiscipline, as a succinct chapter on sexual hygiene in Dr Zhuang Weizhong's *Questions and answers on the art of health* (1934) illustrates:

> *Question*: What is considered sexual abuse?
>
> *Answer*: The excessive indulgence of sexual desire, the squandering of semen [*jingxue*, a classical medical term], be it through nocturnal emissions or through immoral emissions [*feifa chujing*, a Buddhist term], are all considered to constitute abuse.
>
> *Question*: What are the consequences of the excessive use of sexual desire?
>
> *Answer*: The consequences are sexual neurasthenia [*xing shenjing shuairuo*, a biomedical term], impotence, spermatorrhoea, venereal diseases and the like.
>
> *Question*: How many kinds of venereal diseases are there? What is harmful about them?
>
> *Answer*: There are four kinds of venereal diseases: syphilis, gonorrhoea and soft chancres, the last named being divided into a minor type which leads to disability and a major type which leads to death, sterility or the infection of offspring.
>
> *Question*: What is the harm of diseases like sexual neurasthenia, impotence and spermatorrhoea?
>
> *Answer*: Dejection, the inability to have sexual relations and death.
>
> *Question*: How should youth cherish sex?
>
> *Answer*: They should preserve their body like jade, avoid any excitement and restrain their behaviour, and to preserve their health, the married couple should know how to restrain sexual desire.[63]

The dangerous potential of sexuality – seen as a biological urge to be resisted – tested the social responsibility of the adolescent.

63 Zhuang Weizhong, *Jiankangshu wenda* (Questions and answers on the art of health), Shanghai: Dahua shuju, 1934, pp. 165–7.

Rationality and voluntary self-discipline became paramount. The medical distinction between 'involuntary depletions' and 'wilful masturbation' underlined the importance of self-regulation: 'Involuntary stimulation leading to an improper emission is called "hack and cut" (*zhuofa*), popularly called "masturbation" (*shouyin*); self-pollution during sleep is called "loose and leak" (*yixie*); it is also called "emission during a dream" (*mengyi*), or "losing essence" (*yijing*),' Yu Fengbin wrote in 1915.[64] The pathogenesis of nocturnal emissions – already widespread in *yangsheng* medical texts of the late imperial period – highlighted the dominance of the mind over the body, where reason in a slumber could create havoc. 'The mind' was represented as a relatively independent entity which increased in strength with the advance of 'civilization'. Emphasis on the power of the mind, thought to indicate individual responsibility in the control over bodily fluids, was so important that many medical authorities failed to establish clear distinctions between physiological gonorrhoea and voluntary discharges. Fear of pathological emissions, called 'spermatorrhoea' (*yijing*) from the 1920s onwards, was perhaps the most obsessive theme of medical literature on sex in Republican China.

Masturbation was described as a bad habit (*exi, huai xiguan*) acquired by a weak mind like addiction to cigarettes and alcohol. If it was not given up (*jiechu*) at an early stage, addiction would set in, eventually leading to irreparable bodily harm. 'Bad habits' could gradually establish their ascendancy over the body and consume it from inside. The nerve cells through which habitual information was channelled gradually grew larger, and repetition implanted that information into the nervous system, which was thought to be particularly vulnerable during the years of adolescence. The idea of 'habits' – borrowed from psychological literature – contrasted ill-considered gestures to disciplined rationality. Since onanism was not the result of a congenital defect or a biological fault, the masturbator had the power to discipline his desires and to regain control over a transient fad,

64 Yu Fengbin, *Xingyu weisheng pian* (Talks on sexual hygiene), Shanghai: Shangwu yinshuguan, 1915, pp. 7–8.

to overcome a vice acquired through a momentary aberration.[65] The compulsive masturbator was a social outcast, recognizable by his pale and haggard features. Voluntary depletion not only threatened the body which the individual had inherited from his progenitors, but it was also a threat to the body of society. 'Habit', 'instinct' and 'impulse' were the terms opposed to 'reason' and 'reflection', and the absence of self-control indicated a breach of moral principles, which was far more dangerous. Exhaustion of spinal nerves, atrophy of sexual glands, decay of the digestive system, dysfunction of the bladder and decline of sight: describing the pathology of onanism, Yu Fengbin, president of the prestigious Chinese Medical Association from 1920 to 1922, associated criminality and masturbation by claiming that 'the most pitiable is the one who cannot exercice self-control. Those who commit crimes are people who cannot keep themselves under control. They are a nuisance to society and the state.'[66] The booklet of scientific vulgarization entitled *Growth of adolescents* (1940) digressed at length on the control of seminal fluid, the maintenance of bodily rectitude and even the disciplining of emotions.[67]

Spreading according to a clearly defined social geography, sexual deviancy was thought to characterize the new spaces of modernity where the 'lower classes' were packed, for instance army barracks and factories, all contaminated by collective masturbation (*qunji shouyin*).[68] At the other end of the social scale, individual isolation was thought to lead to sexual abuse among children of rich households, an idea upheld by the use of popular sayings such as 'A person leading an idle life is given

65 The theme of self-discipline is pursued further in Frank Dikötter, 'Sexualité, discipline et modernité en Chine', *Equinoxe. Déviances, intolérances et normes*, no. 13 (April 1994), pp. 171–83.

66 Yu, *Xingyu*, p. 12.

67 Zhou Shang and Ye Hua, *Nannü qingnian de changcheng* (Growth of adolescents), Shanghai: Shangwu yinshuguan, 1940.

68 Xie Yunshou, *Xingbing zhi mi* (Guide to venereal diseases), Shanghai: Shehui yibaoguan chubanbu, 1933, pp. 116–17.

to evil'; literary clichés like 'to live in seclusion' (*youju yishi*) also interspersed the anti-masturbatory rhetoric. Vigilance became necessary: 'Without a long period of observation, it is not possible for parents and teachers to single out masturbators. Tell-tale signs are a pallid complexion, listlessness and bags under the eyes', wrote Li Baoliang in his *Sex knowledge*, published in 1937. The quest for solitude was interpreted as a pathological sign which required the intervention of the social group: 'There is not one masturbator who does not like solitude, so if a young man often gets excited at the idea of living in a room alone, masturbation may be suspected and parents as well as teachers should severely watch them.' The final step was to inspect bedding for suspicious stains.[69]

Once the habit became established, the body took over, leaving the victim a passive spectator of his own depletion. As Yu Fengbin recalled:

> The error of a moment may become the regret of a lifetime. As a child, I used to be careless and masturbate often. As an adult, I now regret this bitterly. [. . .] I have had constant nocturnal emissions. For some obscure reason, my condition has recently got worse. When I go to the toilet, semen actually seeps out with the urine. Since I have contracted this disease, my memory has gradually faded, my comprehension has degenerated and my vision is impaired.[70]

Medical foundation of disciplinary injunctions, the pathological diagnosis of masturbation was as popular with the medical profession in China as in the West. Dr Yuan Guorong, an eminent specialist and prolific writer on spermatorrhoea, admitted to having fallen victim to 'the habit' himself when young. Suffering from daily discharges at the age of fifteen, he described himself at the age of twenty-five as 'neurasthenic, sallow, worn to a shadow, dim-sighted, dizzy, suffering from lumbago, loss of memory, fits of terror and dullness of mind'. When he was

69 Li, *Xing de zhishi*, p. 65.
70 Yu, *Xingyu*, p. 7.

reduced to skin and bone, life seemed to be slowly slipping through his fingers until he was finally cured by a medical master a few years later.[71] Other recitals of symptoms claimed that masturbation eroded the memory, obstructed mental faculties and retarded physical development, eventually leading to early death (*yaowang*). First, the nervous system was affected: fatigue, palpitations, irregular blood circulation, indigestion and loss of appetite were some of the most obvious symptoms. Gradual decay of the nervous system impaired the normal functioning of the brain, leading to insanity and hypochondria. 'They may feel elated at one point, dejected at another. Most of them are restless and frightened at the idea of disease. They suffer from irrational terror at the slightest feeling of unhappiness. They are afraid of boarding a train, walking through busy streets, going up high buildings and entering dark places':[72] the city, a site of modernity beset with dangerous temptations, could lead to a sense of alienation and to sexual transgressions. According to Dr Li Yongnian, who wrote in the journal *Healthy Life*, self-abuse resulted in exhaustion of the nerves in the spinal column, atrophy of the sex glands, collapse of the digestive system, malfunctioning of the bladder and worsening of eyesight – among other symptoms.[73] The outcome was death, the untimely extinction of life after a long process of dissipation: according to a 'famous Beijing physician', Zhang Jingsheng claimed, some young persons whom he treated could have died as the result of a suicidal obsession with their reproductive organs.[74] Solitary pleasures led to death, that of the individual and of the species. Medical advertisements, instrumental in transforming discursive formations into actual practice, became an area where representations of masturbatory depletion were put to commercial use. Thriving

71 Yuan Guorong, *Yijingbing zhimi* (Guide to spermatorrhoea), Hong Kong: Yuan Guorong yiwusuo, 1940 (15th edn).
72 Pan Gongzhan, 'Liangxing shenghuo yu xingjiaoyu' (Human sexual life and sexual education), *Jiaoyu zazhi*, 15, no. 8 (Aug. 1923), p. 22105.
73 Li Yongnian, 'Shouyin de haichu' (The harm of masturbation), *Jiankang shenghuo*, 22, no. 3 (March 1940).
74 Chang, *Sex histories*, p. 17.

on a medical discourse which represented masturbation as a threat to the individual and the future health of the species, newspapers carried advertisements for medicines preventing nocturnal discharges, while loss of semen, publicized as 'the common failing of unmarried youth', could be cured with 'tablets for the brain and the kidneys' (*naoshending*).[75] As in Victorian England,[76] quack doctors manipulated contemporary medical terminology for their own purposes, contributing to the spread of modernizing notions of human agency, causality and individual responsibility.

Semen was a form of capital which had to be carefully managed in the interests of the nation and future generations. It was said that masturbation caused impotence and premature ejaculation, and in the latter the seed was sterile. An alarmist rhetoric described how the genital organs could decompose from within. Although a superficial examination would not show them to be any different from those of a normal person, the testicles of the masturbator could shrink or become clogged with stale sperm, while the urethra could suffer from inflammation. Semen itself disintegrated: 'The secretions inherent to the testes gradually decrease, the spermatozoa also diminish in quantity, the semen becomes thinner in consistency and often contains underdeveloped and weak spermatozoa. This type of spermatozoon is abnormally transparent and has an impaired power of movement, it has no feeling, it lacks vitality and dies quickly, its membrane is shortened, the head is small, the whole body is bent as if it had been snapped, and it has a curled tail.'[77] A sterile sexual practice, masturbation caused permanent infertility and deprived the nation from man's most precious contribution.

75 For instance, in the *Shenbao* of 17 March 1935.

76 Sally Shuttleworth, 'Medical discourse and popular advertising in the mid-Victorian era' in Mary Jacobus, E.V. Keller and Sally Shuttleworth, *Body/Politics: Women and the discourses of science*, London: Routledge, 1990, pp. 47–68.

77 Zhao Jianxin, *Yiniao ji yijing* (Enuresis and spermatorrhoea), Shanghai: Shangwu yinshuguan, 1931 (1st edn 1921), p. 24.

Medical literature focused on internal physiological mechanisms, urging the adolescent to monitor his bodily functions closely. Accumulation of smegma under the foreskin, constipation leading to intestinal pressure, excessive bed-covering and unusual postures – all caused slight increases in temperature that could only stir up the 'sexual instincts'. Constipation, medical literature often stressed, was an excitant, with the proximity of excrement to the sexual organs causing increased heat. A new regime of table manners also found its place in medical discourses against masturbation: at school and at home, the defiling hand should be kept on the table. 'Sleeping flat on one's back or on one's front are ill-considered positions. Those who frequently have nocturnal emissions should sleep on one side with both legs slightly bent. Those who are inclined to sleep on their back could tie a towel around the waist with the knot at the back, which will waken them whenever they turn over on to the back. One will thus gradually acquire the habit of sleeping on the side.'[78] In reply to the letter of a reader who was tormented by the evil habit, one periodical advised tying the hands to the sides of the bed at night.[79] Yu Fengbin suggested that the patient should cool the restive organ with cotton-wool soaked in cold water. A last resort was to immerse the penis in a glass of ice-cold water. Although many of these prescriptions clearly reflected older theories of 'cold heat', new representations of the body located sources of energy within the body. Cold water, it was believed, would invigorate the body, activating hidden energies. More radical was the leather sheath lined with stings on the inside: it should cover the organ at night and would force any unsolicited erection to detumesce immediately.[80] The popular *Home medicine* prescribed a medication based on potassium bromide to counteract nocturnal emissions and masturbation.[81]

78 Yu, *Xingyu*, p. 9.

79 'Xingyu tongxun' (Communications on sexual education), *Xinwenhua*, 1, no. 4 (April 1927), p. 8.

80 Yu, *Weisheng*, p. 54.

81 Chen Jiwu, *Jiating yixue* (Home medicine), Shanghai: Shangwu yinshuguan, 1930 (1st edn 1915), pp. 217–18.

Very similar prescriptions, of course, can be found in the medical literature published in Europe in the nineteenth century. The persistent panic about the medical consequences of masturbation, which appeared in the wake of the publication of *De l'onanisme* by the Swiss physician Tissot in 1758, is well documented by historians and has been described in great detail.[82] The second half of the nineteenth century in particular was marked by growing numbers of respected specialists lending their prestige to the campaign against masturbation. The extent to which the solitary vice was taken seriously is demonstrated by the remedies which some medical men prescribed, including mechanical restraints and metal contrivances. Yet even in that half-century of medical terror about the potentially fatal consequences of self-abuse, no unanimity or consensus existed among physicians. As early as 1881, moreover, some prominent medical voices denied observing any ill-effects following upon masturbation.[83] A new perspective on masturbation appeared in the early twentieth century, and sex educators disseminated a far less gruesome view of its outcome. Many writers even claimed that it was a relatively harmless practice, and denounced instead the guilt induced by old scaremongering myths. After the 1920s, masturbation was sometimes advocated in print as an occasional hygienic outlet.[84] One of the first to explode contemporary

82 For an introduction, see E.H. Hare, 'Masturbatory insanity: The history of an idea', *Journal of Mental Science*, no. 108 (1962), pp. 1–25; Robert H. MacDonald, 'The frightful consequences of onanism: Notes on the history of a delusion', *Journal of the History of Ideas*, no. 28 (1967), pp. 423–31; Jr. Engelhardt and H. Tristam, 'The disease of masturbation: Values and the concept of disease', *Bulletin of the History of Medicine*, no. 48 (1974), pp. 234–48; R.P. Neuman, 'Masturbation, madness and the modern concepts of childhood and adolescence', *Journal of Social History*, 8, no. 3 (spring 1975), pp. 1–27; Thomas W. Laqueur, 'The social evil, the solitary vice and pouring tea' in Michel Feher, with Ramona Naddaff and Nadia Tazi (eds), *Fragments for a history of the human body*, vol. 3, New York: Zone Books, 1989, pp. 334–43.
83 Peter Gay, *The bourgeois experience: Education of the senses*, Oxford University Press, 1984, p. 299.
84 Lesley A. Hall, 'Forbidden by God, despised by men: Masturbation, medical warnings, moral panic, and manhood in Great Britian, 1850–1950', *Journal of the History of Sexuality*, 2, no. 3 (Jan. 1992), pp. 376–8.

medical myths about onanism, Havelock Ellis radically criticized the received wisdom in his *Auto-Erotism*, part of his *Studies in the Psychology of Sex* published in 1899. Tellingly, his view of masturbation had virtually no influence in Republican China, although he was undoubtedly the most popular foreign writer on sexual matters in that country.[85] Few voices opposed the macabre imagination of those who crusaded against the evil habit. Cheng Hao, an isolated author who suggested that masturbation could 'eliminate excess secretions' and 'calm the sexual nerves',[86] was lambasted by the medical fraternity:[87] even 'spiritual masturbation' (*jingshen shouyin*), it was argued, could cause physiological damage.[88] If the right to individual pleasure was never recognized, sex and procreation were conflated in medical discourses which represented masturbation as a sterile deviation which had to be eradicated.

Control of the body was also expressed in a reconceptualization of bodily postures. Broadly similar to developments in modern Europe,[89] shifts in representations of the body and the comparison of the human organism to a machine brought about a revolution in deportment in China. Gestures and postures were to be reformed, since physical uprightness was thought to be equivalent to moral rectitude. A good posture and balance, it was argued, would improve the national spirit: the body and the country both had to be steeled in face of the enemy. At home and at school, the reluctant child was increasingly forced to stand

85 For instance Fei Yunhe, *Nannü nengli zhi yanjiu (*H. Ellis, *Man and woman: Secondary sexual characteristics)*, Shanghai: Shangwu yinshuguan, 1926; Pan Guangdan, *Xing xinlixue* (Havelock Ellis, *Psychology of sex*), Beijing: Sanlian shudian, 1988 (1st edn 1946).
86 Cheng, *Renlei*, p. 157.
87 Yan Shi, 'Liangbu guanyu xingzhishi de shuji' (Two books relating to sexual knowledge), *Xinnüxing*, 1, no. 1 (Jan. 1926), pp. 53–8. Reply of the author in 'Xingzhishi shuji de taolun' (A debate about books on sexual knowledge), *Xinnüxing*, 1, no. 2 (Feb. 1926), pp. 109–111.
88 Chen Weibo, 'Lian'ai yu xingjiao' (Love and sex), *Xinnüxing*, 1, no. 8 (Aug. 1926), p. 569.
89 See Georges Vigarello, *Le corps redressé. Histoire d'un pouvoir pédagogique*, Paris: Delarge, 1978.

up, sit up and straighten up. Numerous 'health guides for youth' carefully introduced young readers to the new gestures: the head thrown up, the chest thrown out, the stomach drawn in. A strict upright posture was prescribed to youngsters under the Guomindang's New Life Movement in the 1930s, and today it is still the characteristic way in which young party members are portrayed in communist propaganda. On the other hand, a bearing which denoted indolence was attacked and every effort was made to correct slovenly gestures: these became the marks of physical degeneration and spiritual decay. Lack of discipline in a person's posture was condemned, and laziness was a social evil. The reformer Jiang Zhiyou (1866–1929), also author of an influential *Inquiry into the Chinese race*,[90] propagated the new discoveries on the 'disease of laziness' in Liang Qichao's *New People's Journal* at the turn of the century;[91] Gan Yonglong expatiated on the same 'disease'.[92] After 1900 there was an emphasis on physical training and martial vigour, and this ranged from Luo Zhenyu's recommendation to turn Confucian temples into physical training centres[93] to Mao Zedong's writings on physical exercise.

The latter was thought to cultivate a sense of discipline, to tire the body into submission, and to eliminate excess fluids in the form of sweat. These prescriptions were of course designed for the wealthier social formations of the big cities; farmers hardly needed to add to the physical hardship they already endured. The consumption of alcohol and cigarettes was also discouraged, as both were believed to have aphrodisiac effects. Dietary habits were important. Zhang Dianjie wrote: 'Food with stimulants should be given up. For example tea, coffee, chocolate and cocoa all contain salt of a toxic nature. They can impede

90 See Dikötter, *The discourse of race*, p. 120.

91 Jiang Guanyun, 'Kuleiai zhi laiduobing fa' (Kuleiai's method of curing the disease of laziness), *Xinmin congbao*, no. 33 (May 1903), p. 10.

92 Gan Yonglong, 'Duoweibing zhi yizhong' (Laziness is a kind of disease), *Dongfang zazhi*, 8, no. 2 (March 1912), pp. 5–7.

93 Paul Bailey, *Reform the people: Changing attitudes towards popular education in early 20th century China*, Edinburgh University Press, 1990, p. 76.

digestion, harm the brain, overstimulate the liver and kidneys and dilate the blood vessels. Thus, it is best to eliminate them entirely.'[94] In the opinion of this more traditionally inclined medical writer, for whom the regulation of diet was essential, keeping the sexual drive under control was like 'riding a wild horse which wants to kick'; in order to force the 'devil of desire' to retreat, moderation in eating was crucial. Using terms derived from traditional medicine, he inveighed against the use of salt, which was thought to increase the production of body fluids and to cause diarrhoea. The consumption of new products like coffee and chocolate, which symbolized an allegiance to modernity, could only increase the pressure of seminal fluid in a body already deregulated by evil habits. Other authors advised against eating excessive quantities of meat, which was claimed to arouse sexual appetite. Young people were counselled to consume milk, eggs, fruit and a little fish – which must have seemed like a feast in times when famine regularly swept the countryside. Reading habits were also vital in the containment of evil: literature of high quality gave nourishment to the mind, and produced a fiery and upright temperament which would 'keep bestial instincts under the control of the higher faculties'.[95] Reason was contrasted to temptation, the mind opposed the flesh, and force of will would rule the lower instincts. Good literature and good company were encouraged, and young people were urged to ignore coarse language and vulgar jokes. The presence of edifying portraits of national heroes on the walls would instil a sense of restraint into the young man, while the Confucian values of frugality, hard work, modesty in dress and the separation of sexes would keep lustful thoughts at bay. A few minutes sitting quietly (*jingzuo*, a Buddhist term) could cause improper thoughts to evaporate. In the adolescent, dress, diet, gestures, manners, emotions, speech, and thought were all to be disciplined for the building of 'character' (*xingge*).

Methods of establishing a diagnosis for female masturbation

94 Zhang, *Qingnian*, p. 35.
95 Yu, *Xingyu*, p. 10.

also appeared in medical journals.[96] The signs of defilement by hand were thought to be lassitude, facial pallor, premature wrinkling, expressionless eyes and digestive problems; the woman who masturbated suffered from increased leucorrhoea and from painful periods. Masturbation could also cause uncontrolled growth of the clitoris, a sign of physical degeneration which brought the female a step closer to the hermaphrodite, a monstrous form of masculinization which disturbed gender boundaries.[97] Unlike some Western countries, however, the campaign against female masturbation never reached the stage where strait-jackets, handcuffs and specially designed underwear were used to keep the patient under control. The reason for this paucity in China of debates on female masturbation was not so much a lack of interest in female deviation, or a degree of tolerance towards it, but the relative lack of personal status granted to adolescent girls. As we have seen in the earlier chapters, women were rarely recognized as active sexual agents. Sexuality was a male drive which needed a male type of discipline.

The actual incidence of auto-erotism in Republican China can only remain a matter for conjecture. One might speculate that the rising number of single men in the inner cities, the institutionalization of boarding schools for higher education, the multiplication of dormitories not only in schools, but also in the army and at factories, the postponement of the age of marriage, the decrease in the social acceptability of prostitution and the high incidence of venereal disease are some of the factors which may have contributed to an increase in solitary sexual behaviour. Research carried out by Zhou Tiaoyang in 1931 among university students in Beijing pointed at a rate of 86%, although social pressure and internalized notions of guilt must have influenced

96 Bao Tianbai, 'Nüzi shouyin zhi zhenduanfa' (The methods to diagnose female masturbation), *Jiating yiyao*, 2 (Aug. 1933), pp. 19–21.

97 Gu, *Fangzhongyi*, pp. 170–1; on the hermaphrodite, see Frank Dikötter, 'The neuter sex: Hermaphroditism, medical science and gender boundaries in China' in Frank Dikötter and Leslie Hall (eds), *The body and beyond: The creation and violation of bodily boundaries* (forthcoming).

the figures downwards.[98] A few years earlier, an American woman physician remarked on the frequency of masturbation at boarding schools and on the fact that the practice aroused no sense of shame, although her comments are clearly part of a disciplinary discourse which cannot be taken at face value.[99] The extent to which individual practices were transformed by medical discourses is also a matter for speculation. At first, normative pressures would have been internalized by the generation of students who went through the new educational system set up after the fall of the empire. New notions of sexual discipline, however, may have combined with a more tolerant set of informal customs in the early Republic, thus increasing awkwardness and anxiety among students. *Sinking*, a tale written by Yu Dafu about a student in Japan who relieved his sexual urges by masturbation, connected the idea of a 'weak nation' with his own condition as a 'weakling'. This novelette struck a sympathetic chord with many students, who represented Yu Dafu as the embodiment of a contemporary malaise (*shidaibing*). The subject of this autobiographical story, who was described as paranoid, believed that people were always staring at him, a symptom which seems to have been shared by other alienated students of that era.[100] Every time the protagonist 'sinned' (ethical and medical terms mingle), he would 'go to the library to look up references on the subject' to find that all books condemned the practice as 'harmful'.[101] Although this type of circumstantial evidence makes it impossible to draw any satis-

98 Zhang Mingyuan, ' "Shouyin you hai" bian' (Analysis of the belief that masturbation is harmful) in *Xingjiaoyu yu yousheng* (Sexual education and eugenics), Shanghai: Shanghai kexue jishu chubanshe, 1987, vol. 2, pp. 58–9.
99 F.J. Heath, 'Venereal diseases in relation to prostitution in China', *Social Pathology*, 1, no. 6 (1925), p. 283.
100 Sun, 'Out of the wilderness', pp. 175–82.
101 Joseph S.M. Lau, S.T. Hsia and Leo Ou-fan Lee (eds), *Modern Chinese stories and novellas, 1919–1949*, New York: Columbia University Press, 1981, pp. 125–41; Rey Chow analyses the story in detail in her *Woman and Chinese modernity: The politics of reading between West and East*, Minneapolis: University of Minnesota Press, 1991, pp. 138–45.

factory conclusions about the transformation of sexual practices by discursive formations, historical changes in sexual behaviour are clearly a terrain which deserves to be fully investigated.

If real sexual practices are often beyond the realm of the historian, there is ample evidence to suggest that the fear of wasting caused by loss of semen may be common to a large number of social groups. We have highlighted the continuities between traditional notions of seminal depletion and biomedical concepts of masturbation in Republican China, but spermatorrhoeic aetiologies can also be found in other contemporary societies. Between Tissot's famous medical work on onanism and the beliefs of a small Indian village near Bihar, Alain Bottéro has found a surprising overlap of diagnosis and symptomatology as well as conceptual analogies concerning the physiology of semen. As he has convincingly demonstrated, different cultures agree in considering the loss of seminal fluid to be a primary cause of disease: semen as the elixir of longevity and the warrant of vitality is a widely shared belief which cannot be confined to modernity alone.[102]

More important to our purposes, however, is that medical literature on adolescent physiology recognized the youth as a relatively autonomous agent who could monitor, control and discipline his bodily fluids. 'Youth' as a social category was culturally constructed by biologizing discourses in Republican China.

102 Alain Bottéro, 'Consumption by semen loss in India and elsewhere', *Culture, Medicine and Psychiatry*, 15 (1991), pp. 303–20.

7

EPILOGUE: THE REGULATION OF SEXUALITY IN THE PEOPLE'S REPUBLIC

Republican China was a crucial period of change during which modernizing élites increasingly referred to human biology instead of imperial cosmology as an epistemological foundation for social order. As in other secular nations, imagined or real biological differences were essentialized in the construction of categories like 'race', 'woman' and 'youth'; social groups were equated with biological units, the presumed biological endowments of human beings were given primacy, and cultural variety was thought to reflect more profound differences in nature. The construction of sexuality as a biological drive which formed the very core of the individual led to the emergence of a wide range of identities like the menstruating girl, the hysterical housewife, the menopausal harpy, the masturbating adolescent and the syphilitic husband. Moreover, the naturalization of desire introduced a polarity between a relatively autonomous individual, based on the idea of self-discipline, and the coercive intervention of civil society, justified in the name of the collective health of future generations. Sexual discourses constructed a conceptual link between individual, conjugal couple, population and state in which the discipline of the individual founded the power of the state. Finally, sexual desire, represented as a natural drive for heterogenital intercourse, was seen as a mechanism intended to ensure the reproduction of the species only: medical discourses drew a line between procreative and nonprocreative acts. Sex, in other words, was never dissociated from procreation.

The emergence and articulation of a biologizing approach in early Republican China, intimately linked to specific modes of power and knowledge, was to a great extent the result of the introduction of new discursive repertoires from modernizing nations. However, it is hypothesized that the discursive formations which were shaped in this period were also the outcome of a number of cultural reorientations which may have taken place as long before as the seventeenth and eighteenth centuries. Instead of describing the rise of normative naturalism as a derivative discourse from 'the West', this book recognizes that the roots of modernizing representations may have to be sought in a rich and diverse past in China itself.

The structures of meaning shaped through discourses on sex before 1949 were located in a burgeoning civil society in Republican China. The most important development after the foundation of the People's Republic in 1949 by the Chinese Communist Party was the dissemination of these discursive formations to other levels of culture. In Republican China, some philanthropic institutions were established and forms of discipline appeared to shape the sexuality of the poor, but it was only under socialist rule after 1949 that public policies were inaugurated to deal with the sexual practices of the less privileged strata of society.

The institutionalization of discourses on sex through official publications has been analyzed in detail by Harriet Evans.[1] Promoting the structure, repertoire and boundaries of Republican discursive formations, official propagandists in the CCP added little to an approach which emphasized discipline and restraint. The official socialist discourse constructed sexuality as an area of state control, and premarital or extramarital sexual practices like adultery, masturbation and homosexuality were declared to be 'shameless' or 'abnormal'. Through official publications the state attempted to regulate sexuality and establish mechanisms of control in the interests of marital and social welfare. By identifying sexuality as a domain for intervention, it expanded the available possibilities for direct interference into gender and family relationships. In its representation of gender distinctions, which were seen as biologically determined structures, official discourse

1 Harriet Evans, 'The official construction of female sexuality and gender in the People's Republic of China, 1949–1959', Ph.D. dissertation, University of London, 1991.

continued to give women a clearly subordinate role in the service of male-associated interests. The discursive link established between individual sexuality and state power was even more evident through narratives of self-abuse. In a public speech about the evil consequences for Chinese adolescents of bad habits, Huang Shuze observed: 'Young friends, I say that the force to overcome this kind of bad habit exists. Where is this force? This force is in our state's concern for the physical health of youth; it is in the responsibility you should have for the state and for the cause of socialism; it is in the socialist education you have received; it is in your yearning for a beautiful future; the force is within yourself.'[2] A popular *Common knowledge of physiological hygiene for youth*, published in 1982 and still on the open shelves in some public libraries at the beginning of the 1990s, described how 'evil habits' could dim the mind and become harmful for 'production, study and work', even transforming 'sturdy and lively youth' into 'spiritless and weak people, similar to opium addicts'. The medical effects included neurasthenia and hypochondria in men and vaginal infections in women.[3] Even a short article on the alleged medical consequence of masturbation, published as part of a book on *Sexual education and eugenics* (1987), was followed by a contribution on 'kidney deficiency' and the 'evil effects' of losses of semen on the health of youth.[4] A survey conducted in the mid-1980s found that 65.7% of students thought that masturbation was dangerous to health, an indication of the extent to which social practices may have been moulded by normative discourses.[5]

2 Huang Shuze, 'Zenyang cai neng duanjue shouyin xiguan?' (How can we stop the evil habit of masturbation?), *Zhongguo qingnian*, 1955, no. 13, p. 38.
3 *Qingnian shengli weisheng changshi* (Common knowledge of physiological hygiene for youth), Beijing: Zhongguo qingnian chubanshe, 1982, vol. 5, pp. 32–4.
4 Zhang Mingyuan, ' "Shouyin you hai" bian' (Analysis of the belief that masturbation is harmful) and Chen Zelin, 'Shouyin yu "shenkui"' (Masturbation and 'kidney deficiency') in *Xingjiaoyu yu yousheng* (Sex education and eugenics), Shanghai kexue jishu chubanshe, 1987, vol. 2, pp. 57–69.
5 Chen Huichang, 'Yifen zhongxuesheng xing wenti xiankuang diaocha'

In contrast to the Republican period, moreover, medical technologies have been mobilized in the official campaign against undisciplined sexuality in young people. Extreme methods of 'scientific control' are used, including psychological and medical treatment for young people who are thought to suffer from 'sexual hyperfunction' (*xing kangjin de ren*) and 'sexual addiction' (*xingpi de ren*). One article recommended the regulation of the level of sex hormones for dangerous sex criminals and for sexually active young girls.[6] The increase in so-called 'juvenile sex crime'[7] and sexually transmitted diseases[8] during the 1980s was also an argument used in favour of sex education, notably by professor Wu Jieping, and authority in the field of sexology who had benefited from a close relationship with Zhou Enlai. Other leading experts also pressed for the establishment of sex education programmes, notably Zhou Jianren, who had risen under the communist regime to be vice-chairman of the Standing Committee of the National People's Congress. His appeals for sex education were widely publicized in the official press, just as such appeals had permeated independent periodicals during the Republic: the state was promoted as an agent responsible for providing the individual with the knowledge necessary to discipline his sexual economy and regulate the flow of his bodily fluids. Hardliners in the party also fulminated against the 'deterioration of the racial spirit' caused by homosexuality, a 'Western social disease'. Considered a crime which should be eliminated or a mental illness susceptible to treatment by electric shock therapy, homosexuality incurs summary arrest and long prison sentences,

(Investigation into sex problems of a group of middle school students) in *Xingjiaoyu yu yousheng* (Sex education and eugenics), Shanghai: Shanghai kexue jishu chubanshe, 1987, vol. 2, pp. 33–6.

6 Børge Bakken, 'Modernizing morality in China', *East Asian History*, no. 2 (1991), p. 127.

7 For a discussion of 'sex crime', see Jean-Louis Rocca, *L'empire et son milieu. La criminalité en Chine populaire*, Paris: Plon, 1991, pp. 243–66.

8 Documented in Chen Fan (ed.), *Xingbing zai Zhongguo* (Venereal disease in China), Beijing: Shiyue wenyi chubanshe, 1990.

while many lesbians end up in the Shanghai Women Delinquents Correction Institution.[9]

The married couple, promoted as a harmonious family model by a few scholar-officials in the eighteenth century, and heralded by civil society as the 'natural' foundation of social order after the fall of the empire, became the only legal basis for human procreation after 1949. The socialist regime, in a distant echo of late Qing reformers like Yan Fu and Kang Youwei, linked the health of the population to the sexual economy of couples. The careful monitoring of bodies and the regulation of procreative behaviour was seen as the proper foundation for a strong state and a healthy nation. Fidelity between spouses, according to a recent report, is not only highly emphasized in official discourse, but also by most of the urban population.[10] If the transformation of individual expectations is an indication of the power of normative discourses, the coercive means deployed by a totalitarian state to impose social discipline are often intimidating. The harsh implementation of a birth control programme, which has led to abortions and mass sterilizations being forced on rural women,[11] somehow brings to mind the dogmatic vision of social order first outlined by Wang Shiduo a century before in the intimacy of a private diary.

The public administration of sexuality for the sake of future generations was a public concern prominently articulated by modernizing élites in Republican China. After the reforms initiated by Deng Xiaoping, these disciplinary discourses were partly implemented through a programme of eugenics. On 25 November 1988, the *People's Daily* announced that the Standing Committee of the National People's Congress of Gansu Province had passed the country's first law prohibiting 'mentally retarded

9 Ruan Fangfu, *Sex in China: Studies in sexology in Chinese culture*, New York: Plenum Press, 1991, p. 171.

10 Zha Bo and Geng Wenxiu, 'Sexuality in urban China', *The Australian Journal of Chinese Affairs*, no. 28 (July 1992), pp. 1–20.

11 Steven W. Mosher, *Broken earth: The rural Chinese*, London: Robert Hale, 1984, pp. 224 ff.

people' from having children. Chen Muhua, Vice-President of the Standing Committee of the National People's Congress and President of the Women's Federation, declared: 'Eugenics not only affects the success of the state and the prosperity of the race, but also the well-being of the people and social stability.'[12] Actively promoted by a small group of high CPC functionaries centred around Li Peng, a bill on eugenics to prevent 'inferior births' was recently presented to the NPC Standing Committee.[13] Publications based on scientifically discredited theories – such as Pan Guangdan's *Eugenic principles* – appear regularly.[14]

The strict economy of reproduction, in short, has caused the exclusion of all forms of sexuality that are not directly conducive to procreation. Economically profitable and politically conservative, the regulation of sexuality in the name of the nation has been the ultimate objective of legal sanctions, social controls and medical norms in China. In contrast to discourses on sexuality in Europe in the twentieth century, sex has not been dissociated from procreation. In its conflation of sex with reproduction, moreover, official discourse has not considered each person's particular and unique preferences to be significant and has refused to confer any rights to pleasure upon individuals. Instead of a distinction between individual sexual *preferences* ('heterosexuality' or 'homosexuality'), lines have been drawn between procreative and nonprocreative *acts* (e.g. 'sodomy') that should be administered in the name of a higher entity, be it 'the nation', 'the state' or 'future generations'. Official discourse, in other words,

12 'Zhiming renshi zuotan zhichu: tuixing yousheng ke bu rong huan' (Public figures point out that eugenic policies are of great urgency), *Dagongbao*, 30 Jan. 1991, p. 12.

13 *Summary of World Broadcasts*, 22 Dec. 1993, G/2–3.

14 Pan Guangdan, *Yousheng yuanli*, Tianjin: Tianjin renmin chubanshe, 1981, first published in 1948 and based mainly on Paul Popenoe and R.H. Johnson's *Applied eugenics*, New York, 1926; this publication was favourably reviewed in demographic journals like Hu Jize, 'Yao dong yidian yousheng-xue (jieshao Pan Guangdan de *Yousheng yuanli*) (We should understand some eugenics: Introducing Pan Guangdan's *Eugenic principles*), *Renkouxue*, 1986, no. 3, pp. 74–6.

has thrived on the deployment not so much of 'sexuality' as a multiplicity of individual variations, but on 'sex' as a procreative act to be performed in the legal site of domesticity.

With the gradual decline of communist authority since the mid-1980s, human sexuality has also become the subject of heated debate outside official circles. In an eerie revival of the New Culture Movement, which shook educated society seventy years earlier, intellectuals and academics from a variety of fields have identified human sexuality as a cultural domain where forces of good and evil are in contention.[15] Narratives of 'repression', denunciations of 'backwardness' and promises of 'pleasure' place the intellectual in a position of privilege in which his knowledge is set against established power. Whatever their claims to enlightenment, however, intellectuals in the PRC who crusade for 'sexual liberation' often speak the same language when dealing with sexuality as the regime from which they most wish to distance themselves. Both invent sexual desire as a 'natural' instinct, construct personal identities through the prism of sexuality and represent gender distinctions as biologically determined structures. Although a variety of voices have clearly appeared since the relative relaxation of official control over the cultural domain, the underlying structures of meaning with which human sexuality has been endowed have not yet been vigorously challenged. The degree of convergence between state and intellectuals in the recent proliferation of debates on sexuality is perhaps the best illustration of how profoundly culture and society have been transformed in China since the fall of the empire.

15 One example is Jiang Xiaoyuan, *Zhongguoren de xingshenmi* (The Chinese mystery of sex), Taibei: Boyuan chuban youxian gongsi, 1990; for an analysis of the literature, see Harriet Evans, 'Policing the body: Gender and the scientific construction of sex in the People's Republic of China', *Signs* (forthcoming).

BIBLIOGRAPHY

PRIMARY SOURCES

Bao Shichen 包世臣, 'Gengzhen zazhu er' 庚辰杂著二 (Notes on agriculture), *Qimin sishu* 齊民四術 (Works on economy), 1888.

Bao Tianbai 包天白, 'Nüzi shouyin zhi zhenduanfa' 女子手淫之診斷法 (The methods to diagnose female masturbation), *Jiating yiyao*, 2 (Aug. 1933), pp. 19–21.

Bao Zuxuan 鮑祖宣, *Changji wenti* 娼妓問題 (The problem of prostitution), Shanghai: Nüzi shudian, 1935.

'Bengang yixuejie chouzu Xianggang youshenghui' 本港醫學界籌組香港優生會 (Medical circles in Hong Kong organize a Hong Kong Eugenics Society), *Xianggang gongshang ribao*, 21 May 1936, 3:3.

Bingzhi 秉志, *Shengwuxue yu minzu fuxing* 生物學與民族複興 (Biology and the revival of the nation), Shanghai: Zhongguo wenhua fuwu she, 1946.

Cai Luxian 蔡陸仙., *Taichan kebing wenda* 胎產科病問答 (Questions and answers about obstetric problems), Shanghai: Huadong shuju, 1937.

Cai Qiao 蔡翹, *Shenglixue* 生理學 (Physiology), Shanghai: Shangwu yinshuguan, 1929.

Cao Guanlai 曹觀來, *Qingchun shengli tan* 青春生理談 (Chats about the physiology of youth), Taibei: Zhengzhong shuju, 1982 (1st edn 1936).

Cao Tingdong 曹庭棟, *Laolao hengyan* 老老恒言 (Health manual for elderly people), orig. 1784, 1878 edn.

Chai Fuyuan 柴福沅, *Xingxue ABC* 性學ABC (ABC of sexology), Shanghai: Shijie shuju, 1928.

'Chanfu weisheng' 產婦衛生 (Hygiene during parturition), *Dagongbao*, 24 April 1934, 3:11.

Chang Daozhi 常道直, 'Xingjiaoyu gailun' 性教育概論 (Outline of sex education), *Jiaoyu zazhi*, 15, no. 8 (Aug. 1923).

Chen Changheng 陳長衡, *Sanminzhuyi yu renkou zhengce* 三民主義與人口政策 (The Three Principles of the People and population policies), Shanghai: Shangwu yinshuguan, 1930.

Chen Da 陳達, *Renkou wenti* 人口問題 (Population problems), Shanghai: Shangwu yinshuguan, 1934.

Chen Dongyuan 陳東原, 'Xing de xisheng yu jiefang' 性的犧牲與解放 (The sacrifice and liberation of sex), *Funü zazhi*, 14, no. 6 (June 1928).

Chen Duxiu 陳獨秀, 'Maersaisi renkoulun yu Zhongguo renkou wenti' 馬尔賽斯人口論與中國人口問題 (The demographic theory of Malthus and the population problem in China) in Chen Duxiu, *Chen Duxiu wenzhang xuanbian* 陳獨秀文章選編 (Selected writings of Chen Duxiu), Beijing: Sanlian shudian, pp. 505–6.

——, 'Chen Duxiu da Mo Fuqing' 陳獨秀答莫芙卿 (Reply of Chen Duxiu to Mo Fuqing) in Chen Duxiu, *Chen Duxiu shuxin ji* 陳獨秀書信集 (Collected correspondance of Chen Duxiu), Beijing: Xinhua chubanshe, 1987.

Chen Fan 陳凡, *Xingbing zai Zhongguo* 性病在中國 (Venereal disease in China), Beijing: Shiyueyi chubanshe, 1990.

Chen Hu'an 陳笏庵, *Taichan mishu* 胎產秘書 (The secrets of childbirth), Shanghai: Huiwentang xinji shuju, 1923 (Qing publication).

Chen Huichang 陳會昌, 'Yifen zhongxuesheng xing wenti xiankuang diaocha' 一份中學生性問題現況調查 (Investigation into sex problems of a group of middle school students) in *Xingjiaoyu yu yousheng* (Sex education and eugenics), Shanghai: Shanghai kexue jishu chubanshe, 1987, vol. 2, pp. 33–6.

Chen Jiwu 陳繼武, *Jiating yixue* 家庭醫學 (Home medicine), Shanghai: Shangwu yinshuguan, 1930 (1st edn 1915).

Chen Jianshan 陳兼善, *Renlei naosui zhi jinhua* 人類腦髓之進化 (The evolution of the human brain), Shanghai: Zhengzhong shuju, 1947.

——, *Taijiao* 胎教 (Prenatal education), Shanghai: Shangwu yinshuguan, 1926.

——, 'Yichuan yu cixiong' 遺傳與雌雄 (Heredity and sex determination), *Jiaoyu zazhi*, 15, no. 2 (Feb. 1923), pp. 21141–62.

Chen Laoxin 陳勞薪, 'Guanyu *Xingyu yu xing'ai*' 關於性欲與性愛 (About *Sexual desire and sexual love*), *Xinnüxing*, 2, no. 2 (Feb. 1927), pp. 207–9.

——, *Dongwu de shengzhi* 動物的生殖 (The reproduction of animals), Shanghai: Beixin shuju, 1929.

Chen Shiduo 陳士鐸, *Shishi milu* 石室秘錄 (Writings of Chen Shiduo), orig. 1687, 1805 edn.

Chen Shu 陳述, *Xingbing changshi* 性病常識 (Elementary knowledge of venereal diseases), Harbin: Guanghua shudian, 1948.

Chen Tianbiao 陳天表, *Renkou wenti yanjiu* 人口問題研究 (Research on population problems), Shanghai: Liming shuju, 1930.

Chen Weibo 陳威伯, 'Lian'ai yu xingjiao' 戀愛與性交 (Love and sex), *Xinnüxing*, 1, no. 8 (Aug. 1926), pp. 574–67.

Chen Yinghuang 陳映璜, *Renleixue* 人類學 (Anthropology), Shanghai: Shangwu yinshuguan, 1928 (1st edn 1918).

Chen Yucang 陳雨蒼, *Shenghuo yu shengli* 生活與生理 (Life and physiology), Taibei: Zhengzhong shuju, 1958.

——, *Renti de yanjiu* 人體的研究 (Research on the human body), Shanghai: Zhengzhong shuju, 1937 (repr. 1965 in Taiwan).

Chen Zejiang 陳澤江, 'Tai cheng nannü zhi yuanyin' 胎成男女之原因 (The reason for sex determination) in Zhu Zhensheng, *Qiuyun yu biyun* (Birth control), Shanghai: Xingfu shuju, 1933, pp. 12–14.

Chen Zelin 陳澤霖, 'Shouyin yu "shenkui"' 手淫與"肾亏" (Masturbation and 'kidney deficiency') in *Xingjiaoyu yu yousheng* (Sex education and eugenics), Shanghai: Shanghai kexue jishu chubanshe, 1987, vol. 2, pp. 67–9.

Chen Zhen 陳楨, *Putong shengwuxue* 普通生物學 (General biology), Shanghai: Shangwu yinshuguan, 1924.

Cheng Hao 程浩, *Fukexue* 婦科學 (Gynaecology), Shanghai: Shangwu yinshuguan, 1950 (9th edn, 1st edn 1939).

——, *Jiezhi shengyu wenti* 節制生育問題 (Questions about birth control), Shanghai: Yadong tushuguan, 1925.

——, *Renlei de xingshenghuo* 人類的性生活 (The sexual life of mankind), Shanghai: Yadong shuju, 1934.

——, 'Xingzhishi shuji de taolun' 性知識書籍的討論 (Debate about books regarding sex knowledge), *Xinnüxing*, 1, no. 2 (Feb. 1926), pp. 109–11.

Chu Renhuo 褚人获, *Jianhuji* 堅瓠集 (Collected writings of Chu Renhuo), orig. 1690.

Cousland, P.B., *An English-Chinese lexicon of medical terms compiled for the terminology committee*, Shanghai: Medical Missionary Association, 1908.

Dashengpian 達生篇 (Obstetrics), Shanghai: Foxue shuju, 1934 (orig. 1715).

Dai Qiling 戴棣齡, *Shenglixue dayi* 生理學大意 (General physiology), Shanghai: Shangwu yinshuguan, 1931.

Dawson, E.R., *The secret of sex: The discovery of a new law of nature*, New York: Cochrane, 1909.

Ding Fubao 丁福保, 'Lun nanzi zongyu zhi hai' 論男子縱欲之害 (About the evil of young men indulging in carnal desires), *Zhongxi yixuebao*, no. 21 (Feb. 1912), pp. 1–2.

——, 'Lun nüzi zongyu zhi hai' 論女子縱欲之害 (About the evil of young girls indulging in carnal desires), *Zhongxi yixuebao*, no. 21 (Feb. 1912), pp. 3–4.

——, 'Lun shouyin zhi hai' 論手淫之害 (About the evil of masturbation), *Zhongxi yixuebao*, no. 21 (Feb. 1912), pp. 6–7.

Ding Shu'an 丁淑安 and Zhao Efen 周咢芬, *Jianyi chankexue* 簡易產科學 (Easy obstetrics), Beijing: Cicheng yinshuachang, 1948.

Doncaster, L., *The determination of sex*, Cambridge University Press, 1912.

Dong Renjian 董任堅, *Xing de jiaoyu* 性的教育 (Sex education), Shanghai: Ertong shuju, 1933.

Du Zhanzhen 杜占眞, *Youerqi zhi xingjiaoyu* 幼兒期之性教育 (Sex education for children), Shanghai: Jiaoyu duanboshe, 1936.

Du Zuozhou 杜佐周, 'Xingyu jiaoyu' 性欲教育 (Sex education), *Zhonghua jiaoyujie*, 15, no. 12 (June 1926), pp. 1–8.

—— and Qian Yishi 錢亦石, *Xingjiaoyu zhinan* 性教育指南 (T.W. Shannon, *Guide to sex instruction*), Shanghai: Zhonghua shuju, 1934.

Fan Shouyuan 范守淵, *Qingnian weisheng jianghua* 青年衛生講話 (Guide to youth hygiene), Shanghai: Zhengzhong shuju, 1947.

Faust, Ernest C., 'Social diseases in China', *Social Pathology*, 1, no. 6 (June 1925), pp. 274–7.

Fei Hongnian 費鴻年, 'Liangxing de benxing ji qi zuoyong' 倆性的本性及其作用 (The essence of both sexes and their function), *Xueyi*, 7, no. 5 (Jan. 1926).

——, *Renlei xingyuan lun* 人類性源論 (The origin of sex in man), Shanghai: Shangwu yinshuguan, 1927.

——, *Shengwu de qiyuan* 生物的起源 (The morphology and physiology of fertilization), Shanghai: Shangwu yinshuguan, 1926.

Fei Yunhe 費雲鶴, *Nannü nengli zhi yanjiu* 男女能力之研究 (Havelock Ellis, *Man and woman: Secondary sexual characteristics*), Shanghai: Shangwu yinshuguan, 1926.

Frazier, C.N., 'The prevention and control of syphilis', *China Medical Journal*, 51. no. 9 (Sep. 1937), pp. 1043–6.

Fu Shan 傅山, *Fu Qingzhu nüke* 傅青主女科 (Fu Shan's gynaecology), Shanghai: Shanghai kexue jishu chubanshe, 1991.

Gan Yonglong 甘永龍, 'Duoweibing zhi yizhong' 惰爲病之一種 (Laziness is a kind of disease), *Dongfang zazhi*, 8, no. 2 (March 1912), pp. 5–7.

Gao Shan 高山, 'Xing de jinhua' 性的進化 (The evolution of sex), *Funü zazhi*, 10, no. 9–10 (Sep.–Oct. 1924).

Gao Xisheng 高希聖, *Chan'er zhixian ABC* 產兒制限 ABC (ABC of birth control), Shanghai: Shijie shuju, 1929.

'Gaowan zahua' 睪丸杂話 (Chats about testicles), *Dagongbao*, 20 March 1937, 3:1.

Ge Shaolong 戈紹龍, *Nüzi weishengxue* 女子衛生學 (Science of hygiene for women), Shanghai: Youzheng shuju, 1918.

Gear, Harry Sutherland, 'The incidence of venereal diseases in hospital patients in China', *China Medical Journal*, 49, no. 10 (Oct. 1935), pp. 1122–35.

Geddes, Patrick and J.A. Thomson, *The evolution of sex*, London: Scott, 1889.

Gu Mingsheng 顧鳴盛, *Fangzhong yi* 房中醫 (Medicine for the bed-chamber), Shanghai: Wenming shuju, 1916 (1930, 15th edn).

——, *Zhongxi hezuan fuke daquanshu* 中西合纂婦科大全書 (Great compendium of Chinese and Western gynaecology), Shanghai: Dadong shuju, 1932.

Gu Shaoyi 顧紹衣, 'Xiujue yu qingyu zhi guanxi' 嗅覺與情欲之關係 (The relationship between olfaction and desire), *Dongfang zazhi*, 15, no. 9 (Sep. 1918), pp. 99–104.

Gu Shi 顧實, *Rensheng erbainian* 人生二百年 (Man may live two hundred years), Shanghai: Shangwu yinshuguan, 1929 (1st edn 1916).

Gu Shouban 顧壽白, *Neifenmi* 内分泌 (Internal secretions), Shanghai: Shangwu yinshuguan, 1923.

——, *Qihou yu jiankang* 氣候與健康 (Climate and health), Shanghai: Shangwu yinshuguan, 1924.

Gu Zhonghua 顧鍾驊, *Shengwuxue wenti xiangjie* 生物學問題詳解 (Detailed explanations of problems in biology), Beijing: Zhengzhong shuju, 1936.

——, *Xing yu shengzhi* 性與生殖 (Sex and reproduction), Shanghai: Zhengzhong shuju, 1936.

Gui Zhiliang 桂質良, *Nüren zhi yisheng* 女人之一生 (A woman's life), Beijing: Zhengzhong shuju, 1936.

Guo Quanqing 郭泉清, *Shiyong biyunfa* 實用避孕法 (Using birth control), Shanghai: Jiazazhi she, 1948.

Guo Renji 郭人驥 and Li Renlin 酈人麟, *Nüxing yangsheng jian* 女性養生鑑 (Mirror of health for women), Shanghai: Shangwu yinshuguan, 1928 (1st edn 1922).

Guo Taihua 郭太華, 'Biyunfa lüeshu' 避孕法略述 (Brief discussion of birth control methods), *Shenbao*, 21 Sep. 1934, 5:20.

Guo Yuyu 郭豫育 and Guo Daxiong 郭大雄, *Xing* 性 (F.A.E. Crew, *An introduction to the study of sex*), Shanghai: Shangwu yinshuguan, 1936.

'Heyuan liushisi sui lao'ou Deng Chen shi chan zi' 河源六十四歲老嫗鄧陳氏產子 (Old lady Deng born Chen from Heyuan gives birth to a son at the age of sixty-four), *Xianggang gongshang*, 3 May 1936, 2:4.

Heape, Walter, *Sex antagonism*, London: Constable, 1913.

Heath, F.J., 'Venereal diseases in relation to prostitution in China', *Social Pathology*, 1, no. 6 (1925), pp. 278–84.

Heimburger, L.F., 'The incidence of syphilis at the Shantung Christian University dispensary', *China Medical Journal*, 41, no. 6 (June 1927), pp. 541–50.

Hirschfeld, Magnus, *Die Weltreise eines Sexualforschers*, Brugg: Bözberg, 1933.

Hobson, Benjamin, *A medical vocabulary in English and Chinese*, Shanghai: Shanghai Mission Press, 1858.

—— and Chen Xiutang 陳修堂, *Quanti xinlun* 全體新論 (Outline of anatomy and physiology), 1850.

Hodge, S.R., 'Syphilis in China', *China Medical Journal*, 21, no. 5 (May 1907), pp. 237–241.

Hong Liangji 洪亮吉, *Hong Beijiang shiwenji* 洪北江詩文集 (Poems and writings of Hong Liangji), Taibei: Shijie shuju, 1964.

Hu Dingan 胡定安, *Shengyu changshi* 生育常識 (Common knowledge about childbirth), Shanghai: Dadong shuju, 1933.

Hu Dunfu 胡敦復, 'Shengsi zhi xin fenjie' 生死之新分界 (The new border between life and death) *Dongfang zazhi*, 9, no. 12, vol. 10, no. 3 (June–Sep. 1913).

Hu Jize 胡紀澤, 'Yao dong yidian youshengxue (jieshao Pan Guangdan de *Yousheng yuanli*)' 要懂一點優生學（介紹潘光旦的優生原理） (We should understand some eugenics: Introducing Pan Guangdan's *Eugenic principles*), *Renkouxue*, 1986, no. 3, pp. 74–76.

Hu Yuzhi 胡愈之, 'Changsheng xinlun' 長生新論 (A new debate about the prolongation of life), *Dongfang zazhi*, 14, no. 7 (July 1917), pp. 109–13.

Hu Zhengxiang 胡正祥, 'Meidu' 梅毒 (Syphilis), *Kexue*, 5, no. 2 (Feb. 1920), pp. 177–96.

Hu Zhenyuan 胡珍元, *Renti de shenghuo* 人體的生活 (Life of the human body), Shanghai: Shijie shuju, 1931.

Huang Gongjue 黃公覺, 'Xingjiaoyu gailun' 性教育概論 (Introduction to sexology), *Jiaoyu zazhi*, 15, no. 8 (Aug. 1923), pp. 22071–6.

Huang Shi 黄石, 'Shenma shi taijiao' 甚麼是胎教 (What is prenatal education), *Funü zazhi*, 17, no. 11 (Nov. 1930), pp. 19–28.

——, 'Guanyu chanyu de mixin yu fengsu' 關於產育的迷心與風俗 (About superstitions and customs on birth), *Funü zazhi*, 16, no. 10 (Oct. 1930), pp. 97–105.

Huang Shuze 黄樹則, 'Zenyang cai neng duanjue shouyin de huai xiguan?' 怎樣才能斷絕手淫的壞習慣 (How can we stop the evil habit of masturbation?), *Zhongguo qingnian*, 1955, no. 13, p. 38.

Huang Zifang 黄子方, *Weisheng changshi wenda* 衛生常識問答 (Elementary questions and answers about hygiene), Shanghai: Shangwu yinshuguan, 1937.

Jianmeng 健孟, 'Meidu shi zhongzu shuaitui de yuanyin' 梅毒是種族衰頹的原因 (Syphilis is the cause of racial decline), *Dongfang zazhi*, 19, no. 7 (April 1922), pp. 85–6.

——, 'Minzu zhi shuaitui' 民族之衰頹 (The decline of the race), *Dongfang zazhi*, 18, no. 21 (Nov. 1921), pp. 1–3.

Jiang Guanyun 蔣觀雲, 'Kuleiai zhi laiduobing fa' 庫雷唉治懶惰病法 (Kuleiai's method of curing the disease of laziness), *Xinmin congbao*, no. 33 (May 1903), p. 10.

Jiang Shaoyuan 江紹原, 'Xue yu tiangui' 血與天癸 (Blood and menstruation), *Gongxian*, 2, no. 7 (May 1928), pp. 5–24.

Jiang Xiangqing 蔣湘青, *Renti celiangxue* 人體測量學 (The science of body measurements), Shanghai: Qinfen shuju, 1935.

Jiang Xiaoyuan 江曉原, *'Xing' zai gudai Zhongguo: dui yizhong wenhua xianxiang de tansuo* 性在古代中國：對一種文化現象的探索 ('Sex' in ancient China: Exploration of a cultural phenomenon), Shanxi: Kexue jishu chubanshe, 1988.

——, *Zhongguoren de xingshenmi* 中國人的性神秘 (The Chinese mystery of sex), Taibei: Boyuan chuban youxian gongsi, 1990.

Jiao Xun 焦循, *Diaogu ji* 雕菰集 (Collected works of Jiao Xun), Shanghai: Shangwu yinshuguan, 1936.

Jifan 寄凡, 'Shouyin zhi weihai' 手淫之危害 (The danger of masturbation) in Zhu Zhensheng, *Qiuyun yu biyun* (Birth control), Shanghai: Xingfu shuju, 1933, pp. 20–22.

Jin Ke'nan 金克難, 'Nei fenmi yu shengli de guanxi' 内分泌與生理的關係 (The physiological functions of inner secretions), *Xinwenbao*, 31 August 1934, 3:2, also in *Zhongyang ribao*, 7, 14, 21 and 28 Sep. 1934.

——, 'Women keyi changsheng busi ma?' 我們可以長生不死嗎 (Can we live eternally?), *Zhongyang ribao*, 5 and 12 Oct. 1934, 3:2.

Jin Zizhi 金子直, *Minzu weisheng* 民族衛生 (Racial hygiene), Shanghai: Shangwu yinshuguan, 1930.

Jin Zhonghua 金仲華, *Qingnian yu shenghuo* 青年與生活 (Youth and life), Shanghai: Kaiming shudian, 1933.

Kang Youwei 康有爲, *Datongshu* 大同書 (One World), Beijing: Guji chubanshe, 1956.

——, 'Qing jin funü chanzu zou' 請禁婦女纏足奏 (Memorial with a request for a ban on the binding of women's feet) in Jian Bozan *et al.* (eds), *Wuxu bianfa* (The Hundred Days), Shanghai: Shenzhou guoguang she, 1953, vol. 2, pp. 242–4.

Ke Xiangfeng 柯象峯, *Xiandai renkou wenti* 現代人口問題 (Modern population problems), Shanghai: Zhengzhong shuju, 1934.

'Kexue de changshengshu' 科學的長生術 (The scientific technique of prolonging life), *Dongfang zazhi*, 18, no. 7 (July 1921), pp. 70–80.

Lai, Daniel G. and Suchen Wang Lai, 'Incidence of syphilis among Chinese civilian patients in Swatow district', *China Medical Journal*, 43, no. 1 (Jan. 1929), pp. 22–7.

——, 'Incidence of syphilis among the Chinese soldiers at Swatow', *China Medical Journal*, 43, no. 8 (Aug. 1929), pp. 557–67.

Lamson, H.D., 'Educated women and birth control in China', *China Medical Journal*, 44, no. 12 (Dec. 1930), pp. 1100–9.

——, *Social pathology in China*, Shanghai: The Commercial Press, 1935.

Lan Hu 藍瑚, *Xing zhishi wenda* 性知識問答 (Answers and questions about sex knowledge), Kunming: Yunnan renmin chubanshe, 1958.

Lei Yuxian 雷遜先, 'Xing de zhishi zenyang shouyu ertong' 性的知識怎樣授於兒童 (How to impart sex knowledge to children), *Zhonghua jiaoyujie*, 13, no. 8 (Feb. 1924).

Lennox, W.G., 'Neurosyphilis among Chinese', *China Medical Journal*, 37, no. 8 (Aug. 1923), pp. 663–71.

Li Baoliang 李寶梁, *Xing de zhishi* 性的知識 (Sex knowledge), Shanghai: Zhonghua shuju, 1937.

Li Jianyi 李健頤, 'Funü shengyu chizao zhi yuanyin' 婦女生育遲早之原因 (The reason for differences in the reproductive age of girls) in Zhu Zhensheng, *Qiuyun yu biyun* (Birth control), Shanghai: Xingfu shuju, 1933, pp. 16–17.

Li Meishi 李梅士, 'Sanminzhuyi de renkoulun' 三民主義的人口論 (The Three Principles of the People and demographic theory), *Xiandai Zhongguo zazhi*, 2, no. 1–2 (Aug. 1928).

Li Sanwu 李三无, 'Xingyu jiaoyu yanjiu' 性欲教育研究 (Research into sex education), *Xinjiaoyu*, 5, no. 12 (Aug. 1922), pp. 29–42.

Li Shizhen 李時珍, *Bencao gangmu* 本草綱目 (Compendium of materia medical), Beijing: Renmin weisheng chubanshe, 1981.

Li Yu 李漁, *Xianqing ouji* 閑情偶集 (Prose works of Li Yu), Hangzhou: Zhejiang guji chubanshe, 1985.

Liao Shicheng 廖世承, 'Xingjiaoyu yu zhongxuexiao' 性教育與中學校 (Sex education and middle schools), *Jiaoyu zazhi*, 15, no. 11 (Nov. 1923), p. 12.

Liaowu 了悟, 'Yige chunü de xingjiaoyu wenti' 一個處女的性教育問題 (The problem of sex education for a virgin), *Xinnüxing*, 3 (March 1928), pp. 269–70.

Lin Yutang, *My country and my people*, New York: John Ray, 1935.

Lin Zhaoyin 林昭音, *Nannü xing zhi fenxi* 男女性之分析 (Analysis of male and female sex), Shanghai: Shangwu yinshuguan, 1925.

Liu Chongyan 劉崇燕 and Yao Changxu 姚昶緒, *Xingbing* 性病 (Venereal diseases), Shanghai: Shangwu yinshuguan, 1929.

Liu Piji 劉丕基, *Renjian wujie de shengwu* 人間誤解的生物 (Misinterpretations in everyday biology), Shanghai: Shangwu yinshuguan, 1928.

——, *Shengwu nanti jieda* 生物難題解答 (Explanations of difficult problems in biology), Shanghai: Shangwu yinshuguan, 1935.

Liu Ruocun 劉若村, *Shaonü xingzhishi shijiang* 少女性知識十講 (L.D. Steinhardt, *Ten sex talks to girls*), Shanghai: Zhonghua shuju, 1946.

Liu Wang Liming 劉王立明, *Kuaile jiating* 快樂家庭 (The happy family), Shanghai: Shangwu yinshuguan, 1931.

Liu Xiulan 劉秀蘭, 'Yuejing zhi shengli de jieshi' 月經之生理的解釋 (Explanation of the physiology of menstruation), *Funü zazhi*, 10, no. 5 (May 1925), pp. 850–2.

Liu Yicang 劉一倉, 'Nüzi xingyu zhi zhenxiang' 女子性欲之眞相 (The true nature of female sexual desire) in *Xing de wenti* (The problem of sex), Shanghai: Xinghua shuju, 1933, pp. 30–6.

Lu Feikui 陸費逵, 'Seyu yu jiaoyu' 色欲與教育 (Sexual desire and education), *Jiaoyu zazhi*, 3, no. 9 (Sep. 1911), pp. 3175–8.

Lu Xun, *Selected writings*, Yang Xianyi and Gladys Yang, transl., Beijing: Foreign Languages Press, 1980.

'Lun Zhongguo zhi luan youyu renkou zhi zhonggua' 論中國之亂由於人口之衆寡 (A large population causes political unrest in China), *Dongfang zazhi*, 1, no. 6 (June 1904), pp. 115–20.

'Lun Zhongguo zhi luan yu renkou zhi guanxi' 論中國之亂與人口之關係 (The relationship between overpopulation and political unrest), *Dongfang zazhi*, 4, no. 7 (July 1907), pp. 129–32.

Ma Chonggan 馬崇淦, *Jiehun zhidao* 結婚指導 (Marriage guide), Shanghai: Qinfen shuju, 1931.

MacBride, E.W., *Textbook of embryology*, London: Macmillan, 1914.

Maxwell, J.L., 'Some notes on syphilis among the Chinese', *China Medical Journal*, 27, no. 6 (Dec. 1913), pp. 379–86.

'Minzu gaizao wenti' 民族改造問題 (The problem of race reform), *Zhongyang ribao*, 20 Aug. 1935.

Mou Hongyi 牟鴻彝, *Hualiubing de yufang ji zhiliao* 花柳病的預防及治療 (The prevention and treatment of venereal diseases), Shanghai: Beixin shuju, 1934.

——, *Xing shenjing shuairuozheng* 性神經衰弱症 (Sexual neurasthenia), Shanghai: Beixin shuju, 1951.

Nannü xingbing zhinan 男女性病指南 (Guide to venereal diseases), Hong Kong: Xianggang shuju, n.d., 1920s.

'Nüxing yingyou de yousheng zhishi' 女性應有的優生知識 (Basic eugenics for women), *Shishi xinbao*, 16 Nov. 1934, 2:4.

'Nüxing youyu nanxing lun' 女性優於男性論 (About women being superior to men), *Shenbao*, 21 March 1936, 6:15.

Oldt, F., 'Purity Campaign in Canton', *China Medical Journal*, 37, no. 9 (Sep. 1923), pp. 776–82.

Pan Gongzhan 潘公展, 'Bageluo de liangxing jiaoyuguan' 巴哥羅的倆性教育觀 (Bigelow's views on sex education), *Jiaoyu zazhi*, 12, no. 10–12 (Oct.–Dec. 1920).

——, 'Liangxing jiaoyu' 倆性教育 (Education for both sexes), *Jiaoyu zazhi*, 12, nos 10 to 12 (Nov. 1920 to Jan. 1921).

——, 'Liangxing shenghuo yu xingjiaoyu' 倆性生活與性教育 (Human sexual life and sex education), *Jiaoyu zazhi*, 15, no. 8 (Aug. 1923), pp. 22097–114.

Pan Guangdan 潘光旦, *Renwen shengwuxue luncong* 人文生物學論叢 (Writings on human biology), Shanghai: Xinyue shudian, 1939.

——, *Xing xinlixue* 性心理學 (Havelock Ellis, *Psychology of sex*), Beijing: Sanlian shudian, 1988 (1st edn 1946).

——, *Yousheng yuanli* 優生原理, Tianjin: Tianjin renmin chubanshe, 1981.

——, *Zhongguo zhi jiating wenti* 中國之家庭問題 (Problems of the Chinese family), Shanghai: Xinyue shuju, 1940 (1st edn 1928).

Peiyu 配嶽, 'Yanshou xinshu' 延壽新術 (A new technique for prolonging life), *Funü zazhi*, 7, no. 2 (Feb. 1922), pp. 37–42.

Peter, W.W., 'Fighting venereal disease openly', *China Medical Journal*, 35, no. 1 (Jan. 1924), pp. 1–29.

Qi Senhuan 祁森煥, 'Ertong xingjiaoyu zhi shishi' 兒童性教育之實施 (The implementation of sex education for children), *Jiaoyu zazhi*, 15, no. 8 (Aug. 1923).

Qi Sihe 齊思和 (ed.), *Huang Juezi zoushu – Xu Naiji zouyi: hekan* 黃爵滋奏疏 許乃濟奏議合刊 (Combined publication of the memorials of Huang Juezi and Xu Naiji), Beijing: Zhonghua shuju, 1959.

Qian Yiqing 錢挹青, *Xingyixue* 性醫學 (Sexual medicine), Shanghai: Shangwu yinshuguan, 1935.

Qingnian shengli weisheng changshi 青年生理衛生常識 (Common knowledge of physiological hygiene for youth), Beijing: Zhongguo qingnian chubanshe, 1982.

Qu Shaoheng 瞿紹衡, 'Guanyu taipan ji qidai zhi tanhua' 關于胎盤及臍帶之談話 (About the placenta and the umbilical cord), *Shenbao*, 16 July 1934, 6:21.

Ren Guang 任广, *Xing de shengli yu weisheng* 性的生理與衛生 (R.T. Trall, *Sexual physiology and hygiene*), Shanghai: Beixin shuju, 1927.

'Renjun zhanzheng' 人菌戰爭 (The struggle between bacteria and man), *Dagongbao*, 15 Dec. 1936, 3:11.

'Renshen xuzhi' 妊娠須知 (Basic knowledge of childbirth), *Wuhan ribao*, 2 Feb. 1935, 3:2.

'Renzhong gailiang xiansheng jiang you kexue yinghai chuxian' 人種改良先聲將有科學嬰孩出現 (First signs of race improvement: Imminent appearance of scientific babies), *Xianggang gongshang ribao*, 18 Jan. 1935.

Ru Qiu 如丘, 'Kuaigan de shengli' 快感的生理 (The physiology of orgasm), *Xuesheng zazhi*, 15, no. 12 (Dec. 1928), pp. 15–18.

Ruan Yuan 阮元, *Yanjingshi ji* 揅經室集 (Collected works of Ruan Yuan), Shanghai: Shangwu yinshuguan, 1937.

Sanger, Margaret, *Margaret Sanger: An autobiography*, New York: Norton, 1938, reprint by New York: Dover, 1971.

——, *My fight for birth control*, New York: Farra and Rinehart, 1931.

——, *Nüzi yingyou de zhishi* 女子應有的知識 (What every girl should know), Shanghai: Shangwu yinshuguan, 1931.

——, *Shengyu jiezhifa* 生育節制法 (Family limitation), Shanghai: Zhonghua jieyu yanjiushe, 1922.

'Shaoxing yi laoshuang chansheng huluxing rouqiu' 紹興一老孀產生葫蘆形肉球 (Old widow from Shaoxing gives birth to flesh loaf shaped like bottle gourd), *Beiping chenbao*, 5 June 1935, p. 3.

Shen Jian'an 沈健安, 'Renshenshi weishengfa' 姙娠時衛生法 (Hygienic rules during pregnancy), *Shenbao*, 15 April 1934, 6:21.

Shen Jin'ao 沈金鰲, *Fuke yuchi* 婦科玉尺 (Health manual for women), orig. 1773, 1784 edn.

Shen Junqi 沈奮淇, *Jixie rensheng* 機械人生 (Mechanic life), Shanghai: Wentong shuju, 1946.

Shen Yong 沈勇, *Xingyuan* 性源 (The origin of sex), Shanghai: Dadong shuju, 1931.

Shen Youpeng 沈又彭 (*zi* Yaofeng), *Nüke jiyao* 女科輯要 (Essentials of gynaecology), orig. 1764, 1850 edn.

Shen Zhaoqiu 沈肇球, 'Jinyu zhi lihai' 禁欲之利害 (The advantages and disadvantages of sexual abstinence) in *Xing de wenti* (The problem of sex), Shanghai: Xinghua shuju, 1933, pp. 12–20.

Shen Zhijian 沈志堅, *Women de shenti* 我們的身體 (Our body), Shanghai: Xin Zhongguo shuju, 1935.

Sheng Langxi 盛朗西, 'Xingjiaoyu zai xinxuezhi kechengshang de weizhi' 性教育在新學制課程上的位置 (The position of sex education in the curriculum of the New Learning system), *Jiaoyu zazhi*, 15, no. 8 (Aug. 1923), p. 17.

'Shengli qitan – qishi lao'ou luansheng erzi' 生理奇談 七十老嫗孿生二子 (Strange tales of physiology – old woman gives birth to two sons at age seventy), *Dagongbao*, 2 April 1934, 2:5.

Shi Chengli 史成禮, *Xingkexue zixun* 性科學資詢 (Sexological counselling), Shengyang: Liaoning renmin chubanshe, 1988.

'Shouyun zhi yuanli' 受孕之原理 (Principles of impregnation), *Xunhuan ribao*, 15 Oct. 1935, 4:1.

Song Jiazhao 宋嘉釗, *Taijiao* 胎教 (Prenatal education), Shanghai: Zhonghua shuju, 1914 (11th edn 1923).

Song Yuan Ming Qing mingyi lei'an 宋元明清醫類案 (Cases from famous physicians from the Song, Yuan, Ming and Qing dynasties), Taibei: Da Zhongguo tushu gongsi, 1971.

Stratz, Carl Heinrich, *Die Rassenschönheit des Weibes*, Stuttgart: Ferdinand Enke, 1901.

Su Yizhen 蘇儀貞, *Funü shengyu lun* 婦女生育論 (About women bearing children), Shanghai: Zhonghua shuju, 1922.

——, *Nüxing weisheng changshi* 女性衛生常識 (Elementary knowledge of female hygiene), Shanghai: Zhonghua shuju, 1941 (1st edn 1935).

Sun Benwen 孫本文, *Renkoulun ABC* 人口論ABC (ABC of population theories), Shanghai: Shijie shuju, 1928.

Sun Simo 孫思邈, *Beiji qianjin yaofang* 備急千金要方 (Book of remedies), orig. 652, 1805 edn.

Suo Fei 索非, *Renti kexue tanxie* 人體科學談屑 (Trivial talks on the science of the human body), Shanghai: Kaiming shudian, 1941.

'Tan jiewen' 談接吻 (About the kiss), *Xianggang gongshang*, 10 Feb. 1935, 2:1.

Tan Sitong 譚嗣同, *Renxue* 仁學 (A study of benevolence), Shanghai: Zhonghua shuju, 1958.

'Tantan nüren de yuejing' 談談女人的月經 (About female menstruation), *Beiping chenbao*, 27 Jan. 1935, p. 13.

Tang Peng 湯鵬, *Fu Qiuzi* 浮邱子 (Works of Tang Peng), Changsha: Yuelu shushe, 1987.

Tang Zhou 湯周, 'Renti jixie yu motoche de bijiao' 人體機械與摩托車的比較 (A comparison of the mechanics of the body to the motorcycle), *Xuesheng zazhi*, 15, 12 (Dec. 1928), pp. 19–25.

'Tongxin' 通信 (Letters from readers), *Xinnüxing*, 1, nos 1–9 (Jan.–Sept. 1926); 2, nos 1–7 (Jan.–July 1927).

'Tongxun' 通訊 (Letters from readers), *Xinwenhua*, 1, nos 1–4 (Jan.–April 1927).

Wan Quan 萬全, *Guangsi jiyao* 廣嗣紀要 (Essentials for multiplying offspring) in *Wan Mizhai yixue quanshu* (The collected medical works of Wan Quan), orig. 1549, 1778 edn.

Wan Quan 萬全, *Wan shi jiachuan yangsheng siyao* 萬氏家傳養生四要 (Four essential's of Wan Quan's family notes on nourishing life), Wuhan: Hubei kexue jishu chubanshe, 1984.

Wang Chengpin 汪誠品, *Qingchun de xingjiaoyu* 青春的性教育 (Sex education for youth), Shanghai: Xiongdi chubanshe, 1939.

Wang Chuanying 王傳英 (tr.), 'Xin taijiao' 新胎教 (New prenatal education), *Funü zazhi*, 4, no. 1–2 (Jan.–Feb. 1918).

Wang Jianshan 王兼善, *Shengli ji weishengxue* 生理及衛生學 (Physiology and hygiene), Shanghai: Shangwu yinshuguan, 1927 (1st edn 1914).

Wang Jungang 王君綱, *Xing de jueding* 性的決定 (The determination of sex), Shanghai: Nüzi shudian, 1933.

Wang Qishu 王其澍, *Jinshi shengwuxue* 近世生物學 (Modern biology), Shanghai: Shangwu yinshuguan, 1925.

Wang Shiduo 汪士鐸, *Wang Huiweng yibing riji* 汪悔翁乙丙日記 (Diary of Wang Shiduo), Taibei: Wenhai chubanshe, 1967.

Wang Shoucheng 王守成, *Gongmin shengwuxue* 公民生物學 (A textbook of civic biology), Shanghai: Shangwu yinshuguan, 1928 (1st edn 1924).

Wang, T.H., James Y. Shen and C.C. Chung, 'An inquiry into the prevalence of syphilis in Nanking', *China Medical Journal*, 51, no. 6 (June 1937), pp. 983–8.

Wang Wenbin 王文彬, *Xing de zhishi* 性的知識, Beijing: Renmin weisheng chubanshe, 1980 (1st edn 1956).

Wang Yang 汪洋, 'Renlei faqingqi zhi xing de tezheng' 人類發情期之性的特徵 (The sexual characteristics of humans during the heat period) in *Xing de wenti* (The problem of sex), Shanghai: Xinghua shuju, 1933, pp. 36–48.

——, *Shengyu guwen* 生育顧問 (Advice on childbirth), Shanghai: Zhongyang shuju, 1933.

Wang Yugang 汪于岡, *Xing shenjing shuairuo ziliao fa* 性神經衰弱自療法 (Self-treatment of sexual neurasthenia), published and distributed by the author, 1932.

Weisheng jiaoyubu 衛生教育部 (eds), *Chanfu baojian xuzhi* 產婦保健須知 (Information on health for lying-in women), Shanghai: Zhonghua pingmin jiaoyu cujinhui, no date (1930s).

'Wen' 吻 (The kiss), *Xianggang gongshang*, 1 Feb. 1936, p. 7.

Wieger, Léon, *Moralisme officiel des écoles, en 1920*, Hien-hien, 1921.

Winiwarter, Hans von, *Recherches sur l'ovogenèse de l'ovaire des mammifères (lapin et homme)*, Liège: Vaillant-Carmanne, 1900.

Wu Lien-teh, 'Problem of venereal diseases in China', *China Medical Journal*, 41, no. 1 (Jan. 1927), pp. 28–36.

Wu Yan 吳衮, *Weisheng xinlun* 衛生新論 (New hygiene), Shanghai: Zhongguo tushu gongsi heji, 1922 (1st edn 1907).

Wu Yingchao 吳影超, *Shehui de shengwu jichu* 社會的生物基础 (The biological basis of society), Shanghai: Shijie shuju, 1930.

Wu Yuying 吳矞英, *Shengli weisheng gangyao* 生理衛生綱要 (Essentials of physiological hygiene), Shanghai: Guangyi shuju, 1929.

Wu Zelin 吳澤霖 and Ye Shaochun 葉紹純, *Shijie renkou wenti* 世界人口問題 (Problems of the world population), Shanghai: Shangwu yinshuguan, 1938.

Wu Zhenzi 吳振兹, 'Women wei shenme yao yanjiu youshengxue' 我們爲什麼要研究優生學 (Why we should study eugenics), *Xuesheng zazhi*, 15, no. 9 (Sep. 1928), pp. 31–6.

Xi Huimin 奚惠民, *Nannü xingbing zhiliao quanshu* 男女性病治療全書 (Compendium on the treatment of venereal diseases), Shanghai: Shangye shuju, 1935.

Xishen 西神 (tr.), 'Renshenzhong zhi jingshen ganying' 姙娠中之精神感應 (Spiritual impressions during pregnancy), *Funü zazhi*, 2, no. 10 (Oct. 1916), pp. 13–15.

Xia Shenchu 夏慎初, *Xingbingxue* 性病學 (The science of venereal diseases), Shanghai: Zhenliao yibao she, 1933.

Xiancun shengwu ziran fashengshuo zhipiping wenlu 現存生物自然發生說之批評文錄 (Documents criticising the theory of spontaneous generation), Canton: Zhongshan daxue shengwuxi, 1933.

Xie Yunshou 謝筠壽, *Xingbing zhi mi* 性病之迷 (Guide to venereal diseases), Shanghai: Shehui yibaoguan chubanbu, 1933.

Xing de wenti 性的問題 (The problem of sex), Shanghai: Xinghua shuju, 1933.

'Xingzhishi shuji de taolun' 性知識書籍的討論 (A debate about books on sex knowledge), *Xinnüxing*, 1, no. 2 (Feb. 1926), pp. 109–16.

Xu Guangqi 徐光啓, *Nongzheng quanshu jiaozhu* 農政全書校注 (Complete book on agricultural management with annotations), Shanghai: Guji chubanshe, 1979.

Xu Shilian 許仕廉, *Renkoulun gangyao* 人口論綱要 (Essentials of population theory), Shanghai: Zhonghua shuju, 1934.

——, *Zhongguo renkou wenti* 中國人口問題 (The Chinese population problem), Shanghai: Shangwu yinshuguan, 1930.

Xu Songming 徐誦明, 'Meidu yu jiehe' 梅毒與結核 (Syphilis and tuberculosis), *Dongfang zazhi*, 18, no. 16 (Aug. 1921), pp. 116–20.

Xu Zheshen 徐哲身, *Xingfang mijue* 行房秘訣 (Secrets of the bedchamber), Shanghai: Xinxin shudian, 1938.

Xu Zi 徐鼒, *Weihuizhai wenji* 未灰齋文集 (Collected writings of Xu Zi), Taibei: Wenhai chubanshe, 1970.

Xue Deyu 薛德焴, *Shengwu de mudi shi baozhong* 生物的目的是保種 (The goal of organisms is the preservation of the race), Shanghai: Xinya shuju, 1933.

Y.S., 'Renshenqi zhong funü ying zhi zhi changshi ji qi weisheng' 妊娠期中婦女應知之常識及其衛生 (Common knowledge for pregnant women and hygiene), *Funü zazhi*, 16, no. 10 (Sep. 1930), pp. 77–95.

Yan Fu 顏復, 'Baozhong yuyi' 保種余儀 (Afterthoughts on the preservation of the race) in *Yan Fu ji* (Collected works of Yan Fu), Beijing: Zhonghua shuju, 1986.

Yan Shi 晏始, 'Liangbu guanyu xingzhishi de shuji' 兩部關於性知識的書籍 (Two books relating to sex knowledge), *Xinnüxing*, 1, no. 1 (Jan. 1926), pp. 53–8.

Yan Yukuan 嚴與寬, *Jieyu de lilun yu fangfa* 節育的理論與方法 (The debate and the methods of birth control), Shanghai: Dadong shuju, 1933.

Yang Guanxiong 楊冠雄, *Xingjiaoyu fa* 性教育法 (Method of sex education), Shanghai: Liming shuju, 1930.

Yang Mingding 楊銘鼎 (tr.), *Nannü qingnian xingwenti* 男女青年性問題 (M. Scholtz, *Sex problems of man in adolescence*), Shanghai: Zhonghua shuju, 1933.

Yang Yuechuan 楊月川, 'Lun *Sunüjing*' 論素女經 (About the Classic of the Plain Girl) in *Xing de wenti* (The problem of sex), Shanghai: Xinghua shuju, 1933, pp. 1–12.

Yao Changxu 姚昶緒, *Taichan xuzhi* 胎產須知 (Essentials of obstetrics), Shanghai: Shangwu yinshuguan, 1929 (1st edn 1920).

——, *Xingbing wenda* 性病問答 (Answers and questions on venereal diseases), Shanghai: Dahua shuju, 1935.

Yao Dehong 姚德鴻, 'Wu yi haoqi qu kaishi, bu yi fasheng er aonao' 勿以好奇去开始 不以發生而懊惱 (Not to start out of curiosity, not to get upset if it happens) in *Xingjiaoyu yu yousheng* (Sex education and eugenics), Shanghai: Shanghai kexue jishu chubanshe, 1987, vol. 2, pp. 63–7.

Ye Żuozhou 葉作舟, 'Funü yu xiesidiliya' 婦女與歇私的里亞 (Women and hysteria), *Funü zazhi*, 13, no. 10 (Sep. 1927), pp. 8–11.

'Yibailingqi sui lao Huafu Xu Tianlang huaiyun qishiwu nian jin shi yu chan' 一百零七歲老華婦許添烺懷孕七十五年今始欲產 (Old Chinese woman aged one hundred and five pregnant for seventy-five years and about to give birth), *Xingzhou ribao*, 30 March 1936, 2:5.

'Yichuan yu yousheng' 遺傳與優生 (Heredity and eugenics), *Shishi xinbao*, 11 Jan. 1935.

'Yige Meiguo yisheng de jianjie sishi sui you kaishi shi lian'aiqi' 一個美國醫生的見解四十歲又開始戀愛期 (According to an American doctor the period of love begins again at the age of forty), *Zhongyang ribao*, 29 July 1936, 3:3.

Yi Jiayue 易家鉞, *Jiating wenti* 家庭問題 (Problems of the family), Shanghai: Shangwu yinshuguan, 1920.

——, 'Zhongguo de xingyu jiaoyu wenti' 中國的性欲教育問題 (The problem of sex education in China), *Jiaoyu zazhi*, 15, no. 8 (Aug. 1923), pp. 22149–70.

'Yixue xin faxian wuling nütong huaiyun' 醫學發現五齡女童懷孕 (New medical discovery of pregnant young girl of five years), *Xianggang gongshang*, 23 Oct. 1935, 4:2.

'Yong dianliu jueding sheng nan sheng nü wenti' 用電流決定生男生女問題 (Resolving the question of the sex of the embryo with the use of electric currents), *Guangming ribao*, 31 Aug. 1934, 4:1.

You Yi 尤怡, *Jinkui yaolüe xindian* 金匱要略心典 (Commentaries on the Golden Chamber), orig. 1726, reprint 1881.

Yu Fengbin 俞鳳賓, *Geren weisheng pian* 個人衛生篇 (Personal hygiene), Shanghai: Shangwu yinshuguan, 1931 (1st edn 1917).

—, *Weisheng conghua* 衛生叢話 (Chats on hygiene), Shanghai: Shangwu yinshuguan, 1927.

—, *Xingyu weisheng pian* 性欲衛生篇 (Talks on sexual hygiene), Shanghai: Shangwu yinshuguan, 1915.

— and Cheng Hanzhang 程瀚章, *Weisheng yaoyi* 衛生要義 (A short discourse on hygiene), Shanghai: Shangwu yinshuguan, 1930.

Yu Jiaju 余家菊, 'Xingyu de jiaoyu' 性欲的教育, (Sex education) *Zhonghua jiaoyujie*, 10, no. 3 (Oct. 1920), pp. 33–43.

'Yu nan yu nü de rengong renshenfa' 育男育女的人工姙娠法 (Artificial pregnancy and a method to choose the sex of the child), *Gongshang ribao*, 11 July 1935, 4:1.

Yu Xijian 于熙儉, *Xingshenghuo de kongzhi* 性生活的控制 (L.D. Weatherhead, *The mastery of sex*), Shanghai: Qingnian xiehui shuju, 1936.

Yu Zhengxie 俞正燮, *Guisi leigao* 癸巳類稿 (Collection of notes), Shanghai: Shangwu yinshuguan, 1957.

Yu Zi 玉子 (ed.), *Renti de jianghua* 人體的講話 (Talks about the human body), Shanghai: Guangyi shuju, 1933.

Yuan Guorong 袁國榮, *Yijingbing zhimi* 遺精病指迷 (Guide to spermatorrhoea), Hong Kong: Yuan Guorong yiwusuo, 1940 (15th edn).

'Yuejing de mixin yu chuanshuo' 月經的迷心與傳說 (Superstitions and myths about menstruation), *Dagongbao*, 20 March 1937, 3:11.

'Yuejing de yuanyin' 月經的原因 (The causes of menstruation), *Dagongbao*, 20 March 1937, 3:11.

Yun Daiying 惲代英, 'Lun shehuizhuyi' 論社會主義 (About socialism), *Shaonian Zhongguo* (Young China), 2, no. 5 (Oct. 1922), pp. 1–6.

Yun Tieqiao 惲鐵樵, *Shengli xinyu* 生理新語 (New language of physiology), Shanghai: published by the author, 1928.

Zeng Xiangtian 曾香田, *Fuke zhigui* 婦科指歸 (Guide to gynaecology), 1895.

Zeng Yingshi 曾英士, 'Tan dao shouyin' 談到手淫 (About masturbation), *Xuesheng zazhi*, 14, no. 7 (July 1927), pp. 55–58.

'Zhanzai yixue de lichang mantan chunü de qingjing' 站在醫學的立場漫談處女的清淨 (Virginity discussed from a medical perspective), *Xunhuan ribao*, 17 Feb. 1937, 1:1.

Zhan Wenhu 詹文滸, *Liangxing wenti* 倆性問題 (Problems of the two sexes), Shanghai: Shijie shuju, 1930.

Zhang Dianjie 張殿傑, *Qingnian weisheng bidu* 青年衛生必讀 (Essentials of hygiene for youth), Shanghai: Wenming shuju, 1922.

Zhang Jingcheng 張景澄, 'Sishi sui yihou aiqing de huoyan zai chi' 四十歲以後愛情的火焰再熾 (The flame of love will blaze again after the age of forty), *Dagongbao*, 1 March 1936, 3:12.

Zhang Jingsheng 張競生, 'Di sanzhong shui yu luanqiu ji shengji de dian he youzhong de guanxi' 第三種水與卵珠及生機的電和優種的關係 (The third kind of fluid and the egg in their relationship to the current of vitality and eugenics), *Xinwenhua*, 1, no. 2 (Feb. 1927), pp. 23–48.

—— (Chang Ching-sheng), *Sex histories: China's first modern treatise on sex education*, tr. by H.S. Levy, Yokohama: Levy, 1967.

——, *Xinwenhua shi* 新文化史 (The history of *New Culture*), Shanghai: Xinwenhua she, 1927.

——, 'Xin yinyi yu zhen kexue' 新淫義與真科學 (New pornography and genuine science), *Xinwenhua*, 1, no. 1 (Jan. 1927), pp. 104–9.

——, 'Xingshi zhi shi' 性史之史 (The history of *Sex histories)*, *Xinwenhua*, 1, no. 1 (Jan. 1927), pp. 125–6.

——, 'Zenyang bian xingyu zui fazhan yu qi liyi' 怎樣便性欲最發展與其利益 (How to best develop sexual desire and its benefits), *Xinwenhua*, 1, no. 1 (Jan. 1927), pp. 33–41.

——, 'Zhang Jingsheng zizhuan 張競生自轉, 1–4' (The autobiography of Zhang Jingsheng, chapters 1 to 4), *Dacheng*, nos 19–22 (1975).

'Zhang Jingsheng de qilun sheng nan sheng nü juezhu yu fumu de jingli' 張競生的奇論生男生女決諸於父母的精力 (Zhang Jingsheng's strange claim that sex of the embryo depends on parents' vigour), *Xingzhou ribao*, 25 May 1936, 5:17.

Zhang Jixiu 張寄岫, *Funü zhuance* 婦女專冊 (Special handbook for women), Shanghai: Shangwu yinshuguan, 1937.

Zhang Luwei 張履慰, *Shengli weisheng nanti xiangjie* 生理衛生難題詳解 (Detailed explanations of difficult problems in physiological hygiene), Shanghai: Dafang shuju, n.d.

Zhang Mingyuan 張明園, '"Shouyin you hai" bian' 手淫有害編 (Analysis of the belief that masturbation is harmful) in *Xingjiaoyu yu yousheng* (Sex education and eugenics), Shanghai: Shanghai kexue jishu chubanshe, 1987, vol. 2, pp. 57–62.

Zhang Qiutao 張秋濤, *Qingnian jiankang zhidao* 青年健康指導 (Health guide for youth), Shanghai: Dadong shuju, 1933.

Zhang Xichen 章錫琛, 'Du *Funü wenti zatan*' 讀婦女問題杂談 (Reading *Talks about women's problems*), *Xinnüxing*, 1, no. 6 (June 1926), pp. 433–7.

——, 'Renshou erbaisui shuo' 人壽二百歲説 (The theory of man living two hundred years), *Dongfang zazhi*, 10, no. 10 (April 1914), pp. 1–4.

——, '*Xinnüxing* yu xing de yanjiu' 新女性與性的研究 (*New Woman* and research on sex), *Xinnüxing*, 2, no. 3 (March 1927), pp. 237–41.

Zhang Xinsheng 張新生, 'Lüe tan Zhongguo gudai taijiao xueshuo' 略談中國古代胎教學説 (The theory of prenatal education briefly considered), *Shaanxi shida xuebao*, 1982, no. 4, pp. 109–115.

Zhang Yinlin 張蔭麟, 'Hong Liangji ji qi renkoulun' 洪亮吉及其人口論 (Hong Liangji and his population theory), *Dongfang zazhi*, 23, no. 2 (Jan. 1926), pp. 69–73.

Zhang Zhongshu 張忠恕 *et al.* (eds), *Taijiao yu yousheng* 胎教與優生 (Prenatal education and eugenics), Shanghai: Wenhui chubanshe, 1987.

Zhang Ziping 張資平, *Renlei jinhualun* 人類進化論 (The theory of human evolution), Shanghai: Shangwu yinshuguan, 1930.

Zhang Zongyuan 章宗元, 'Lun gujin shengjijie zhi jingzheng' 論古今生計界之競爭 (About competition over the means of livelihood in past and present), *Dongfang zazhi*, 3, no. 9 (Oct. 1906).

Zhao Jianxin 趙建新, *Yiniao ji yijing* 遺尿及遺精 (Enuresis and spermatorrhoea), Shanghai: Shangwu yinshuguan, 1931 (1st edn 1921).

Zhao Shifa 趙士法, *Geren weishengxue* 個人衛生學 (Personal hygiene), Nanjing: Nanjing shudian, 1933.

Zhao Yintang 趙蔭堂, *Xingjiaoyu de shier bian* 性教育的示兒編 (M. Sanger, *What every boy and girl should know*), Shanghai: Beixin shuju, 1929.

Zhen He 眞和, 'Yuejing zhi weisheng' 月經之衛生 (Hygiene of the menses), *Funü zazhi*, 4, no. 12 (Dec. 1918), pp. 4–6.

'Zhengchang yuejing de texing' 正常月經的特徵 (The characteristics of normal periods), *Dagongbao*, 29 May 1937, 3:11.

Zheng Zuoxin 鄭作新, *Putong shengwuxue* 普通生物學 (General biology), Taibei: Zhengzhong shuju, 1961 (1st edn 1944).

Zhihou 志厚, 'Jiaoyushang zhi seyu wenti' 教育上之色欲問題 (The problem of sexual desire in education), *Jiaoyu zazhi*, 6, no. 12 (Dec. 1914), pp. 61–66.

'Zhiming renshi zuotan zhichu: tuixing yousheng ke bu rong huan' 知明人士座談指出：推行優生刻不容緩 (Public figures point out that eugenic policies are of great urgency), *Dagongbao*, 30 January 1991, p. 12.

Zhongguo yixue da cidian 中國醫學大辭典 (Encyclopedia of Chinese medicine), Shanghai: Shangwu yinshuguan, 1921.

Zhou Guangqi 周光琦, *Xing yu fanzui* 性與犯罪 (Sex and crime), Shanghai: Zhengzhong shuju, 1946.

Zhou Jianren 周建人, 'Erzhong daode' 二種道德 (Two kinds of morality), *Xinnüxing*, 1, no. 1 (Jan. 1926), pp. 1–10.

——, 'Shanzhongxue de lilun yu shishi' 善種學的理論與實施 (The theory of eugenics and its implementation), *Dongfang zazhi*, 18, no. 2 (Jan. 1921), pp. 63–4.

——, 'Shengwu zhi qiyuan' 生物之起源 (The origin of biology), *Xinqingnian*, 6, no. 4 (April 1919).

——, *Xingjiaoyu* 性教育 (Sex education), Shanghai: Shangwu yinshuguan, 1931.

——, 'Xingjiaoyu de jige yuanli' 性教育的幾個原理 (Some principles of sex education), *Jiaoyu zazhi*, 15, no. 8 (Aug. 1923), pp. 22091–6.

——, 'Xingjiaoyu de lilun yu shiji' 性教育的理論與實際 (Theory and practice of sex education), *Jiaoyu zazhi*, 14, no. 8 (Aug. 1922), pp. 20195–8.

——, 'Xingjiaoyu yu jiating guanxi de zhongyao' 性教育與家庭關係的重要 (The importance of sex education for family relations), *Funü zazhi*, 8, no. 9 (Sep. 1922), pp. 2–5.

——, 'Xingjiaoyu yundong de weiji' 性教育運動的危機 (The crisis of the movement for sex education), *Xinnüxing*, 2, no. 2 (Feb. 1927), pp. 135–9.

——, *Xing yu rensheng* 性與人生 (Sex and life), Shanghai: Kaiming shudian, 1927.

——, *Xing yu yichuan* 性與遺傳 (J.G. Kerr, *Sex and heredity*), Shanghai: Kaiming shudian, 1928.

Zhou Shang 周尚 and Ye Hua 葉華, *Nannü qingnian de changcheng* 男女青年的長成 (Growth of adolescents), Shanghai: Shangwu yinshuguan, 1940.

Zhou Taixuan 周太玄, *Shengwuxue qianshuo* 生物學淺說 (Elementary biology), Shanghai: Shangwu yinshuguan, 1930.

——, *Shengwuxue yu changshou* 生物學與長壽 (Biology and longevity), Shanghai: Shangwu yinshuguan, 1927.

Zhou Tianchong 周天冲, 'Jiating xingjiaoyu shili' 家庭性教育示例 (Typical examples for sex education in the family), *Zhonghua jiaoyujie*, 14, no. 11 (May 1925).

Zhou Yizhao 周燁昭, 'Ping Zhang Jingsheng boshi de suowei "mei de xingyu"' 評張競生博士的所謂美的性欲 (Appraising Professor Zhang Jingsheng's so-called 'beautiful sex'), *Xinnüxing*, 2, no. 3 (March 1927), pp. 543–52.

Zhou Yueran 周越然, *Xingzhishi* 性知識 (Sex knowledge), Shanghai: Tianma shudian, 1936.

Zhu Kongzhao 朱孔昭, *Funü weisheng* 婦女衛生 (Hygiene for women), Shanghai: Shijie shuju, 1933.

Zhu Wenyin 朱文印, 'Taijiao yu youshengxue' 胎教與優生學 (Prenatal education and eugenics), *Funü zazhi*, 17, no. 8 (Aug. 1931), pp. 11–19.

Zhu Xi 朱洗, *Cixiong zhi bian* 雌雄之變 (The changes of female and male), Shanghai: Wenhua shenghuo chubanshe, 1945.

——, *Danshengren yu renshengdan* 蛋生人與人生蛋 (The evolution of sex), Shanghai: Wenhua shenghuo chubanshe, 1939.

——, *Women de zuzong* 我們的祖宗 (Our forefathers), Shanghai: Wenhua shenghuo chubanshe, 1940.

——, *Zhong nü qing nan* 重女輕男 (Women over men), Shanghai: Wenhua shenghuo chubanshe, 1941.

Zhu Yunping 朱雲平, *Xingjiaoyu gailun* 性教育概論 (Outline of sex education), Shanghai: Shijie shuju, 1941.

Zhu Yunying 朱雲影, *Renlei xingshenghuo shi* 人類性生活史 (The history of man's sexual life), Shanghai: Zhengzhong shuju, 1936.

Zhu Zhenjiang 祝枕江, *Rufang ji qita* 乳房及其他 (About breasts and other things), Shanghai: Kaiming shudian, 1933.

Zhu Zhensheng 朱振聲, *Qiuyun yu biyun* 求孕與避孕 (Birth control), Shanghai: Xingfu shuju, 1933.

——, 'Shengzhiqi bu fayu' 生殖器不發育 (Underdeveloped sexual organs) in Zhu Zhensheng, *Qiuyun yu biyun* (Birth control), Shanghai: Xingfu shuju, 1933, pp. 24–25.

Zhuang Qi 莊启, *Zhanhou Ouyou jianwenji* 戰後歐遊見聞記 (Record of a journey to Europe after the war), Shanghai: Shangwu yinshuguan, 1926.

Zhuang Weizhong 莊畏仲, *Jiankangshu wenda* 健康術問答 (Questions and answers on the art of health), Shanghai: Dahua shuju, 1934.

SECONDARY SOURCES

Adams, Mark, *The wellborn science: Eugenics in Germany, France, Brazil and Russia*, Oxford University Press, 1990.

Ahern, Emily Martin, 'The power and pollution of Chinese women', in Arthur P. Wolf (ed.), *Studies in Chinese society*, Stanford University Press, 1985, pp. 269–90.

Anderson, Benedict, *Imagined communities*, London: Verso, 1991.

Ariès, Philippe, *Centuries of childhood: A social history of family life*, New York: Vintage, 1962.

Bailey, Paul, *Reform the people: Changing attitudes towards popular education in early 20th century China*, Edinburgh University Press, 1990.

Bakken, Børge, 'Modernizing morality in China', *East Asian History*, no. 2 (1991).

Banton, Michael, *Racial theories*, Cambridge University Press, 1987.

Bastid, Marianne, 'Currents of social change' in D. Twitchett and J.K. Fairbank (eds), *The Cambridge history of China*, vol. 11, part 2, Cambridge University Press, 1980, pp. 535–602.

Beahan, Charlotte L., 'In the public eye: Women in early twentieth-century China' in R.W. Guisso and S. Johannesen, *Women in China: Current directions in historical scholarship*, New York: Philo Press, 1981, pp. 215–38.

Bergère, Marie-Claire, *The golden age of the Chinese bourgeoisie, 1911–1937*, Cambridge University Press, 1989.

——, 'The Chinese bourgeoisie, 1911–37' in J.K. Fairbank (ed.), *The Cambridge history of China*, vol. 12, part 1, Cambridge University Press, 1986, pp. 722–825.

Birken, Lawrence, *Consuming desire: Sexual science and the emergence of a culture of abundance, 1871–1914*, Ithaca: Cornell University Press, 1988.

Bodde, Derk, 'Age, youth and infirmity in the law of Ch'ing China' in Jerome A. Cohen, R. Randle Edwards and Fu-mei Chang Chen (eds), *Essays on China's legal tradition*, Princeton University Press, 1980, pp. 137–69.

Borell, Merriley, 'Organotherapy, British physiology and the discovery of the internal secretions', *Journal of the History of Biology*, 9, no. 2 (fall 1976), pp. 235–68.

Borthwick, Sally, 'Changing concepts of the role of women from the late Qing to the May Fourth Period' in D. Pong and E. Fung (eds), *Ideal and reality: Social and political change in China (1860–1949)*, Lanham: University Press of America, 1985, pp. 63–92.

Bottéro, Alain, 'Consumption by semen loss in India and elsewhere', *Culture, Medicine and Psychiatry*, 15 (1991), pp. 303–20.

Bourdieu, Pierre, *Language and power*, London: Polity Press, 1991.

Brandt, Allan M., *No magic bullet: A social history of venereal disease in the United States since 1880*, Oxford University Press, 1985.

Brokaw, Cynthia, *The ledgers of merit and demerit: Social change and moral order in late imperial China*, Princeton University Press, 1991.

Burleigh, Michael, and Wolfgang Wippermann, *The racial state: Germany 1933–1945*, Cambridge University Press, 1991.

Cahill, Suzanne, 'Sex and the supernatural in medieval China', *Journal of the American Oriental Society*, 105, no. 2 (1985).

Caplan, Pat (ed.), *The cultural construction of sexuality*, London: Tavistock, 1987.

Carlson, Eric T., 'George M. Beard and neurasthenia' in E.R. Wallace and C. Pressley (eds), *Essays in the history of psychiatry*, Columbia, SC: W.S. Hall Psychiatric Institute, 1980, pp. 50–7.

Chan Sin-wai, *An exposition of benevolence: The Jen-hsüeh of T'an Ssu-t'ung*, Hong Kong: Chinese University Press, 1984.

Chang Hao, *Chinese intellectuals in crisis: Search for order and meaning, 1890–1911*, Berkeley: University of California Press, 1987.

Chen Fan 陳凡 (ed.), *Xingbing zai Zhongguo* 性病在中國 (Venereal diseases in China), Beijing: Shiyue wenyi chubanshe, 1990.

Chen Guying *et al.* 陳鼓應 (eds), *Ming Qing shixue sichao shi* 明清實學思潮史 (The history of practical scholarship under the Ming and the Qing), Shandong: Qilu shushe, 1989.

Ch'en, Jerome, *China and the West: Society and culture, 1815-1937*, London: Hutchinson, 1979.

Chen Jingzhi 陳敬之, 'Zhang Jingsheng lao er bu si' 張競生老而不死 (Immortal Zhang Jingsheng), *Changliu*, 27, no. 3 (1963).

Chen Yongsheng 陳永生, 'Qingmo minchu woguo xuexiao xingjiaoyu shulüe' 清末民初我國學校性教育述略 (Brief account of sex education in China's schools during the early twentieth century), *Zhonghua yishi zazhi*, 23, no. 1 (Jan. 1993), pp. 6–11.

Cheng Chung-ying, 'Reason, substance, and human desires in seventeenth-century neo-Confucianism' in William T. de Bary, *The unfolding of neo-Confucianism*, New York: Columbia University Press, 1975, pp. 469–510.

Chow, Rey, *Woman and Chinese modernity: The politics of reading between West and East*, Minneapolis: University of Minnesota Press, 1991.

Chow Tse-tsung, *The May Fourth Movement*, Cambridge, MA: Harvard University Press, 1960.

Cohen, Paul, *Discovering history in China: American historical writing on the recent Chinese past*, New York: Columbia University Press, 1984.

Cohen, Myron L., 'Cultural and political inventions in modern China: The case of the Chinese "peasant"', *Daedalus*, 122, no. 2 (1993), pp. 151–70.

Corbin, Alain, *Les filles de noces. Misère sexuelle et prostitution aux XIXe–XXe siècles*, Paris: Aubier, 1978.

—, *The foul and the fragrant: Odor and the French social imagination*, Cambridge, MA: Harvard University Press, 1986.

—, 'L'hérédosyphilis ou l'impossible rédemption. Contribution à l'histoire de l'hérédité morbide' in *Le temps, le désir et l'horreur*, Paris: Aubier, 1991, pp. 141–70.

Croizier, Ralph C., *Traditional medicine in modern China: Science, nationalism, and the tension of cultural change*, Cambridge, MA: Harvard University Press, 1968.

Dikötter, Frank, 'Body, discipline and modernity in late imperial China', paper presented at the Annual Conference of the Association for Asian Studies, History Panel, Boston, 24–27 March 1994.

—, 'Birth control and eugenics in Republican China', paper presented at the Contemporary China Institute, London, 11 Dec. 1990.

—, 'Eugenics in Republican China', *Republican China*, 15, no. 1 (Nov. 1989), pp. 1–18.

—, 'The neuter sex: Hermaphroditism, medical science and gender boundaries in China' in Frank Dikötter and Leslie Hall (eds), *The body and beyond. The creation and violation of bodily boundaries* (forthcoming).

—, 'Sexualité, discipline et modernité en Chine', *Equinoxe. Déviances, intolérances et normes*, no. 13 (April 1994), pp. 171–83.

—, *The discourse of race in modern China*, London: C. Hurst/Stanford University Press/Hong Kong University Press, 1992.

—, 'The discourse of race and the medicalization of public and private space in modern China (1895–1949)', *History of Science*, 29 (Dec. 1991), pp. 411–20.

—, 'The cultural history of sexually transmitted diseases in China', *Genitourinary Medicine*, 69 (Oct. 1993), 341–5.

—, 'The limits of benevolence: Wang Shiduo (1802–1889) and

population control', *Bulletin of the School of Oriental and African Studies*, 55, no. 1 (Feb. 1992), pp. 110–15.

Drège, Jean-Pierre, *La Commercial Press de Shanghai, 1897–1949*, Paris: Presses Universitaires de France, 1978.

—— and Hua Chang-ming, *La révolution du livre dans la Chine moderne. Wang Yunwu, éditeur*, Paris: Publications Orientalistes de France, 1979.

Duval, Jean, *A study of prostitution in Shanghai at the end of the Qing dynasty as it appears in the 'Shanghai novels'*, Paris: VERLCA, 1972.

Ebrey, Patricia, 'Women, marriage and the family in Chinese history' in Paul Ropp (ed.), *Heritage of China: Contemporary perspectives on Chinese civilization*, Berkeley: University of California Press, 1990, pp. 197–223.

Elman, B.A., *Classicism, politics, and kinship: The Ch'ang-chou school of New Text Confucianism in late imperial China*, Berkeley: University of California Press, 1990.

——, *From philosophy to philology: Intellectual and social aspects of change in late imperial China*, Cambridge, MA: Harvard University Press, 1984.

——, 'The revaluation of benevolence (*jen*) in Ch'ing dynasty evidential research' in Richard J. Smith and D.W.Y. Kwok (eds), *Cosmology, ontology, and human efficacy: Essays in Chinese thought*, Honolulu: University of Hawaii Press, 1993, pp. 59–80.

Elvin, Mark, 'Female virtue and the state in China', *Past and Present*, no. 104 (1984).

Engelhardt, Jr. and H. Tristam, 'The disease of masturbation: Values and the concept of disease', *Bulletin of the History of Medicine*, no. 48 (1974), pp. 234–48.

Engelstein, Laura, *The keys to happiness: Sex and the search for modernity in fin-de-siècle Russia*, Ithaca: Cornell University Press, 1992.

Evans, Harriet, 'The official construction of female sexuality and gender in the People's Republic of China, 1949–1959', Ph.D dissertation, University of London, 1991.

——, 'Policing the body: Gender and the scientific construction of sex in the People's Republic of China', *Signs* (in preparation).

Fee, Elisabeth, 'Nineteenth-century craniology: The study of the female skull', *Bulletin of the History of Medicine*, 53, no. 3 (1979), pp. 415–33.

Feher, Michel, with Ramona Naddaff and Nadia Tazi (eds), *Fragments for a history of the human body*, 3 vols, New York: Zone Books, 1989.

Foucault, Michel, *The history of sexuality*, Harmondsworth: Penguin, 1984.

Fout, John C. (ed.), *Forbidden history: The state, society, and the regulation of sexuality in modern Europe*, University of Chicago Press, 1992.

Furth, Charlotte, 'Androgynous males and deficient females: Biology and gender boundaries in sixteenth- and seventeenth-century China', *Late Imperial China*, 9, no. 2 (Dec. 1988), pp. 1–31.

—, 'Blood, body and gender: Medical images of the female condition in China, 1600–1850', *Chinese Science*, 7 (Dec. 1986), pp. 43–66.

—, 'Concepts of pregnancy, childbirth, and infancy in Ch'ing dynasty China', *Journal of Asian Studies*, 46, no. 1 (Feb. 1987), pp. 7–35.

—, 'From birth to birth: The growing body in Chinese medicine', paper presented at the Conference on Childhood in Premodern China, University of Virginia, May 1990.

—, 'Rethinking van Gulik: Sexuality and reproduction in traditional Chinese medicine', paper presented at the Conference on Engendering China, Harvard University, February 1992.

—, 'Talk on Ming-Qing medicine and the construction of gender', paper presented at the Institute of History and Philosophy, Taibei, 26 Nov. 1992.

— and Ch'en Shu-yueh, 'Chinese medicine and the anthropology of menstruation in contemporary Taiwan', *Medical Anthropology Quarterly*, vol. 6, no. 1 (March 1992), pp. 27–48.

Gallagher, Catherine and Thomas W. Laqueur (eds), *The making of the modern body: Sexuality and society in the nineteenth century*, Berkeley: University of California Press, 1987.

Gay, Peter, *The bourgeois experience: Education of the senses*, Oxford University Press, 1984.

—, *The bourgeois experience: The tender passion*, Oxford University Press, 1986.

Gélis, Jacques, *History of childbirth: Fertility, pregnancy and birth in early modern Europe*, London: Polity Press, 1991.

Girardot, Norman J., *Myth and meaning in early Taoism: The theme of chaos (hundun)*, Berkeley: University of California Press, 1983.

Gosling, F.G., *Before Freud: Neurasthenia and the American medical community, 1870–1910*, Chicago: University of Illinois Press, 1987.

Gronewold, S., *Beautiful merchandise: Prostitution in China 1860–1936*, New York: Harrington Park Press, 1986.

Gulik, R.H. van, *Sexual life in ancient China*, Leiden: Brill, 1974.

Hall, Lesley A., 'Forbidden by God, despised by men: Masturbation, medical warnings, moral panic, and manhood in Great Britian, 1850–1950', *Journal of the History of Sexuality*, 2, no. 3 (Jan. 1992), pp. 365–87.

——, *Hidden anxieties: Male sexuality, 1900–1950*, Oxford University Press, 1991.

Halliday, M.A.K., *Language as social semiotic: The social interpretation of language and meaning*, London: Edward Arnold, 1978.

Hare, E.H., 'Masturbatory insanity: The history of an idea', *Journal of Mental Science*, no. 108 (1962), pp. 1–25.

Hayford, Charles W., *To the people: James Yen and village China*, New York: Columbia University Press, 1990.

Henderson, J.B., *The development and decline of Chinese cosmology*, New York: Columbia University Press, 1984.

Hendrick, Harry, *Images of youth: Age, class, and the male youth problem, 1880–1920*, Oxford: Clarendon Press, 1990.

Henriot, Christian, 'Medicine, VD and prostitution in pre-revolutionary China', *Social History of Medicine*, 5, no. 1 (April 1992), pp. 95–120.

Hershatter, Gail, 'Courtisans and streetwalkers: The changing discourses on Shanghai prostitution, 1890–1949', *Journal of the History of Sexuality*, 3, no. 2 (1992), pp. 245–69.

——, 'The hierarchy of Shanghai prostitution, 1919–1949', *Modern China*, 15, no. 4 (1989), pp. 463–97.

——, 'Prostitution and the market in women in early twentieth-century Shanghai' in Rubie S. Watson and Patricia B. Ebrey (eds), *Marriage and inequality in Chinese society*, Berkeley: University of California Press, 1991, pp. 256–85.

——,'Regulating sex in Shanghai: The reform of prostitution in 1920 and 1951' in Frederic Wakeman and Yeh Wen-hsin (eds), *Shanghai Sojourners*, Berkeley: Center for Chinese Studies, 1992, pp. 145–86.

——, 'Sex work and social order: Prostitutes, their families, and the state in twentieth-century Shanghai', paper presented at the Conference on Family Process and Political Process in China, Taibei, 3–5 Jan. 1992.

Hinsch, Bret, *Passions of the cut sleeve: The male homosexual tradition in China*, Berkeley: University of California Press, 1990.

Hoeppli, R. and Chiang I-hung, 'The doctrine of spontaneous generation of parasites in old-style Chinese and Western medicine: A comparative study', *Peking Natural History Bulletin*, no. 19 (1950).

Hu Xiansu 胡先驌, 'Huashengshuo yu shengming zhi qiyuan' 化生説與生命之起源 (The origins of generation theories and destiny), *Kexue*, 12, no. 5 (May 1927), pp. 571–83.

Huang Kewu 黃克武, 'Cong *Shenbao* yiyao guanggao kan minchu Shanghai de yiliao wenhua yu shehui shenghuo, 1912–1926' 從申報醫藥廣告看民初上海的醫療文化與社會生活 (Medical culture and social life in the early Republican era as seen through the medical advertisements of the *Shenbao*, 1912–1926), Zhongyang yanjiuyuan jindaishi yanjiusuo jikan, 17, no. 2 (Dec. 1988), pp. 141–94.

Jones, Susan Mann, 'Hung Liang-chi (1746–1809): The perception and articulation of political problems in late eighteenth-century China', Ph.D. dissertation, Stanford University, 1972.

Kevles, D.J., *In the name of eugenics: Genetics and the use of human heredity*, New York: Alfred Knopf, 1985.

Ko, Dorothy, 'Pursuing talent and virtue: Education and women's culture in seventeenth- and eighteenth-century China', *Late Imperial China*, 13, no. 1 (June 1992), pp. 9–39.

Kwok, D.W.Y., *Scientism in Chinese thought, 1900–1950*, New Haven: Yale University Press, 1965.

Laqueur, Thomas W., '"Amor veneris, vel dulcedo appeletur"' in Michel Feher, with Ramona Naddaff and Nadia Tazi (eds), *Fragments for a history of the human body*, vol. 3, New York: Zone Books, 1989, pp. 90–131.

——, *Making sex: Body and gender from the Greeks to Freud*, Cambridge, MA: Harvard University Press, 1990.

——, 'The social evil, the solitary vice and pouring tea' in Michel Feher, with Ramona Naddaff and Nadia Tazi (eds), *Fragments for a history of the human body*, vol. 3, New York: Zone Books, 1989, pp. 334–43.

Lau, Joseph S.M., S.T. Hsia and Leo Ou-fan Lee (eds), *Modern Chinese stories and novellas, 1919–1949*, New York: Columbia University Press, 1981.

Lau, M.P. and M.L. Ng, 'Homosexuality in Chinese culture', *Culture, Medicine, and Psychiatry*, 13, no. 4 (Dec. 1989), pp. 465–88.

Le Breton, David, *Anthropologie du corps et modernité*, Paris: Presses Universitaires de France, 1990.

Lee, B.J., 'Female infanticide in China' in R.W. Guisso and S. Johannesen, *Women in China: Current directions in historical scholarship*, New York: Philo Press, 1981, pp. 163–78.

Lee, Leo Ou-fan, 'In search of modernity: Some reflections on a new mode of consciousness in twentieth-century Chinese history and literature' in Paul A. Cohen and Merle Goldman (eds), *Ideas across cultures: Essays on Chinese thought in honor of Benjamin I. Schwartz*, Cambridge, MA: Harvard University Press, 1990, pp. 109–136.

Leung, Angela•K., 'Autour de la naissance. La mère et l'enfant en Chine aux XVIe et XVIIe siècles', *Cahiers Internationaux de Sociologie*, 76 (Jan.-June 1984), pp. 51–70.

—, 'L'amour en Chine. Relations et pratiques sociales aux XIIIe et XIVe siècles', *Archives des Sciences Sociales des Religions*, 56, no. 1 (1983), pp. 59–76.

—, 'To chasten the society: The development of widow homes in the Ch'ing, 1773–1911', paper presented at the Conference on Family Process and Political Process in China, Taibei, 3–5 January 1992.

Leutner, M., *Geburt, Heirat und Tod in Peking: Volkskultur und Elitekultur vom 19. Jahrhundert bis zur Gegenwart*, Berlin: Reimer, 1989.

Levy, Marion J., *The family revolution in modern China*, New York: Atheneum, 1949.

Lin Yutang, *History of the press and public opinion in China*, Oxford University Press, 1937.

Linck, Gudula, *Frau und Familie in China*, München: Verlag C.H. Beck, 1988.

Link, Perry, *Mandarin ducks and butterflies: Popular fiction in early twentieth-century Chinese cities*, Berkeley: University of California Press, 1981.

Lung, C.F., 'A note on Hung Liang-chi, the Chinese Malthus', *Tien-hsia Monthly*, 1 (1935), pp. 248–250.

Luo Dunwei 羅郭偉, 'Wusi renwu zongheng tan: Zhang Jingsheng' 五四人物縱横談：張兢生 (Free talks about Zhang Jingsheng, a figure of the May Fourth Movement), *Changliu*, 7, no. 6 (1953).

MacDonald, Robert H., 'The frightful consequences of onanism: Notes on the history of a delusion', *Journal of the History of Ideas*, no. 28 (1967), pp. 423–31.

McMahon, Keith, 'A case for Confucian sexuality: The eighteenth-century novel, *Yesou puyan*', *Late Imperial China*, 9, no. 2 (Dec. 1988), pp. 32–55.

—, *Causality and containment in seventeenth-century Chinese fiction*, Leiden: Brill, 1988.

Mann, Susan, '*Fuxue* (Women's Learning) by Zhang Xuecheng (1738–

1801): China's first history of women's culture', *Late Imperial China*, 13, no. 1 (June 1992), pp. 40–62.

——, 'Grooming a daughter for marriage: Brides and wives in the mid-Ch'ing period' in Rubie S. Watson and Patricia B. Ebrey (eds), *Marriage and inequality in Chinese society*, Berkeley: University of California Press, 1991, pp. 204–30.

——, 'Widows in the kinship, class and community structures of Qing dynasty China', *Journal of Asian Studies*, 46, no. 1 (Feb. 1987), pp. 37–56.

Martin, Emily, *The woman in the body: A cultural analysis of reproduction*, Milton Keynes: Open University Press, 1987.

Mayr, Ernst, *The growth of biological thought: Diversity, evolution, and inheritance*, Cambridge, MA: Belknap Press, 1982.

Medvei, V.C., *A history of endocrinology*, Lancaster: MTP, 1982.

Meijer, M.J., 'Homosexual offenses in Ch'ing law', *T'oung Pao*, 71 (1985), pp. 109–33.

Micale, Mark S., 'Hysteria and its historiography: A review of past and present writings', 2 parts, *History of Science*, 27 (1989), pp. 223–61 and 319–51.

Mitterauer, Michael, *A history of youth*, London: Blackwell, 1992.

Moscucci, Ornella, *The science of woman: Gynaecology and gender in England, 1800–1929*, Cambridge University Press, 1990.

Mosher, Steven W., *Broken earth: The rural Chinese*, London: Robert Hale, 1984.

Mosse, G.L., *Nationalism and sexuality: Respectability and abnormal sexuality in modern Europe*, New York: Howard Fertig, 1985.

Neuman, R.P., 'Masturbation, madness and the modern concepts of childhood and adolescence', *Journal of Social History*, 8, no. 3 (spring 1975), pp. 1–27.

Ng, On-cho, '*Hsing* (nature) as the ontological basis of practicality in early Ch'ing Ch'eng-Chu Confucianism: Li Kuang-ti's (1642–1718) philosophy', *Philosophy East and West*, 44, no. 1 (Jan. 1994), pp. 79–109.

Ng, Vivien W., 'Ideology and sexuality: Rape laws in Qing China', *Journal of Asian Studies*, 46, no. 1 (Feb. 1987), pp. 57–70.

——, '*Jiating baofa*: Family life education or instructions for sex-free living?', paper presented at the Conference on Engendering China, Harvard, February 1992.

Nivard, Jacqueline, 'L'évolution de la presse féminine chinoise de 1898 à 1949', *Études Chinoises*, 5, nos 1–2 (1986), pp. 157–84.

——, 'Histoire d'une revue féminine chinoise: Funü zazhi 1915–1931', Paris: EHESS, Ph.D. dissertation, 1983.

Ono Kazuko, *Chinese women in a century of revolution, 1850–1950*, edited by Joshua A. Fogel, Stanford University Press, 1989.

Ortner, Sherry B. and Harriet Whitehead (eds), *Sexual meanings: The cultural construction of sexuality*, Cambridge University Press, 1981.

Oudshoorn, Nelly, 'Endocrinologists and the conceptualization of sex', *Journal of the History of Biology*, 23, no. 2 (fall 1990), 163–87.

——, 'On measuring sex hormones: The role of biological assays in sexualizing chemical substances', *Bulletin of the History of Medicine*, 64, no. 2 (summer 1990), pp. 243–61.

Parker, Andrew, Mary Russo, Doris Sommer and Patricia Yaeger (eds), *Nationalisms and sexualities*, London: Routledge, 1989.

Parkin, David, 'Latticed knowledge and the impossibility of eliminating dispersal', manuscript, May 1993.

Pauly, P.J., 'Review article: The eugenics industry – Growth or restructuring?', *The Journal of the History of Biology*, 26, no. 1 (Spring 1993), pp. 131–45.

Payne, R.K., 'Sex and gestation, the union of opposites in European and Chinese alchemy', *Ambix*, 36, part 2 (July 1989), pp. 66–81.

Pomata, Gianna, 'Uomini mestruanti: Somiglianza e differenza fra i sessi in età moderna', *Quaderni Storici*, no. 1, pp. 51–103.

Porter, Roy, *Health for sale: Quackery in England, 1660–1850*, Manchester University Press, 1989.

Proctor, Robert N., *Racial hygiene: Medicine under the Nazis*, Cambridge, MA: Harvard University Press, 1988.

Quétel, Claude, *The history of syphilis*, London, Polity Press, 1990.

Rawski, Evelyn S., *Education and popular literacy in Ch'ing China*, Ann Arbor: University of Michigan Press, 1979.

Rawski, T.G., *Economic growth in prewar China*, Berkeley: University of California Press, 1989.

Reynolds, D.C., 'The advancement of knowledge and the enrichment of life: The Science Society of China in the early Republic, 1914–1930', Ph.D. dissertation, University of Wisconsin, 1986.

Rocca, Jean-Louis, *L'empire et son milieu. La criminalité en Chine populaire*, Paris: Plon, 1991.

Ropp, Paul, 'The seeds of change: Reflections on the condition of women in the early and mid-Ch'ing', *Signs*, 2, no. 1 (1976), pp. 5–23.

Rosner, Erhard, 'Le développement de la terminologie médicale moderne en Chine' in *IVe colloque international de sinologie, Chantilly 1983*, Paris, 1991, pp. 272–87.

Rowe, W.T., 'Modern Chinese social history in comparative perspective' in Paul Ropp (ed.), *Heritage of China: Contemporary perspectives on Chinese civilization*, Berkeley: University of California Press, 1990, pp. 242–62.

—, 'The public sphere in modern China', *Modern China*, no. 3 (July 1990), pp. 309–29.

—, 'Women and the family in mid-Ch'ing social thought: The case of Ch'en Hung-mou', *Late Imperial China*, 13, no. 2 (Dec. 1992), pp. 1–41.

Ruan Fangfu, *Sex in China: Studies in sexology in Chinese culture*, New York: Plenum Press, 1991.

Russett, Cynthia Eagle, *Sexual science: The Victorian construction of womanhood*, Cambridge, MA: Harvard University Press, 1989.

Saari, Jon L., *Legacies of childhood: Growing up Chinese in a time of crisis, 1890–1920*, Cambridge, MA: Harvard University Press, 1990.

Sabban, Françoise, 'Un savoir-faire oublié. Le travail du lait en Chine ancienne', *Zinbun (Memoirs of the Research Institute for Humanistic Studies)*, no. 21 (1987), pp. 31–65.

Santangelo, Paolo, 'Destiny and retribution in late imperial China', *East and West*, 42, nos 2–4 (Dec. 1992), pp. 377–442.

Satyendra, Indira, 'Metaphors of the body: The sexual economy of the *Chin P'ing Mei tz'u-hua*', *Chinese Literature*, 15 (1993), pp. 85–97.

Schiebinger, Londa, 'Skeletons in the closet: The first illustrations of the female skeleton in nineteenth-century anatomy', *Representations*, 14, no. 2 (spring 1986), pp. 42–82.

Schipper, Kristofer, *Le corps Taoïste*, Paris: Fayard, 1982.

Schwarcz, Vera, *The Chinese enlightenment*, Berkeley: University of California Press, 1986.

Scott, Joan W., 'Gender: A useful category of historical analysis', *American Historical Review*, 91, no. 5 (1986), pp. 1053–75.

Sheridan, James, 'The Warlord era: Politics and militarism under the Peking government, 1916–28' in J.K. Fairbank (ed.), *Cambridge history of China*, vol. 12, part 1, Cambridge University Press, 1986, pp. 284–321.

Shields, Stephanie A., 'The variability hypothesis: The history of a biological model of sex differences in intelligence', *Signs: Journal of Women and Culture in Society*, no. 7 (1982).

Shuttleworth, Sally, 'Medical discourse and popular advertising in the mid-Victorian era' in Mary Jacobus, E.V. Keller and Sally Shuttleworth (eds), *Body/Politics: Women and the discourses of science*, London: Routledge, 1990, pp. 47–68.

Sicherman, Barbara, 'The paradox of prudence: Mental health in the Gilded Age' in Andrew Scull (ed.), *Madhouses, mad-doctors, and madmen: The social history of psychiatry in the Victorian age*, Philadelphia: University of Pennsylvania Press, 1981, pp. 218–40.

Sissa, Giulia, 'Subtle bodies' in Michel Feher, with Ramona Naddaff and Nadia Tazi (eds), *Fragments for a history of the human body*, vol. 3, New York: Zone Books, 1989, pp. 133–57.

Sontag, Susan, *Illness as metaphor and Aids and its metaphors*, New York: Doubleday, 1990.

Starobinski, Jean, 'Sur la chlorose', *Romantisme*, no. 31 (1981), pp. 113–30.

Stoddart, D.M., *The scented ape: The biology and culture of human odour*, Cambridge University Press, 1990.

Su Ru-chiang, 'Birth control in China', unpubl. MA dissertation, University of Chicago, 1946.

Sun, E.Z., 'The growth of the academic community, 1912–1949' in J.K. Fairbank and A. Feuerwerker (eds), *The Cambridge history of China*, vol. 13, part 2, Cambridge University Press, 1986, pp. 361–420.

Sun Lung-kee, 'Out of the wilderness: Chinese intellectual odysseys from the "May Fourth" to the "Thirties"', Ph.D. dissertation, Stanford University, 1985.

Swain, Gladys, 'L'âme, la femme et le corps. Les métamorphoses de l'hystérie à la fin du XIXe siècle', *Le Débat*, no. 24, March 1983.

Thompson, Laurence G., *Ta t'ung shu: The one world philosophy of K'ang Yu-wei*, London: Geo. Allen and Unwin, 1958.

T'ien Ju-k'ang, *Male anxiety and female chastity: A comparative study of Chinese ethical values in Ming-Ch'ing times*, Leiden: Brill, 1988.

Trillat, Étienne, *Histoire de l'hystérie*, Paris: Seghers, 1986.

Vicinus, Martha, 'Sexuality and power: A review of current work in the history of sexuality', *Feminist Studies*, 8, no. 1 (spring 1982), pp. 132–56.

Vigarello, Georges, *Le corps redressé. Histoire d'un pouvoir pédagogique*, Paris: Delarge, 1978.

——, *Concepts of cleanliness: Changing attitudes in France since the Middle Ages*, Cambridge University Press, 1988.

Vitiello, Giovanni, '"The dragon's embrace": Ming and Qing homoerotic tales from *The Cut Sleeve*', *T'oung Pao*, 78, nos 4–5 (1992), pp. 341–72.

Volkmar, Barbara, 'Das Kind in der chinesischen Heilkunde', Ph.D. dissertation, University of Freiburg, 1985.

Wakeman, Frederic and Yeh Wen-hsin (eds), *Shanghai sojourners*, Berkeley: Center for Chinese Studies, 1992.

Waltner, Ann, *Getting an heir: Adoption and the construction of kinship in late imperial China*, Honolulu: University of Hawaii Press, 1990.

——, 'The moral status of the child in late imperial China: Childhood in ritual and in law', *Social Research*, 53, no. 4 (winter 1986), pp. 667–87.

Wang Jintao 王劲濤 (ed.), *Zhongguo yiji tiyao* 中國醫籍提要 (Essential of Chinese books on medicine), Changchun: Jilin kexue jishu chubanshe, 1984.

Wang Shengduo 王聲多, 'Maersaisi renkoulun zai Zhongguo de liuchuan he lunzheng' 馬尔賽斯人口論在中國的流傳和論爭 (The spread and debate on the population theory of Malthus in China), *Shehui kexue yanjiu*, no. 6, (Nov. 1986), pp. 17–21.

Wang Shihe 王世和, 'Feng Menglong yu jihua shengyu' 馮夢龍與計划生育 (Feng Menglong and birth control), *Renkouxue*, 1985, no. 4, p. 54.

Wang Shunu 王書奴, *Zhongguo changji shi* 中國娼妓史 (History of Chinese prostitution), Shanghai: Sanlian shudian, 1988.

Watson, Rubie S. and Patricia B. Ebrey (eds), *Marriage and inequality in Chinese society*, Berkeley: University of California Press, 1991.

Weeks, Jeffrey, *Sex, politics and society: The regulation of sexuality since 1800*, London: Longman, 1989.

Weindling, Paul J., *Health, race and German politics between national unification and Nazism, 1870–1945*, Cambridge University Press, 1989.

Wu Shenyuan 吳申元, '"Renman zhi huan": jindai Zhongguo renkou sixiang de "redian"' "人滿之患" 近代中國人口思想的熱點 (The peril of overpopulation: a 'hot point' in modern Chinese demographic thought), *Renkouxue*, 1987, no. 3, pp. 92–93.

Wu Wenwei 吳文蔚, 'Zhong Xi xingxue liang boshi: Zhang Jingsheng yu Jin Sai' 中西性學倆博士：張競生與金賽 (Two doctors of Eastern and Western sexology: Zhang Jingsheng and Kingsley), *Zhongwai zazhi*, 30, no. 4 (1981).

Xiao Yaotian 蕭遙天, 'Wo tan Zhang Jingsheng' 我談張競生 (About Zhang Jingsheng), *Dacheng*, no. 10 (1974).

Xiong Bingzhen 熊秉眞, 'Chuantong Zhongguo yijie dui changcheng yu fayu xianxiang de taolun' 傳統中國醫界對長成與發育現象討論 (Debates about growth and development in traditional Chinese medicine), *Guoli Taiwan shifan daxue lishi xuebao*, no. 20 (July 1992), pp. 27–40.

Yeh Wen-hsin, *The alienated academy: Culture and politics in Republican China, 1919–1937*, Cambridge, MA: Harvard University Press, 1990.

Yip, Ka-che, 'Health and society in China: Public health education for the community, 1912–1937', *Social Science and Medicine*, no. 16 (1982), pp. 1197–1205.

Zha Bo and Geng Wenxiu, 'Sexuality in urban China', *Australian Journal of Chinese Affairs*, no. 28 (July 1992), pp. 1–20.

Zhang Jingyuan, 'Sigmund Freud and modern Chinese literature', Ph.D. dissertation, Cornell University, 1989.

Zhu Xi 朱洗, 'Huashengshuo de jinhua' 化生說的進化 (The evolution of generation theories), *Ziran kexue*, 4, no. 4 (1933).

CHARACTER LIST

ao 凹

Bao Shichen 包世臣
Bao Zuxuan 鮑祖宣
bentunqi 奔豚氣
biantai 變態
bingtai 病態
bu putong de tongxing lian'ai
不普通的同性戀愛

Cai Yuanpei 蔡元培
Cao Guanlai 曹觀來
Cao Tingdong 曹庭棟
Chai Fuyuan 柴福沅
chan'er zhixian 產兒制限
Chen Changheng 陳長衡
Chen Duxiu 陳獨秀
Chen Jianshan 陳兼善
Chen Laoxin 陳勞薪
Chen Muhua 陳慕華
Chen Yucang 陳雨蒼
chengdu 程度
Cheng Hao 程浩
chengqun 成群
chidao 赤道
chidun 遲鈍
chouren 醜人
Chu Cheng 褚澄
Chu Renhuo 褚人獲
congshu 叢書

dapao 打炮
Dai Qiling 戴棣齡
Dai Zhen 戴震
dandu 單獨
dineng 低能
dian 電
diandao 巔倒
Ding Fubao 丁福保
Dongfang zazhi 東方杂誌

echou 惡嗅
elie fenzi 惡劣份子

faluopiaoguan 發羅票管
Fan Shouyuan 范守淵
fan ziran 反自然
feifa chujing 非法出精
Fei Hongnian 費鴻年
feipangbing 肥胖病
fei zhengshi zhi yixing
非正式之異性
fen 分
fenmian 分娩
Feng Menglong 馮夢龍
fengshui 風水
fugaowan 附睾丸
fugu 復古
fuke 婦科
fulan 腐爛
fuluanchao 附卵巢
funü 婦女
Funü zazhi 婦女杂誌
Fu Qiuzi 浮邱子

Fu Shan 傅山

Gan Yonglong 甘永龍
ganshou muqi 感受母氣
Gao Xisheng 高希聖
geren weisheng 個人衛生
gonggong weisheng 公共衛生
gongmin weisheng 公民衛生
Gong Tingzhang 宮廷璋
Gong Zizhen 龔自珍
Gu Mingsheng 顧鳴盛
Gu Shi 顧實
Gu Shoubai 顧壽白
guangchuang 廣瘡
Gui Zhiliang 桂質良
guodu 過渡
guolao 過勞

Hong Liangji 洪亮吉
huchou 胡臭
Hu Dingan 胡定安
Hu Shi 胡適
huajing 滑精
huashengshuo 化生説
huai xiguan 壞習慣
Huang Shuze 黃樹則
Huang Zifang 黃子方
huopo 活潑

ji 癪
jiajing 佳境
jiazhi 價値
Jiang Xiangqing 蔣湘青
Jiang Zhiyou 蔣智由
Jiao Xun 焦循
Jiaoyu zazhi 教育杂誌
jiechu 戒除
jieyu 節欲
jiexing 節性
jindai biecheng 近代別稱
jinhua 進化
Jinkui yaolüe fanglun
金匱要略方論
Jinkui yaolüe lunzhu
金匱要略論注
Jinkui yaolüe qianzhu buzheng
金匱要略淺注补正
Jinkui yaolüe xindian 金匱要略心典
Jinpingmei 金瓶梅
Jin Zhonghua 金仲華
Jin Zizhi 金子直
jingchao 精巢
jingchong 精蟲
jinghao 精耗
jingjie 境界
jingshen shouyin 精神手淫
jingshen wuran 精神污染
jingshi 經世
jingluo 經絡
jingxue 精血
jingzhi budong 靜止不動
jingzuo 靜坐

Kaiming shudian 開明書店
kaozhengxue 考證學
kedou 蝌蚪
kuaigan 快感

laonian shidai 老年時代
laonü 老女
li 理
Li Baoliang 李寶澋
Li Gong 李塨

Li Shizhen 李時珍
Liang Qichao 梁啓超
Lin Yutang 林語堂
linzhuo 淋濁
liuchan 流產
Liu Piji 劉丕基
Liu Yicang 劉一倉
Lu Xun 魯迅
Luo Zhenyu 羅振玉
luanchao 卵巢
luansheng 卵生
Luo Guangdao 羅光道

manxing 漫性
Meichuang bilu 梅瘡筆錄
mengyi 夢遺
mixin 迷心
miuzhong 謬種
Munan 目南

nannü goujing 男女媾精
nannü zhi yu 男女之欲
nanxing qizhi 男性氣質
naoshending 腦腎丁
nei 内
Nie Kesheng 聶克生
nongmin 農民
nüzi qi 女子氣

paichu yu shenti zhi wai 排出於身體之外
paichu yu tiwai 排出於體外
paijing 排精
pailuan 排卵
painiao 排尿
paixie 排泄
Pan Gongzhan 潘公展
Pan Guangdan 潘光旦

qi 氣
Qian Daxin 錢大昕
qianfu ganying 前夫感應
qiaomangyan 雀盲眼
qinfan 侵犯
qingnian 青年
qingnian shidai 青年時代
qunji shouyin 群集手淫

renkou 人口
renkouxue 人口學
renkou yali 人口壓力
renman zhi huan 人滿之患
Rong Yuan 阮元
Rouputuan 肉蒲團
rudong 蠕動
ruanxiagan 軟下疳
ruanxing xiagan 軟性下疳

sangang 三綱
se 色
seqing zhongshu 色情中樞
seyu 色欲
shehui wenti 社會問題
Shenbao 申報
Shen Jin'ao 沈金鰲
shenjingbing 神精病
Shen Junqi 沈奮淇
Shen Mingzong 沈明宗
Shen Youpeng 沈又彭
Shen Yong 沈勇
shengchan 生產
shengjiang 生姜
shengjiang 生僵
shengren zhi lü 生人之律

shi 食
shire 濕熱
shiyu 食欲
shidai 時代
shidaibing 時代病
shi se xing ye 食色性也
shou shen ru yu zhi zhi ru jin 守身如玉執志如金
shouyin 手淫
shujingguan 輸精管
shuluanguan 輸卵管
shuixiang 睡鄉
Sun Simo 孫思邈

taijiao 胎教
taijiaoyuan 胎教院
taisheng 胎生
Tan Sitong 譚嗣同
Tang Peng 湯鵬
Tang Zonghai 湯宗海
tingzhi 停滯
tonglu 通路
tongxingai 同性愛
tongxinglian 同性戀
tu 凸
tujing 途徑
tuihua 退化

wai 外
wangu 頑固
Wan Quan 萬全
Wang Chengpin 王誠品
Wang Fuzhi 王夫之
Wang Jungang 王君綱
Wang Qishu 王其澍
Wang Shiduo 汪士鐸
Wang Shoucheng 王守成
Wang Xianqian 王先謙
Wang Yang 汪洋
Wang Yugang 汪于岡
weihuang 萎黃
weihuangbing 萎黃病
weisheng 衛生
Weisheng baihuabao 衛生白話報
Weisheng shijie 衛生世界
wenming jiehun 文明結婚
Wu Jieping 吳階平
Wu Liande 伍連德

xitong 繫統
xiafu 下腹
xiazhi 下肢
xiangfan er xiangcheng 相反而相成
xiaochong 小蟲
xiaodu 消毒
xiesidili 歇斯底里
Xie Yunshou 謝筠壽
Xingbao 性報
xingbing 性病
xing de kumen 性的苦悶
xingge 性格
xing kangjin de ren 性亢進的人
xingpi 性癖
xingpi de ren 性癖的人
Xing sanribao 性三日報
xing shenjing shuairuo 性神精衰弱
xingyu 性欲
xingyu biantai 性欲變態
xingyu jiaoyu 性欲教育

Xingyu zhoubao 性欲周報
Xing zazhi 性杂誌
Xu Bin 徐彬
Xu Dachun 徐大椿
Xu Guangqi 徐光啓
Xu Naiji 許乃濟
Xu Shilian 許仕廉
Xu Zi 徐鼒
xue 血
Xue Deyu 薛德焴
Xuesheng zazhi 學生杂誌

yasheng 芽生
Yan Fu 顏復
Yan Fuqing 顏福慶
yanyanyixi 奄奄一息
Yan Yuan 顏元
yangchengsuo 養成所
yangmeichuang 楊梅瘡
yangqi 陽氣
yangsheng 養生
yangshui 羊水
yaowang 殀亡
yechou 腋嗅
yeman benneng 野蠻的本能
Yi Jiayue 易家鉞
yijing 遺精
yixie 遺泄
yixingai 異性愛
Yixue weishengbao 醫學衛生報
yindao 陰道
yinhe 陰核
yinjing 陰莖
yinyang ziran zhi dao 陰陽自然之道
yingxiagan 硬下疳
yingxing xiagan 硬性下疳
yonggan 勇敢
youju yishi 幽居一室
youshengxue 優生學
youxing 游行
You Yi 尤怡
Yu Chang 喻昌
Yu Dafu 郁達夫
yudong 欲動
Yu Fengbin 俞鳳賓
Yu Zhengxie 俞正燮
Yuan Guorong 袁國榮
yuanye 元液
Yun Daiying 惲代英

zangfu 臟腑
zangzao 臟躁
zangzaozheng 臟躁症
zaochan 早產
zhanchang 戰場
zhang'ai 障碍
zhang'ai wu 障碍物
Zhang Dianjie 張殿傑
zhangfu qi 丈夫氣
Zhang Jingsheng 張競生
Zhang Xichen 張錫琛
Zhang Ziping 張資平
Zhengzhong shuju 正中書局
Zhang Zongyuan 張宗元
Zhao Shifa 趙士法
zheng 正
zhengdang de zhidao 正當的指導
zhizao 製造
Zhonghua shuju 中華書局
Zhong Xi yixuebao 中西醫學報
zhongjianwu 中間物

zhongxing nanzi 中性男子
zhongzu weisheng 種族衛生
zhongzu zimie 種族自滅
Zhou Jianren 周建人
Zhou Tiaoyang 周調陽
zhunao 主腦
Zhu Xi 朱洗
Zhu Yunying 朱雲影
Zhu Zhenjiang 祝枕江
Zhu Zhensheng 朱振聲
Zhuang Weizhong 莊畏仲
zhuofa 斲伐
ziben 資本
zigong zhi zuoyou guan 子宮之左右管
zigong zhi zuoyou he 子宮之左右核
zixian 子癇
zu'ai 阻碍

INDEX